A DISIMPRISONED EPIC

A DISIMPRISONED EPIC

Form and Vision in Carlyle's *French Revolution*

MARK CUMMING

upp

University of Pennsylvania Press
Philadelphia

Printed in the United States of America

Library of Congress Cataloging-in-Publication Data

Cumming, Mark.
A disimprisoned epic: form and vision in Carlyle's French Revolution / Mark Cumming.
p. cm.
Bibliography: p.
Includes index.
ISBN 0-8122-8117-9
1. Carlyle, Thomas, 1795–1881—Knowledge—History. 2. Carlyle, Thomas, 1795–1881. French revolution. 3. France—History—Revolution, 1789–1799—Historiography. 4. Epic literature, English—History and criticism. 5. History in literature. I. Title.
PR4437 .H5C8 1988 88-18844
824′ .8—dc19 CIP

CONTENTS

ABBREVIATIONS

Collecteanea	*Collecteanea, Thomas Carlyle 1821–1855.* Ed. Samuel Arthur Jones. Canton, PA: The Kirgate Press, 1903.
CW	*The Works of Thomas Carlyle.* Centenary Edition. Ed. H. D. Traill. 30 vols. London: Chapman and Hall, 1896–99.
FR	*The French Revolution: A History.* (Vols. 2, 3, and 4 of *The Works of Thomas Carlyle.*)
Fragments	*Friedrich Schlegel's "Lucinde" and the Fragments.* Trans. Peter Firchow. Minneapolis: University of Minnesota Press, 1971.
Letters	*The Collected Letters of Thomas and Jane Welsh Carlyle.* Ed. Charles Richard Sanders, Kenneth J. Fielding, Clyde de L. Ryals, et al. 15 vols. Durham, NC: Duke University Press, 1970–87.
Prose	Walt Whitman. *Prose Works 1892.* Ed. Floyd Stovall. 2 vols. New York University Press, 1963.
SR	*Sartor Resartus.* Ed. C. F. Harrold. New York: Odyssey, 1937.
Two Note Books	*Two Note Books of Thomas Carlyle, From 23rd March 1822 to 16th May 1832.* Ed. Charles Eliot Norton, 1898. Rpt. Marmaroneck, NY: Paul P. Appel, 1972.

PREFACE

The French Revolution has received far less critical attention than we might expect to have been directed toward a work of such importance; despite its claim to be the heroic prose poem of its time, and despite its undoubted influence on Charles Dickens and other mid-century writers, it has remained remarkably peripheral to our conception of the Victorian era. The reasons for its relative neglect are not hard to find. Long and complex, even by Victorian standards, it has not found a place on university curricula as easily as the more compact *Sartor Resartus* has. And it does not accord with our preexistent categories of academic study, inasmuch as it is too literary for historians, and too historical for students of literature. Though fictive, it is not fiction, in the normal senses of the word, and though poetic, it is not likely to be found in a course on Victorian poetry. It does not readily fit even into the most popular categories of Victorian nonfictional prose: art criticism, social criticism, autobiography, or apologetics. Nevertheless, recent study has moved Carlyle's history in from the margins, to a position more closely resembling the one it held at the end of the nineteenth century—at the center of any understanding of his work and his time.

The French Revolution presents to its modern readers the same two crucial interpretive problems that it offered to those who welcomed its first appearance in 1837. The first—arising from the expectation that Carlyle's text will, as a history, offer an interpretation of the French Revolution—is to establish what the work means, to discern its ideas, perspectives, and, if possible, allegiances. The second—arising from the perception that Carlyle's text is cast in an arresting new form, which transgresses the conventional generic boundaries of a history—is to establish what the work is. For anyone who has read *The French Revolution*, or indeed for anyone who knows Carlyle through *Sartor Resartus*, there can be little surprise that the first problem (What does the work mean?) is inseparable from the second (What is the work's kind?). Carlyle himself protested in response to censorious critics of *The French Revolution* that literary style is not "like a coat" that "can be put off or put on," but "like a *skin*," "the product and close kinsfellow of all that lies under it; exact type of the nature of the beast: *not* to be plucked off without flaying and death" (*Letters* 9: 228). Carlyle's vision of the Revolution embraces both the insurrectionary rhapsody of a Jules Michelet and the reactionary horror of a Hippolyte Taine,[1] and, as he rightly insists, the conceptual complexity of his history is directly registered in the complexity of its form. His reluctance to adopt the political stance of any single party, radical or conservative, is matched by his unwillingness to settle on any single documentary or artistic mode of presentation.

The early reviewers of *The French Revolution*, the adulatory and the vituperative alike, were agreed on one thing: the radically experimental nature of its form. The work's backers resolved to accept Carlyle's underlying premise that form should be accountable to vision; its detractors were similarly ready to acknowledge, though not to accept, its revolutionary nature. When massive changes in literary practice "arrive suddenly and unprepared," Lady Sydney Morgan argued in the *Athenaeum*, "they produce, not reforms merely, but revolutions; and in revolutions, literary as well as political, there occurs between the overthrow of the old and the creation of the new, an epoch of transition in which all monstrous and misshapen things are produced in the unguided search of an unknown and unimagined beauty."[2] The *Literary Gazette* called Carlyle's history, with a similar disgust, "a triple revolution:—1st, allowing the French Revolution itself to be *one*; 2nd, there is the Revolution of Mr. Carlyle, *two*; and 3d, the Revolution of the English language, *three*!"[3] However hostile these reviews are, they gauge with considerable accuracy the artistic and social context of Carlyle's work in an age shaken by massive industrial and economic change, an age caught in the throes of reform and still haunted by the specter of political revolution, an age in which polite fictions and neatly trimmed epics could effect nothing.[4] Lady Morgan's relegation of *The French Revolution* to the class of "monstrous and misshapen things" approximates Carlyle's description of it, in a letter to Ralph Waldo Emerson, as a "wild savage ruleless very bad Book" (*Letters* 9: 82). The *Literary Gazette*, by denouncing the work as "a triple revolution," comes close to Carlyle's statement to John Sterling that his history "is a wild savage Book, itself a kind of French Revolution" (*Letters* 9: 116). The view held by hostile reviewers that the form of *The French Revolution*, as well as its topic, is revolutionary supports Carlyle's own suggestion that it might be "the most radical Book that has been written in these late centuries" (*Letters* 9: 193).

Carlyle's history is not radical in any straightforward political sense, for the conventional labels of radical and conservative are, in his view, hackneyed and inadequate: Carlyle supports the moribund French monarchy only so far as it once represented true order, or cosmos, and he apologizes for the "vital Chaos" of the revolutionaries only so far as, in it, "there is new Order shaping itself free" (*FR* 2: 97). As James Anthony Froude, Carlyle's biographer, correctly observes, he is "neither Tory, nor Whig, nor Radical, nor Socialist, nor any other 'ist.'"[5] What is thoroughly radical in Carlyle's history is his staunch determination to make the form of his text the "exact type" of his subject, the significance of the French Revolution for modern Europe. Because of this determination, Carlyle cannot rest easily in any literary camp, any more than he can affix himself to any political faction. He cannot abide within the cloisters of neoclassicism, the literary counterpart to the lost monarchy and the *ancien régime*, but neither can he entirely reject neoclassicism's striving for clarity and unity. Just as his political vision embraces both royalist and revolutionist as contending parts of a single humanity, his elastic and inclusive form encompasses both the heritage of neoclassicism and the anarchic or romantic or modern kinds of writing which oppose it. The text's problematic suggestion and frustration of generic expectations, its obdurate refusal to be labeled an epic or not an epic, a drama or not a drama, a history or not a history, fittingly reflect the age of flux in which it was written: the epic of the Revolution becomes, through the heroic virtuosity of its form, a revolutionary epic.

Two decades after the publication of his history, Carlyle provocatively defined his revolutionary form in the "Proem" to *Frederick the Great*. There, his fictitious literary theorist Gottfried Sauerteig declares that "All History is an imprisoned Epic," and Carlyle responds to his persona's statement by wishing that Sauerteig "had *dis*imprisoned it in this instance," instead of merely discoursing on "how grand it would be if disimprisoned" (*CW* 12: 17). Carlyle's conception of a disimprisoned epic is a practical embodiment of Sauerteig's thesis, enunciated in various essays of the early 1830s that "History . . . is the true Poetry" and that "Reality, if rightly interpreted, is grander than Fiction" (*CW* 28: 79). Viewed in the context of this thesis, the disimprisonment of epic performs two functions: the first of these, based on Sauerteig's equation of history and poetry, is to present in a highly wrought, continuous form "the Romance of Life" (*CW* 28: 325), which underlies and unites all historical events; the second, based on Sauerteig's assertion of the supremacy of reality over fiction, is to liberate the central romantic vision of epic from the formal restrictions of literary convention. In Sauerteig's eyes, epic machinery is "a miserable, meaningless Deception, kept-up by old use-and-wont alone," while epic deities are mere "Superannuated lumber." Because "the Epic Poems of old time, so long as they . . . had any complete impressiveness, were Histories, and understood to be narratives of *facts*," a believable modern epic must, for Sauerteig, be factually grounded in modern history (*CW* 28: 49–51). Working from the hypothesis that "the true Heroic Poems of these times [are] to be written with the *ink of Science*" (*Two Note Books* 188), and disregarding the Aristotelian separation of poetry from history that had dominated neoclassical criticism of epic, Carlyle chose for his first epic experiment the modern historical theme of the French Revolution.

The very fact that Carlyle was still attempting to define his radical form in the late 1850s reflects the degree to which *The French Revolution* remains an experimental thrust *toward* a disimprisoned epic rather than a complete attainment of it. There is something in the very nature of the form, as Carlyle defines it, which is necessarily perverse, paradoxical, and incomplete, something which resists stasis, confinement, or replication, and which depends for its very existence on the forms it aims to combat. Carlyle's history is a conscious formal experiment, based on a modern aesthetic of mixed and transitional forms derived in part from its author's perception of a radical social crisis in modern life, in part from his reading of modern European literature and criticism in the thirty years before 1837. It must be understood in the context of the experimental aesthetic of nineteenth-century literature, which he both used and helped to create: in Friedrich Schlegel's vision of a new kind of poetry which contains all other kinds but which cannot itself be contained or defined (*Fragments* 175–176), in John Ruskin's assertion that "the demand for perfection is always a sign of a misunderstanding of the ends of art,"[6] and in the formal experiments of writers such as Herman Melville and Walt Whitman.

* * *

In this study I am indebted to a rich tradition of Carlyle scholarship, extending from 1837 to the present. If I have relegated much of my explicit discussion of previous criticism to the notes, it is not to suggest that my argument springs *ex nihilo*. Rather, it is because of a sense that the field of Carlyle scholarship is so intriguing that it threatens to become a subject of critical exploration in itself. To use one of Carlyle's metaphors, tracing the source for a particular critical idea is like trying to find the original image in a hall of mirrors, and the acknowledgment of one source in the text would necessarily entail the discussion of two or three others. My first debt is to nineteenth-century periodical criticism, which, because of its sense of the modernity of Carlyle's text, perceptively defined the issues we continue to investigate. There has been no great divide in criticism of *The French Revolution*: rather than repudiating the initial insights of the early reviewers, contemporary critics continue to explore and substantiate the validity of their predecessors' perceptions. Next, there are the scholars of the first half of this century, such as C. F. Harrold, Carlisle Moore, Emery Neff, and Hill Shine, who did much of the detailed work on which subsequent critical judgments have been founded. They are followed by the authors of a seminal group of studies from the 1950s and 1960s, John Holloway, Kathleen Tillotson, Albert J. LaValley, George Levine, and G. B. Tennyson, who helped to reestablish our sense of Carlyle's modernity and our respect for his literary artistry. Tennyson's study, in particular, remains the best critical book on Carlyle, largely because it perceives the importance of his critical miscellanies to an understanding of his experiments in literary form. I shall be following rather closely Tennyson's method of moving from criticism to art, but because I am looking at Carlyle's early work from the standpoint of *The French Revolution* rather than *Sartor Resartus*, I shall point out some aspects of Carlyle's writing different from those Tennyson identifies. Naturally, I will depict *Sartor Resartus* less as an artistic terminus and more as a transitional work anticipating Carlyle's epic history, and my argument will implicitly challenge Tennyson's assumption that "Carlyle's merit as a literary artist . . . must stand or fall on *Sartor*."[7] Like all current Carlyle scholars, I owe much to the editors of the splendid Duke-Edinburgh edition of the Carlyles' letters. Finally, I am indebted to two scholars who have recently focused our attention on the importance of *The French Revolution*, John Clubbe and John D. Rosenberg. Professor Clubbe has demonstrated the value of taking Carlyle's reading of epic literature as a vital key to his creativity, and Professor Rosenberg has shown the necessity of a detailed reading of individual passages to a full sense of Carlyle's artistry. Both scholars have profitably attempted something I do not attempt, placing *The French Revolution* in the context of the works which follow it in Carlyle's canon.

* * *

I am grateful to the editors of the *Journal of English and Germanic Philology* for permission to reproduce material from my article "Allegory and Phantasmagory in *The French Revolution*," and to the editors of *Victorian Studies* for permission to reproduce material from my article "Carlyle, Whitman, and the Disimprisonment of Epic."

I wish to thank several scholars who have been generous with their criticism and encouragement: John Clubbe, Peter M. Daly, David J. DeLaura, Richard Dellamora, George P. Landow, Barry V. Qualls, John D. Rosenberg, and W. David Shaw.

I acknowledge with pleasure the assistance I received from faculty members of the Department of English at the University of Western Ontario, where I prepared an earlier, much different version of this study as my doctoral dissertation. In particular, I wish to thank Richard M. Stingle and Donald S. Hair, my unfailingly gracious and supportive thesis supervisors, and Thomas J. Collins and Geoffrey Rans. I also wish to thank my undergraduate professors at Wilfrid Laurier University, and especially Jane Campbell, my first guide through the Victorian age.

I am most thankful for the help of my friends and colleagues in the Department of English at Memorial University of Newfoundland, particularly Lawrence Mathews and Nicholas Watson, who generously volunteered their time to read this work in manuscript.

When this study appeared as a dissertation in 1983, it was dedicated "To my parents, Ross and Alice Cumming, with love and gratitude." Since then, my father and mother have died, but the love and the gratitude have not. I am grateful now to those who stand "in the place of parents," Renato and Betty Vecchi of Canandaigua, New York, and Grace Mertz of Wyebridge, Ontario. And I am always thankful for the support of my extended Canadian family, the Cummings, and my extended American family, the Vecchis.

To Linda Mary Vecchi, who has shared with me her great joy and love of life, I say thanks, with words borrowed from Walt Whitman:

> Camerado, I give you my hand!
> I give you my love more precious than money,
> I give you myself before preaching or law;
> Will you give me yourself? Will you come travel with me?
> Shall we stick by each other as long as we live?

A DISIMPRISONED EPIC

ONE

Carlyle Reading

In *The French Revolution*, argued the anonymous reviewer for the *Literary Gazette* in 1837, "There is nothing like a history of the events which took place; but, instead, there is a series of rhapsodical snatches, which may remind readers acquainted with the facts from previous histories and memoirs, what it is that the author is really writing about. By itself, his book is unintelligible."[1] Its critical vituperation notwithstanding, this observation accurately assesses the difficulty of Carlyle's text, which is designed for an especially capable and attentive reader. *The French Revolution* is, according to Carlyle's own description, "ruleless" (*Letters* 9: 82), for it is not governed by any one form of discourse, and it submits to no consistent mode of interpretation. Yet it is intensely dependent on traditional literary associations and inherited codes of reading. As "dense in meaning, as tightly-written, as rich in allusion, as Joyce's *Ulysses*,"[2] Carlyle's history shares with that work a paradox central to modern texts: because of their self-conscious modernity, they direct their audience repeatedly to tradition-laden modes of apprehension, invoked in new and often bizarre contexts. In addition, *The French Revolution*, like many other late-eighteenth- and nineteenth-century texts, enlists its reader as co-worker and co-creator, sharing in the author's imaginative difficulties. It demands the kind of reader sought by Laurence Sterne, who will "give-up the reins of his imagination into his author's hands" (quoted by Carlyle, *CW* 28: 24), or the implied reader of Goethe, who is invited by the deliberate difficulty of the text to help actively in the recreation of the author's vision.[3]

In its density Carlyle's history closely resembles Robert Browning's slightly later poem *Sordello* (1840), written in a form of "brother's speech," where unstated grammatical and logical connections are left to be supplied by an intensely sympathetic reader.[4] After enduring Browning's long and torturous text, Jane Welsh

Carlyle quipped that she was unsure whether Sordello was a man, a city, or a book, but her well-aimed barb might with equal justice have been turned on her husband's history, for after wrestling with its three difficult volumes, the reader can be forgiven for asking what precisely the French Revolution is. Carlyle's history of the Revolution appears to be written for readers so conversant with the event that they need no history of the Revolution. His text seems endlessly to play on some prior (yet nonexistent) history written in comprehensible English. His elliptical wording baffles and frustrates the reader. It is hardly inappropriate that Carlyle anticipates Browning's wording in the final paragraph of his text, when he bids farewell to his reader as to "the disembodied or not yet embodied spirit of a Brother" (*FR* 3: 323). At the end of nine hundred long pages, Carlyle's brotherly reader has been rewarded for his involvement, but he is left battered, exhausted, and not a little exasperated.

Why would a little-known Scot, newly relocated to London and desperately determined to establish himself as a writer, produce such a text? Why would Carlyle, who had been unable to market *Sartor Resartus* as a book, place such demands on his audience in *The French Revolution*?[5] At the time of its first appearance, various explanations were offered. The most caustic critics accused Carlyle of polluting English with Germanisms and of indulging himself in willful obscurity. "Classical absurdities; multitudes of new-coined words; and concocted phrases; illustrations which darken, and expositions which perplex; and a hundred other bewildering follies crush the sense of this work in every page," complained the *Literary Gazette.* Also censorious, but for a different reason, Herman Merivale argued in the *Edinburgh Review* that Carlyle was incapable of encompassing his myriad sources in a coherent picture of events. "His account of the Bastille affair, for example, extracted as it is from the pages of Besenval, Dussaulx, Fauchet, and we know not how many pamphleteers and newswriters more, is full of warlike clamour and riotous hubbub, just about as like the real event as the sieges in *Ivanhoe* and *Old Mortality.* After reading it through, the student would be quite as much puzzled as at the beginning, to know who took the Bastille, and why it surrendered; for the eloquent narrator has all but missed the one military point of the story."[6] Yet while there were those who found Carlyle willfully obscure or incoherent, there were others who found his unintelligibility a definitive and necessary feature of his art. The *Examiner* warmly defended Carlyle by declaring that "Every original thing must speak its own language."[7] And the *Yale Literary Magazine* praised him for the interpretive labor his text demands: the reader of Carlyle cannot expect that complex modern truths can be registered in a simple form or that they "will be instilled into him without labor of his own. It is as if one should read the Novum Organum of Lord Bacon, confident of understanding it, yet bestowing only the same measure of attention with which he would peruse Peveril of the Peak."[8] It is from these critics, with their sense of Carlyle's necessary obscurity, that I shall take my lead, as I attempt to demonstrate how the formal complexity of his text grows from a consciously formulated modern aesthetic, based on his personal model of the process of reading.

I

We cannot understand the formal working of Carlyle's artistic writings without sympathetically encountering what he read, how he read, how he understood the act of interpretation, and how he transmuted his reading into art. Therefore, before we look at *The French Revolution* we must first understand his early reading as a source for his literary inspiration. For Carlyle, reading is the quintessential human activity. The literary act of reading the text is contiguous with the moral act of reading the universe, since both involve the decoding and recreation, in word or action, of the meaning embodied in a system of signs, the book or the world. Despite his lifelong desire to affect the workings of his society by inciting concerted and heroic action, Carlyle's most important achievements were gained in the interpretation and creation of the written word, in his reading of literature and in his verbal recreation of his reading in his art. "Thomas Carlyle was a writer of books, and he was nothing else," observes Augustine Birrell, one of his most discerning nineteenth-century critics. "Beneath this judgement he would have winced, but have remained silent, for the facts are so."[9]

An inevitable initial consideration in assessing Carlyle's reading is its sheer expanse and diversity. Hill Shine's catalogue of *Carlyle's Early Reading* presents 3,184 numbered entries, and its alphabetical index of references reads like an epic catalogue or litany of miscellaneous learning.[10] Take, for instance, this sequence from the P's: Pascal, Passeroni, Paul, Paullini, Pauw, Payne, Peck, Percy, Persius, Pestalozzi, Petitot, Petrarch, Petronius, *Philanthropic Gazette*, Pickering, Pictet, Pinkerton, Piozzi, Pitt, Planche, Plato, Playfair, Plutarch, Polidor, *Poor Laws Report*, Pope, and Porphyry. Or this from the W's: Wieland, Wilkie, *Wilkina- und Niflungasaga*, Williams, Wilmot, Wilson, Winckelmann, *Wise Men of Gotham*, Wither, Wolf, Wollstonecraft, Woltmann, Wolzogen, Wood, Wordsworth, Wright, and *Wyfe of Auchtirmwchty*. The daunting heterogeneity of these references does not lend itself to any simple configuration. What does Alexander Pope have to do with the *Poor Laws Report*, we might ask, and how does Winckelmann connect with the *Wise Men of Gotham*? The sheer mass of references, meanwhile, prompts us to wonder how much of Carlyle's reading appears in his art, and how radically his conception of artistic form is affected by the nature of his own contact with other writers' texts. An immediate suggestion might be that the striking variety of Carlyle's reading contributes in some way to his multifarious aesthetic, that diverse forms internalized through attentive study are later called upon to answer specific creative needs.

In determining the importance of Professor Shine's 3,184 entries to an understanding of Carlyle's writings, we must address the question of his competence and flexibility as a reader. One extreme position, largely antithetical to my own, regards Carlyle as naive, haphazard, or insensitive in his encounters with the literary works of others. A specific instance (and a convincing one) of Carlyle's insensitivity to literary models is offered by William Allingham in his diary, when he bemoans Carlyle's inability to comprehend the principles of verse:

> He has read a vast quantity of Poetry, and admired much that he found there; countless phrases from Shakespeare and Milton are embedded in his writings; he always speaks of Aeschylus, Dante, Shakespeare, Goethe as men of the highest rank. Moreover, he tried hard, tried over and over again, and in many various metres, to write Poetry. In his verse you can hear the sound of an original man, vigour, quaintness, imagery are there, and for a few lines, less or more, the movement may go right, but only by chance; presently it goes all awry. It is not a question of choosing or happening to be rough, or of taking liberties: the Writer, after reading many thousand lines of the best Poets, remains entirely insensible to the

> *structure* of verse, to the indispensable rules derived from the nature of the human mind and ear.[11]

For some, Allingham's indictment of Carlyle for his insensitivity to verse might call in question his openness to any form of literature. And we would not have to look beyond Allingham to find a reason for this insensitivity in the obduracy of Carlyle's mind. Witness the following delightful yet damning anecdote of his refusal, late in life, to quote Shakespeare's epitaph correctly:

> We had been talking, on some previous day or days, about Stratford on Avon, to which I had paid a visit this May. When I quoted the tombstone lines 'Good Friend, for Jesus sake forbear,' etc., C. wished to correct me to 'Sweet Friend,' and would not be gainsaid: indeed he has used the 'Sweet Friend,' etc., several times in his writings and very frequently in conversation, and would not give it up save on compulsion. To-day I brought proof in my pocket in the shape of a photograph of the stone with its inscription clearly legible, and as we sat on a tree-trunk I showed this to him in the quietest possible way—(not the least air of triumph, overt or covert). He looked at the photograph, said nothing or very little ('Ah, well,' perhaps, or the like), and handed it back without any formal retractation [*sic*], though further argument was plainly impossible; and not long afterwards (I mean a few weeks later) he was using his beloved old formula, 'Sweet Friend,' as if nothing had happened, and so continued.[12]

Carlyle's detractors would be well warranted in citing this anecdote as an emblem of his refusal to admit facts incompatible with his inflexible notions. Yet Carlyle's insistent assimilation of borrowed matter to his own rigid conceptual categories is only one of his mental processes, and should be seen in conjunction with his accommodation of his mental patterns to the productions of other minds. If Carlyle was one of the nineteenth century's leading proponents of a puritan world view—if he lived his entire life according to a few precepts learned from James and Margaret Carlyle of Ecclefechan—he was also one of the century's foremost critics of dead creeds and liturgies. And if he rejected eighteenth-century rationalism as a limited and irreligious mode of thought, he equally accepted the truths of such writers as Gibbon and

Voltaire. It is the rich interplay of stubborness with inquisitiveness that makes Carlyle such a fascinating study. Without denying Carlyle's intellectual recalcitrance, and without ignoring the regrettable ossification of his ideas, especially in his later writings, we should acknowledge the breadth of his reading, his reception of works and ideas which were foreign to his fundamental modes of thought, and the liveliness of his critical intelligence, which responded so positively to modern criticism and literature and which framed from them seminal observations on the nature of reading and writing in the modern world.

The telling evidence for Carlyle's openness to literature and criticism lies in his miscellanies, which are neither so incidental nor so negligible as some scholars have insisted, but which are vitally significant exercises in reading. Philip Rosenberg, for example, errs when he dismisses the early essays as "a group of wordy and convoluted studies of German literature with . . . little intrinsic interest." "Because their connection with Carlyle's later works is far from apparent," Rosenberg argues, "they have been on the whole either treated separately as works of philosophy or critical theory—a treatment they hardly merit—or ignored by students who wish to begin with the far more promising *Sartor*."[13] G. B. Tennyson found in his book on *Sartor Resartus* that it is nearly impossible to understand that work without comprehending the miscellanies.[14] And it is not reasonable to think that the preparatory works which had had such a profound effect on the shaping of *Sartor Resartus* should fail to influence *The French Revolution*, written but a few years later. Albert J. LaValley's assessment of the essays is more accurate than Rosenberg's, but still inadequate. The essays "should neither be dismissed . . . nor be salvaged as valuable literary criticism," he writes, for they are "essays in the root sense of the word, attempts at a voice and role. . . . Not primarily critical writings, they are autobiographical acts of self-discovery."[15] Although we benefit from the caveat that there are more systematic and brilliant critical thinkers than Carlyle in the nineteenth century, we need not be so hasty as to dismiss his critical ideas out of hand. As Anne K. Mellor has demonstrated in *English Romantic Irony*, a serious consideration of Carlyle's critical thought in the light of a more renowned contemporary like Friedrich Schlegel can be fruitful.[16]

Carlyle's essays, far from being random judgments on unrelated authors, insistently address the problem of form: how art and nature function symbolically, how a particular kind of art reflects the temper of the age in which it is produced, how an author embodies a vision in a form, and how the reader recreates that vision. Carlyle's overriding concern with form necessitates for him a comprehensive understanding of what it is to read. According to the account of reading presented in the critical miscellanies, the reader must actively and sympathetically recreate, through the inadequate medium of language, the original conception of the author. In order to do this, the reader must come to understand the structural and aesthetic principles according to which the text is shaped. The reader must engage in close, multiple readings of the text, designed to discover its underlying unity, and resist a superficial discussion of its disparate components—the "hop-skip-and-jump style of criticism" favored by some nineteenth-century journals.[17] Faced with daunting texts like *Faust* or the novels of Jean Paul Richter, the reader must abandon or qualify previous generic and evaluative perceptions, since great modern works of art challenge existing literary codes and create the aesthetic assumptions by which they are to be judged. The reader must continually reassess received notions of form, using previous generic codes, perhaps, as fixed points from which to locate the author's new position, but inevitably going beyond them. Furthermore, the reader must recognize that the formal principles inherent in the text are constantly changing: an allegorical sentence might without warning be followed by a symbolic one, and classical poise might unexpectedly give way to romantic confusion.

As we might expect, Carlyle's most sustained accounts of the reading process appear in his essays on Goethe and his contemporaries, the great modern champions of deliberate obscurity, whose works he translated and made popular in the 1820s. Carlyle shares with the modern Germans an insistence that "the merits and characteristics of a Poet are not to be set forth by logic; but to be gathered by personal, . . . deep and careful inspection of his works" (*CW* 26: 209). Like his German models, he attempts to judge the form of a work by reference to its peculiar construction, rather than to preexistent literary codes. As he observes in his article on Goethe's *Helena,* "If an artist has conceived his subject in the secret shrine of his own mind, and knows . . . that it is true and pure, he may choose his own manner of exhibiting it, and will generally be the fittest to choose it well" (*CW* 26: 149). Carlyle follows the Germans in assigning a vigorously active role to the reader, believing like them that the knowledge that can be passively apprehended by the discursive reason is inferior to the less accessible truths embodied in the symbol, which must be tenaciously ferreted out. As Kathleen Wheeler writes, the Germans' fragmentary and symbolic discourses, "by portraying the author's mind in an active grappling which remains uncompleted and indecisive, . . . stir the reader to active thinking," for "the process of the artist's labour to decipher the symbolic language of nature must be repeated as the reader deciphers the 'hieroglyphs' of the aesthetic object."[18] While reading Goethe's *Faust*, Carlyle writes,

> The reader is kept on the alert, ever conscious of his own active coöperation; light breaks on him, and clearer and clearer vision, by degrees; till at last the whole lovely Shape comes forth, definite, it may be, and bright with heavenly radiance, or fading, on this side and that, into vague expressive mystery; but true in both cases, and beautiful with nameless enchantments, as the poet's own eye may have beheld it. We love it the more for the labour it has given us: we almost feel as if we ourselves had assisted in its creation. And herein lies the highest merit of a piece, and the proper art of reading it. We have not *read* an author till we have seen his object, whatever it may be, as *he* saw it. . . .
>
> Everywhere in life, the true question is, not what we *gain*, but what we *do*: so also in intellectual matters, in conversation, in reading, which is more precise and careful conversation, it is not what we *receive*, but what we are made to *give*, that chiefly contents and profits us. (*CW* 26: 149-150)

Carlyle's utterances on reading restate the experimental aesthetic of the modern Germans and undercut any residual sense on our part that he is naive in the art of reading or in the nature of literary form. Indeed, the principles of form and interpretation that Carlyle identifies in his essays have remained central to our understanding of modern writing, whether that of Goethe and Friedrich Schlegel or that of Joyce, Pound, and Eliot.

II

Even if we accept the assumption that Carlyle is a competent and intelligent reader, however, we must yet ascertain how much of his reading is reflected in his own literary works. That he was much concerned with the form of his works is demonstrated by the frequent references to style in his letters and by the painstaking rewriting evident in the few of his manuscripts we now have. But awareness of a problem does not in itself assure its resolution. The question, bluntly stated, is this: did the torment that Carlyle caused himself (and those around him) over the matter of form produce any aesthetically pleasing or valuable results? James Russell Lowell offers a classic nineteenth-century statement of the view that it did not: "With a conceptive imagination vigorous beyond any in his generation, with a mastery of language equalled only by the greatest poets, he wants altogether the plastic imagination, the shaping faculty, which would have made him a poet in the highest sense. He is a preacher and a prophet—anything you will—but an artist he is not, and never can be."[19] Even so sympathetic a critic as John Clubbe expresses only limited approbation of Carlyle's efforts in this area: "Carlyle is an artist, and a very great one," he justly argues, "but without an organizing structure, a shaping model, he increasingly botched the problem of form, always the weakest point in his literary endeavors and the one he most agonized over."[20] Without denying Carlyle's reliance on inherited models, I would go much further than most scholars in asserting both the degree of consciousness and the degree of success in his literary experiments. The critical miscellanies reveal recurrent notions about the nature of form and the nature of modern writing and reading, which resurface, often in the most unexpected contexts, in his creative works. G. B. Tennyson's study of *Sartor Resartus* demonstrates the undeniable resonance between criticism and art that produced that work, and a further examination of the writings that followed in the decade after *Sartor* will reveal even more compellingly Carlyle's artistic resolution of problems raised by his early reading. In his adoption of particular literary kinds and in his recombination of them according to new and aberrant conceptions of artistic unity, Carlyle presents bravura rewritings of the masses of diverse reading indexed by Professor Shine.

For a specific example of the resonance between criticism and art, let us turn to Carlyle's reading of Goethe's *Faust*. In general, Carlyle lauds Goethe for recognizing that poetry must address itself to the present, unencumbered by outdated and spurious enchantments. "The divinities and demons, the witches, spectres, and fairies, are vanished from the world, never again to be recalled," he writes: "but the Imagination which created these still lives, and will forever live in man's soul; and can again pour its wizard light over the Universe, and summon forth enchantments as lovely or impressive, and which its sister faculties will not contradict" (*CW* 23: 29). Carlyle recognizes a central paradox of modern art, that it cannot consort with obsolete phantasms yet urgently needs the "wizard light" of the imagination. In his essay "Goethe's *Helena*," he outlines Goethe's artistic response to this paradox: *Faust*, he notes, negotiates a compromise between an inherited story and mythical apparatus, on the one hand, and the modern theme of salvation in nineteenth-century life, on the other; Goethe cleverly "retains the supernatural vesture of the story, but retains it with the consciousness, on his and our part, that it is a chimera" (*CW* 26: 156). In the language of romantic irony, he creates "an authorial consciousness that is simultaneously affirming and mocking its own creation."[21] Faced with an analogous problem in *The French Revolution*, Carlyle transposes his insights into ironic form, shaped partly by his reading of Goethe, to a new context, by allowing the characters of past mythologies to people his account of modern French history, by turning his Madame Dubarrys, his Marats, and his Marie Antoinettes into witches, demons, and fairies. Despite his fear that literature might become an infinitely recessive verbal universe, "one boundless self-devouring Review" (*CW* 28: 25) with no exterior reference, Carlyle recognizes the multiple perspective of criticism through which we see the critic reading the artist reading other artists and critics, and with his self-reflexive texts, which identify and comment on their own genres, he invites us to a similar recognition of his multilayered writing. Only when we place ourselves in Carlyle's position, and read him reading, do we apprehend the fully ironic nature of his works with their bizarre readings and rewritings of literary forms. And only then do we adequately appreciate him as a conscious artist.

We should not make Carlyle a literary artist by default, only because we find alternative views of him as philosopher and teacher obsolete or repugnant. If we continue to study Carlyle as an artist—important in himself, and not only for his massive influence or for his worth as an exemplum of the Victorian mind—we will have to continue to value the conscious element of his craft, to appreciate his awareness of the literary revolution of his age, and to respect the deliberation which characterizes his artistic responses to that revolution. We should not let the disquieting sense that the tone and emphasis of the late-Victorian adulation of Carlyle are frequently wrong inhibit our own attempts to give him his due of praise.[22] I am not suggesting that we should dress Carlyle in our own image, picture him as a proto-modernist or as a proto-postmodernist, or teach him to utter our critical shibboleths. Such a procedure is offensive, since it takes our thoughts and concerns too smugly as an exclusive norm against which to judge a previous era. Yet I would suggest that many of the seminal observations of the twentieth century's "New" or modernist criticism and "New-New" or post-modernist criticism are anticipated by what Carlyle calls (in the lower case) the "new Criticism" of the early nineteenth century (*CW* 26: 52). Our sense in Carlyle's writings of a dialogic imagination, such as has been brought to our attention by the deserved popularity of Mikhail Bakhtin, may lead us to reexamine the nineteenth-century origins of our present aesthetics of internal dialogue and deliberate self-contradiction.[23] If we discover surprisingly fresh and innovative ideas in Carlyle, if we find a concern with signs and texts which seems arrestingly like our own, we might assume that we have examined his work retrospectively and endowed it with a formal ingenuity and critical profundity that it never in itself possessed. Yet we might with better reason suspect that we have never given full credit either to the author or to his age.

Until recent years, there has persisted a disinclination to respond to Carlyle with enthusiasm and respect. While many critics made perfunctory gestures toward the virtuosity of Carlyle's outlandish style (gestures still too largely reserved for *Sartor Resartus*), they compensated by suggesting not only that he was a racist, a reactionary, and a misogynist (all of which at times and in part he was) but also that he was inevitably and essentially these things. Carlyle fell victim to his own favorite weapon, the stinging or binding epigram: having worked such damage with his squibs on logic mills, Shooting Niagara, and corn-lawing aristocracy, he was himself imprisoned by the labels of hero worshipper, Calvinist without the theology, earnest Victorian, and puritanical Scot—but only imprisoned, for as Birrell notes, "Carlyle cannot be killed by an epigram, nor can the many influences that moulded him be referred to any single source."[24] A resurgent critical interest in Carlyle's artistry, the publication of new biographies, the reediting of the Carlyles' letters, and now, at last, the reediting of Carlyle's works, have all signaled a change in critical temper. As we have reread Carlyle, we have come to a new appreciation of his literary richness and power. We have come to see his badness and heterogeneity as strengths arising from an acute sense of a lost congruity and coherence, and to acknowledge the rifts and self-contradictions which cut across his works not as the symptoms of personal or literary schizophrenia, but as the characteristic marks of a writer who endeavors to address a tormented age in its own voice.[25]

In the following chapters, I shall begin by tracing Carlyle's conception of modern criticism, with particular reference to the issue of form: I shall use "form" in a rather flexible manner that will, I hope, fittingly reflect the range of his interests, both in the definition of specific literary kinds and in the description of the broad principles which generate unity (or disunity) in a literary work. Having discussed Carlyle's responses to neoclassical literary theory, his examinations of traditional genres, and his conception of modern and mixed forms, I shall proceed to demonstrate how his critical ideas are embodied artistically in his literary experiments from *Sartor Resartus* to *The French Revolution*. My discussion of Carlyle's art will involve a series of formal oppositions, which reflect his tendency to encase his thought in binary systems, and his deliberate cultivation of internal contradiction: epic and history, epic and drama, document and myth, satire and elegy, tragedy and farce, emblem and fragment, allegory and phantasmagory. The neatness of these pairings is in part a reflection of the residual systematic bent in Carlyle's mind (an inheritance from his eighteenth-century reading), and in part an illusion created by the agglomeration of pairs which ultimately cannot be aligned in any obvious manner. Some of the terms in these pairings are literary, others extraliterary; some deal with genres, some with modes or subdivisions of genres. A challenging multi-axial work like *The French Revolution* demands that we keep in mind simultaneously several diverse and even contending pairings: Carlyle may establish in close proximity to each other pitched battle between the Aristotelian kinds of epic and drama and textual warfare between the divergent symbolic modes of allegory and phantasmagory. My middle chapters will address the interrelation of these various forms. And in the final chapter, I shall attempt to place *The French Revolution*, the most sustained and complete artistic embodiment of the aesthetic principles that Carlyle derived from his early reading, in the context of other nineteenth-century experiments in epic form. I shall try to show how it goes beyond tradition and impels its reader to rechart the field of nineteenth-century British literature.

TWO

The Critic as Copernicus

In Book Three of *Tristram Shandy*, Laurence Sterne rails against the pedantic connoisseurs of art, whose heads "are stuck so full of rules and compasses . . . that a work of genius had better go to the devil at once, than stand to be prick'd and tortured to death by 'em." Sterne pictures one of these connoisseurs censuring a popular new work: "Oh! 'tis out of all plumb, my Lord," the critic wails, "quite an irregular thing!—not one of the angles at the four corners was a right angle.—I had my rule and compasses, &c. my Lord, in my pocket." "And," he continues, "for the epick poem, your lordship bid me look at;—upon taking the length, breadth, height, and depth of it, and trying them at home upon an exact scale of *Bossu's*,—'tis out, my Lord, in every one of its dimensions."[1] In his essay titled "State of German Literature" Carlyle, the critical defender of many "an irregular thing," including his beloved *Tristram Shandy*, and soon to be the perpetrator of his own irregular masterworks, echoes Sterne and appropriates his metaphor of the critic as geometer when he too caricatures René Le Bossu, author of the unrepentantly systematic and greatly influential *Traité du poëme épique* (1675), as a restrictive arbiter measuring literary genius with his "scale and compasses" (*CW* 26: 50). The recourse of both authors to the figure of Le Bossu reflects not only his importance in charting the most highly regarded of the genres but also his function as an exemplum of what the strict neoclassicists accept and what their detractors insistently reject in generic criticism.

To John Dryden and John Dennis, who disseminated his definitions of epic in Britain, Le Bossu represents method, order, and clarity: the rational division of the creative process into its component parts, the preservation of discrete forms, and the refusal to call a thing by its wrong name. To Sterne and Carlyle and their contemporaries, Le Bossu presents a contrary aspect of art hamstrung by criticism, unity dismembered by arbitrary divisions, and creation mechanized by false rules.[2] His treatise, together with the *Art Poétique* (1674) of Nicholas Boileau, characterizes for them the French neoclassical code, injudiciously imported by the British neoclassicists, which consists of increasingly arid rehearsals of Aristotle's *Poetics*, and which is imprisoned within largely sterile and obsolete concerns: the best kind of machinery for an epic, the proper manner of framing an action to inculcate a particular moral, the relative greatness of epic and tragedy, and the question of whether or not an epic might be permitted to end unhappily. Thus the "exact scale" or ruler which images the neoclassical ideals of measured judgment, impartial evaluation, and accepted norms is denigrated as the instrument of critical prescription and oppression, while the compasses, symbolic representations of symmetry and intellectual distinctions, are rejected as the tracers of specious generic boundaries which must be consciously transgressed by the modern writer.

I

If the representative image of neoclassicism is the enclosing circle, that of the "new Criticism" (as Carlyle calls it in "State of German Literature") is the transgression of the circle's limits. The disavowal of established boundaries in modern writing is well summed up in Friedrich Schlegel's pointed assertion, at the end of the eighteenth century, that "All the classical poetical genres have now become ridiculous in their rigid purity" (*Fragments* 150). Lesser authors might choose to remain within the circumscribed areas assigned to the various literary kinds, Carlyle argues, for they "are men whom Bossu might measure with his scales and compasses as strictly as he pleased." Yet the great modern writers see beyond them and pass them unalarmed: Herder, Schiller, and Goethe "are men of another stature and form of movement, whom Bossu's scale and compasses could not measure without difficulty, or rather not at all" (*CW* 26: 50). Unprofitable inquiries about fixed kinds and catalogues of the parts of discourse are replaced by new speculations on the common properties of poetry and prose, the various possible models for artistic unity, the historical development of genres, and the characteristic forms of modern art. "The grand question is not now a question concerning the qualities of diction, the coherence of metaphors, the fitness of sentiments, the general logical truth, in a work of art, as it was some half-century ago among most critics," Carlyle writes in "State of German Literature," but rather "a question on the essence and peculiar life of the poetry itself" (*CW* 26: 51). The modern emphasis on essence and "peculiar life" repudiates the neoclassical emphasis on itemized ingredients and universal codes.

Yet the new criticism's transgressive impetus is complemented by a desire for a systematic reformulation of the genres that owes much to the methodical tradition of neoclassicism.[3] This desire appears strikingly in Friedrich Schlegel's metaphor of the modern critic as Copernicus remapping the poetic skies, which offers a complementary image to the circles traced by the compasses of Le Bossu. "Most of the ways of conceiving a poetical world are still as primitive as the old pre-Copernican ideas of astronomy," writes Schlegel, adopting Immanuel Kant's metaphor for the modern revolution in philosophy. While Ptolemaic critics, armed with "mere dead pedantry designed for people with limited vision," produce static models of an unchanging poetic universe, modern critics perceive that "in the universe of poetry nothing stands still, everything is developing and changing and moving harmoniously; and even the comets obey invariable laws of motion. But until the course of these heavenly bodies can be calculated and their return predicted, the true world system of poetry won't have been discovered" (*Fragments* 237). Schlegel's metaphor reflects the degree to which the new criticism proceeds not by jettisoning generic distinctions, but by reassessing them, not by ignoring Aristotle, but by rereading him, not by rejecting the circle's clarity and coherence, but by retracing it and enlarging its compass. The new criticism is embodied, as Carlyle argues, "in systems . . . coherent, distinct and methodical, no less than, on their much shallower foundation, the systems of Boileau and Blair" (*CW* 26: 52). Transgression and reformulation work together to further the European revolution in literature and criticism: the ragged efforts of modern writers to escape from imprisoning critical codes effect a necessary development in Europe's striving for an enlarged and renovated literary coherence, just as the chaos of the French Revolution impels society toward a rediscovery of the cosmos lost with the abandoned order of the *ancien régime*. And if clarity and coherence are not possible in the art of the 1830s, it is because the new age of synthesis has not yet fully arrived.

For Carlyle, the most striking manifestation of the European critical revolution and the most concerted attempt to discover a new literary code for the modern age appears in the writings of the

German aestheticians, who make new divisions of the poetic universe, while exposing received categories of discourse to historical revaluation.[4] Friedrich Schiller, in his essay on naive and sentimental poetry, creates a polycentric scheme of classification by adding literary categories to those offered by the standard genres; he suggests a division of literature into the naive and sentimental and further proposes satire, elegy, and idyll as three modes distinct from the genres of the same name. In his correspondence with Goethe, Schiller engages in a prolonged dialogue on the nature of epic and drama, which culminates in their collaborative essay on epic and dramatic poetry.[5] Schiller's explorations in the naive and sentimental are continued in the Schlegels' discussions of the differences between Greek and modern, or classical and romantic, art. August Wilhelm Schlegel, in his lectures on drama, suggests a triadic division of literature (later developed at great length by Hegel in his treatise on aesthetics) into the calm narrative form of epic, the expressive musical form of lyric, and the hybrid form of drama which incorporates elements of both. Friedrich Schlegel, sensing the inadequacy of previous systems of classification, reevaluates the status of generic criticism itself, questioning whether poetry should be divided at all or whether it should be considered an integral body. He isolates the generic complexity of modern literature as a characteristic instance of the radical disparity between ancient and modern art, contending that while the classical genres are fixed, and therefore subject to systematic examination, modern and romantic forms are still developing and elusive. Schlegel's inquiries into the nature of genre produce his innovative generic designations of novels as "the Socratic dialogues of our time," of the dialogue as a "garland of fragments," and of his own essay on Greek poetry as "a mannered prose hymn" (*Fragments* 145, 170, 143). Like Carlyle after him, Schlegel perversely confounds accepted generic categories: "The *Confessions* of Rousseau is in my opinion a most excellent novel," he wryly remarks, "*Héloise* only a very mediocre one."[6] Jean Paul Richter, in his *Vorschule der Aesthetik*, continues the investigations of Schiller and the Schlegels into the difference between ancient and modern poetry. He denigrates facile theories of genre based on Plato's distinction between *mimesis* and *diagesis*, noting acerbically that "mere formalities, at least in poetry, are not forms,"[7] and restates the triadic division of literature into epic, lyric, and drama. He discusses the novel, the ode, the elegy, the idyll, and the fable, as well as their ironic intermingling in modern literature.

Even though Carlyle occasionally expresses dissatisfaction with the Germans' exaltation of art or complains that their methodical examinations of form degenerate into triviality, he respects their systematic bent and heralds their centrality in the shaping of modern literary thought: Germany, he maintains in *German Romance*, has produced "elaborate laws" and "profound systems," whereas Britain has witnessed "Literary anarchy; for the Pandects of Blair and Bossu are obsolete or abrogated, but no new code supplies their place; and, author and critic, each sings or says that which is right in his own eyes" (*CW* 21: 261). Carlyle shares the Germans' sense of generic revaluation, their repudiation of inflexible Ptolemaic models, and their Copernican awareness of newly discovered literary kinds; with them, he works to liberate the emergent forms of nineteenth-century literature from the crystalline spheres of neoclassicism. Carlyle's awareness of the revolutionary implications of modern German criticism manifests itself in the metaphors he uses to describe it. In "Novalis," he portrays the conflict of the new school with the old as a kind of literary warfare, "regular and guerrilla" (*CW* 27: 18). In "Goethe's Works," he renders the meeting between the young Goethe and Johann Christoph Gottsched, the German counterpart of Le Bossu, as a dynastic overthrow. Goethe, perceiving the obsolescence of "the Gottschedic world" of criticism, and acknowledging that "in literature as in philosophy there is neither landmark nor loadstar," is "a young Zeus come to dethrone old Saturn" (*CW* 27: 417–418). The mythic conflict of Olympian moderns and Saturnian neoclassicists reiterates the revolutionary and cosmographic sense embodied in Friedrich Schlegel's Copernican metaphor.

While generic revaluation in Britain is less systematic, Carlyle regards it as a complementary force, different in its degree of development but not in its nature from German literary thought. He insists that the new criticism is not a specific movement deriving from Ludwig Tieck and the Schlegels, or even from Goethe and Schiller, but a larger European phenomenon. Throughout Britain, Carlyle demands in *German Romance*, "who has not lifted up his voice with double vigour in praise of Shakspeare and Nature, and vituperation of French taste and French philosophy? who has not heard of the glories of old English literature; the wealth of Queen Elizabeth's age; the penury of Queen Anne's; and the inquiry whether Pope was a poet?" Even in France, he concludes, "doubts are beginning to be entertained, and even expressed, about Corneille and the Three Unities" (*CW* 21: 261). The innovative forms of German literature have their counterparts in Britain, as Carlyle's critical writings suggest: *Tristram Shandy* and *Don Juan* parallel the novels of Richter and the plays of Tieck as self-conscious fictions, the poems of Ossian and *Childe Harold's Pilgrimage* complement *Werther* as embodiments of the new romantic spirit, and *Tom Jones* stands with *Wilhelm Meister* as an experiment in the epic novel. The Germans' indecorous mingling and transmutation of genres is paralleled by early nineteenth-century innovations in British poetry, where lyric becomes fused with ballad in the lyrical ballad and with drama in the "lyrical drama" *Prometheus Unbound*, and where the epic—for Dryden and other neoclassicists "the greatest work which the soul of man is capable to perform"— is recast in such diverse examples as *The Excursion*, *The Revolt of Islam*, and *Hyperion*.[8]

Carlyle shares with his contemporaries an insistent concern with the historical basis and development of genres.[9] In "Early German Literature" and "Historic Survey of German Poetry," extracted from his aborted history of German literature, he divides literary history into three successive periods with their corresponding literary kinds. The first period is the heroic and chivalric age of fancy, when "knights-errant tilted, and ladies' eyes rained bright influences" (*CW* 27: 275). It is an age of primal innocence and untroubled lyricism, whose characteristic forms are troubadours' songs, epics, and chivalric romances, and whose highest expression is in the *Nibelungenlied*. This age ends with the death of chivalry, when "the world seems to have rhymed itself out" and when "those chivalrous roundelays, heroic tales, mythologies, and quaint love-sicknesses" have become obsolete. At this time, Carlyle writes, the "graceful minuet-dance of Fancy" yields "to the toilsome, thorny pilgrimage of Understanding" (*CW* 27: 280), imagination gives way to didacticism, and poetry disappears, trading its "heavenly vesture and Ariel-harp" for "ferula and horn-book" (*CW* 27: 283). In the didactic age of understanding, whose typical forms are "Apologues, Fables, Satires, Exhortations and all manner of edifying Moralities" (*CW* 27: 283), the spirit of instruction transforms all literary kinds, including epic in the comic beast fable *Reynard the Fox*, comedy in *Till Eulenspiegel*, and tragedy in "the wild mythus of *Faust*" (*CW* 27: 344). Traditional genres reappear in more prosaic garb: "The Madrigal had passed into the Apologue," writes Carlyle, "the Heroic Poem, with its supernatural machinery and sentiment, into the Fiction of practical Life: in which latter species a prophetic eye might have discerned the coming *Tom Joneses* and

Wilhelm Meisters; and with still more astonishment, the *Minerva Presses* of all nations" (*CW* 27: 302). The exclusive didacticism that culminates in the most arid productions of the eighteenth century gives way to a resurgence of the poetic spirit when, "from among Parisian Erotics, rickety Sentimentalism, Court aperies, and hollow Dulness striving in all hopeless courses, we behold the giant spirit of Germany awaken as from long slumber" (*CW* 27: 345–346). The third period—heralded by the formal innovations of modern German literature but not yet fully achieved—is the age of reason, which unites the limited fancy of the first age with the limited understanding of the second.

Carlyle's tripartite schema of literary history links his interest in literary kinds with his central myth of modern life and with his conception of the modern artist's integrative function. His three divisions of literary history correspond to his three divisions of history in general into the age of initial belief, the age of doubt, and the age of renewed belief. His account of generic development, concerned as much with spirit as with form, traces human progress from a harmonious yet incomplete paradise, through a fall into unimaginative rationalism, to a redemption in the regenerate new age, which he describes to Goethe as "a period of new Spirituality and Belief; . . . a new revelation of Nature, and the Freedom and Infinitude of Man, wherein Reverence is again rendered compatible with Knowledge, and Art and Religion are one."[10] Carlyle's use of a Judeo-Christian pattern of apostasy and salvation, his depiction of the reintegration of humanity's constituent elements, and his image of the sleeping giant reawakened, embody central romantic myths of the regenerate modern spirit. His description of the age of reason reflects his conception of the modern artist as the reformulator of divergent literary traditions, working through a necessary stage of heterogeneity and indecorous roughness toward a new completeness and coherence. His account of the historical development of genres manifests the triadic pattern of thesis, antithesis, and synthesis, or unity, plurality, and totality, repeatedly adopted in the generic systems of the modern German aestheticians.[11]

II

Central to Carlyle's tripartite schema of generic development is his obsession with the decline and obsolescence of literary kinds.

According to Carlyle, each genre is born in an age peculiarly suited to it. In its initial stages, congruity exists between its form and its worldview. As time passes, the reality that engenders the genre changes, but the genre itself, retarded in its development by literary conventions and ossified by prescriptive critical codes, does not. Form and worldview no longer correspond. Consequently, the genre must either undergo a radical transformation or succumb to obsolescence, valued only by undiscriminating readers and antiquarians. The epic, to give a predominant specific example, begins for Carlyle as a true account of valorous deeds in a heroic age. The transition from genuine admiration to false convention that begins with Virgil and that is reduced to absurdity by Le Bossu and Boileau renders the form of epic unaccountable to its vision, as invocations to muses, beginnings *in medias res*, and divine machinery become more important than the great deeds of great men. Moreover, the marvelous poetic forms honored by tradition and prescribed by criticism become irrelevant to a rationalistic and prosaic age. In the modern world, the epic spirit must show itself in diverse examples quite unlike the monolithic form described by the neoclassical critics. Carlyle therefore discovers it in a variety of manifestations, historical in Voltaire's *Henriade*, biographical in Boswell's *Johnsoniad*, agrarian in the Corn-Law Rhymer's *Village Patriarch*, civic in Goethe's *Hermann und Dorothea*, comic in his *Reynard the Fox*, and novelistic in his *Wilhelm Meister*.

The epic novel exemplifies for Carlyle the transformation of traditional poetic kinds into modern prose counterparts. Henry Fielding notes the development of this form in his preface to *Joseph Andrews*, arguing that the scope and intention of a work, rather than its metrical or nonmetrical rendition, determines its kind. Schiller refers to it in his correspondence with Goethe, when he comments on the paradoxical relation of poetic spirit and prosaic form in *Wilhelm Meister*. Richter remarks on it when he designates *Don Quixote*, a crucial work for both Fielding and Carlyle, an epic novel. And Hegel identifies the romantic (or novelistic, as opposed to dramatic) novel as the appropriate epic form for modern society, a form which perpetuates a poetic spirit threatened by the hostile prosaic world surrounding it.[12] Carlyle notes this transformation not just in "Early German Literature," where he cites *Tom Jones* and *Wilhelm Meister* as the modern inheritors of heroic poetry, but also in "Biography," where he caustically remarks how "the partially living modern Novel" replaces "the wholly dead modern Epic" (*CW* 28: 52).

Although important, the transformation of the genres most highly valued by neoclassical critics—epic, tragedy, and comedy—remains insufficient to accommodate the needs of modern literature. As a critic and as a translator, Carlyle acquaints himself with a striking array of newly acknowledged or newly appreciated literary kinds not encompassed by Aristotle's *Poetics* and uncanonized by neoclassical treatises on genre. In *German Romance* and in his essays he studies the novel, or *Kunstroman*, the inclusive and characteristically modern form hailed by the German aestheticians, as exemplified in the wild ironic fictions of Richter, the mystical *Heinrich von Ofterdingen* of Novalis and, most significantly, the deeply instructive *Lehrjahre* and *Wanderjahre* of Wilhelm Meister. He examines the various forms of the *Märchen*, the folktales collected and celebrated by the brothers Grimm and the art tales created in response to them by such authors as Johann August Musäus and Tieck. He appreciates the fragment, a form developed by Novalis and the Schlegels, which defines itself not by having a beginning, a middle, and an end, but by signaling, rather perversely, that it lacks at least one of these Aristotelian requisites. He studies diverse forms of fable and allegory, regarding them as incomplete and too exclusively didactic in themselves, but as vital components of a larger, inclusive modern artwork. Finally, he discusses the idyll, the pastoral genre of Theocritus given new prominence by the Germans as a modern prose form, the fantasy-piece, developed by E. T. A. Hoffmann, and the phantasmagory, adapted from the magic lantern-show for the verbal pyrotechnics of Goethe's *Helena*.

Carlyle goes beyond the consideration of these individual genres by explicating the complex modern artworks that incorporate them into a larger mixed form, treating *Helena* as phantasmagory, fantasy-piece, and *Märchen*, and *Wilhelm Meisters Wanderjahre* as allegory, *Kunstroman*, and "*completed fragment*" (*CW* 26: 233). His approbation of artworks which combine diverse kinds reflects the degree to which he shares the Germans' perception of the need to reject unyielding generic categories. Carlyle's preoccupation with mixed forms manifests itself in his predilection for mixed generic designations. He does censure, in his *Life of Schiller*, the Germans' "subdivisions of romantic and heroic and romantico-heroic, and the other endless jargon that encumbers their critical writings" (*CW* 25: 47), yet he employs designations like "romantico-heroic" repeatedly to image the complexity of modern life and the corresponding complexity of modern writing. In "Biography" he calls Rousseau's *Confessions* "an elegiaco-didactic Poem" (*CW* 28: 49), while in "Diderot" he identifies the *Interprétation de la Nature* as a series of "Metaphysico-Baconian phantasmagories" (*CW* 28: 201). "Early German Literature" describes the writings of the medieval author Hugo von Trimberg, caught between traditional lyricism and increasingly prevalent didacticism, as "poetico-preceptorial" (*CW* 27: 287). *The French Revolution*, which uses internal generic designations to highlight its own formal complexity, abounds with such terms as "ludicro-terrific" (*FR* 1: 253) and "comico-tragical" (*FR* 2: 134). Some of Carlyle's mixed designations are incidental and playful, stated ironically or placed within the extravagant discourse of his flamboyant German personae. Others are crucial to an understanding of his critical thought and artistic practice. His description of "The Diamond Necklace" as a "historico-poetico" work (*Letters* 7: 21) points out the transgression of the Aristotelian distinction between the particular interests of history and the general concern of poetry that underlies his experiments in artistic history: this transgression is basic to *The French Revolution*, which counters its historical impulse toward analysis and documentation with its poetic manipulation of literary genres. Carlyle's paradoxical identification of "The Diamond Necklace" as a "True Fiction" (*Letters* 7: 245) underscores his goal of creating a factual account of contemporary history that possesses the shaping power of fiction without betraying its own veracity. His repeated use of "Farce-Tragedy" in *The French Revolution* (*FR* 2: 191 and elsewhere) signals the repudiation of generic decorum that is made necessary by the choice of a complex historical subject.

The transposition and mixture of genres that Carlyle advocates depend upon the principle of Germanic "world-irony" (*CW* 28: 265): the affirmative and inclusive irony of Richter and his compatriots that accepts contradictions, rather than the prohibitive and exclusive irony of Voltaire and the *philosophes* that ridicules them.[13] This world-irony permits the inclusion within a single structure of incongruous and anachronistic modes of thought and presentation. In some works, such as Musäus's modern recreations of the folktale, Carlyle sees structural incongruity as an unintentional or unfortunate element. Musäus, Carlyle argues, writes in a tradition with whose horror and "grim lines of primeval feeling" he is profoundly unsympathetic. Consequently, he does not succeed in shaping the folktale's rough-hewn materials "into a perfect edifice, according to the first simple plan; he has rather pargetted them anew, and decorated them with the most modern ornaments and furniture; and he introduces his guests, with a roguish smile at the strange antic contrast they are to perceive between the movables and the apartment" (*CW* 21: 18). In other works, however, Carlyle views the incongruous relation between the "movables" and the "apartment," or the tenor and the vehicle, as the product of ingenious conscious artistry. Goethe's *Faust,* for instance, turns to advantage the same disparity between literary convention and contemporary vision that hobbles Musäus. "He retains the supernatural vesture of the story," Carlyle maintains, "but retains it with the consciousness, on his and our part, that it is a chimera" (*CW* 26: 156). Mephistopheles, who might with less skillful handling become an unconvincing hobgoblin invoked only to fullfil the play's need for tragic and didactic machinery, becomes in Goethe's treatment a prototype of the Voltairean rationalism that afflicts modern society. "Goethe's Devil is a cultivated personage," Carlyle writes, "and acquainted with the modern sciences; sneers at witchcraft and the black-art, even while employing them, as heartily as any member of the French Institute; for he is a *philosophe,* and doubts most things, nay, half disbelieves even his own existence" (*CW* 26: 156–157). The use of self-conscious machinery, such as Carlyle later adopts in the mythical allusions of *The French Revolution,* makes *Faust* a compelling modern work rather than an antiquarian curiosity or maudlin *Castle Spectre.*

III

The ironic mutation of form effected by the European revolution in literature and criticism means for Carlyle, as for his contemporaries, a radical reassessment of the nature of artistic unity. No modern work, he implies in an early review of *Faust,* can be justly evaluated solely by reference to "the three superannuated *unities* of Aristotle, or the French school" (*Collecteanea* 65). Itemized catalogues of the parts of a work must give way to an integral apprehension of its deeper unity and "peculiar life" (*CW* 26: 51), and analysis of formalities must give way to a synthetic apprehension of form. "The problem is not now to determine by what mechanism Addison composed sentences and struck-out similitudes," he writes in "State of German Literature" (using a distinction between mechanical and organic form reminiscent of A. W. Schlegel and Coleridge), "but by what far finer and more mysterious mechanism Shakspeare organised his dramas, and gave life and individuality to his Ariel and his Hamlet." "What is this unity of theirs," he asks, "and can our deeper inspection discern it to be indivisible, and existing by necessity, because each work springs, as it were, from the general elements of all Thought, and grows up therefrom, into form and expansion by its own growth? Not only who was the poet, and how did he compose; but what and how was the poem, and why was it a poem and not rhymed eloquence, creation and not figured passion? These are the questions for the critic" (*CW* 26: 51–52). Carlyle recognizes that changes in aesthetic perception undermine fixed codes of artistic unity and acknowledges, especially in his studies of Goethe, the principle central to his own literary experiments, that every significant artwork shapes the aesthetic standards by which it is to be judged. His antithetical separation of creation and poetry from craft and rhetoric places him within the critical tradition of Wordsworth, Hazlitt, DeQuincey, and Shelley, and allies him with their preference of renovating nature to suffocating artifice.

In rejecting the hegemony of the neoclassical unities, Carlyle turns to divergent models of artistic composition; in particular, he receives with delight the irregular, nonclassical forms of medieval literature. Carlyle discovers in the grimly splendid *Nibelungenlied* and the starkly noble Icelandic sagas the characteristics of a northern imagination, unrestrained by the decorum of a foreign classicism. From these northern artworks, characterized (as his friend John Ruskin would say) by "wildness of thought" and "roughness of work,"[14] Carlyle defines his own nonclassical aesthetic, with its celebration of an art rude yet eloquent, inelegant yet dignified. His Gothic aesthetic has many parallels in eighteenth- and nineteenth-century writing: Richard Hurd's contention that "Gothic" works such as *The Faerie Queene* should not be judged according to the requirements of "Classic" criticism, and his argument that "the general plan of a work . . . must be governed by the subject-matter itself," rather than by externally imposed standards; William Blake's preference of Gothic "Living Form" to Greek "Mathematic Form"; the general revival of Gothic forms in art, architecture, and literature; the German aestheticians' discussions of the differences between the modern and the classical; and Ruskin's paean in *The Stones of Venice* to the savageness and truth of Gothic art.[15] The divergence of classical and nonclassical conceptions of form appears explicitly in Carlyle's critical vocabulary, and implicitly in his critical metaphors, where the elegance of French artifice contrasts with the roughness of Germanic nature. In his 1831 essay on Schiller, Carlyle opposes "the Versailles gardening and artificial hydraulics" of French neoclassicism to "the true Ginnistan and Wonderland" of modern German aesthetics (*CW* 27: 171). Similarly, in his essay on Voltaire, Carlyle contrasts the French author's style ("the simple artificial symmetry of a parlour chandelier") to the style of Shakespeare ("the deep natural symmetry of a forest oak"). The *Henriade,* he writes, is like "a geometrical diagram by Fermat," whereas *Hamlet* resembles "a cartoon by Raphael." The *Henriade* "is a polished, square-built Tuileries," whereas "*Hamlet* is a mysterious star-paved Valhalla and dwelling of the gods" (*CW* 26: 449). These metaphors point up the aesthetic of necessary roughness which is fundamental to an understanding of Carlyle's work.[16]

When we encounter the heterogeneity and roughness of Carlyle (or, for that matter, of Herman Melville or Walt Whitman), we must ask whether the form is botched because the author is incompetent or negligent, or whether it is botched because a work written in a perplexing, fragmented, transitional age must reflect its time in its shape and texture. Central to Carlyle's conception of modern literature, central to his perception of modern Germany's seminal role in the creation and definition of that literature, is the idea that the nineteenth century must speak with its own voice. If the eighteenth century produced literary works with a beginning, a middle, and an end, the nineteenth century might of necessity create fragments; and if the eighteenth century wrote literature that is "good" and congruous, the nineteenth century might choose to write literature that is "bad" and unruly. When Carlyle recommends *The French Revolution* to Emerson as a "wild savage ruleless very bad Book" (*Letters* 9: 82), he is not merely engaging in boastful self-deprecation; he is, at least in part, being descriptive, for in this context "bad" can have a purely generic, as well as evaluative, significance. A work might fall foul of neoclassical standards of goodness because it disregards its own aesthetic principles, because it fails to match one aspect of its composition harmoniously with another, or because it fails to achieve its own aims; it might equally be "bad" because it deliberately abjures and resists neoclassical standards, and prefers the natural, the Gothic, or the modern to the artificial, the symmetrical, and the contrived.

Carlyle's nonclassical or Gothic aesthetic works in complex harmony with his residual and abiding classical aesthetic, manifested not just in the Johnsonian balance of his earliest prose, but also in his application of classical standards of poetic unity in his criticism. Indeed, for Carlyle as for his German contemporaries, one of the principal justifications for the modern assault on neoclassicism is an attempt to rediscover, without prejudice, what constitutes "classical" literature. Carlyle's championing of alternate models of literary form does not involve a simple rejection of the neoclassical ideal of unity, any more than the Copernican investigations of his German contemporaries involve a simple abandonment of their predecessors' generic categories. For Carlyle, while repudiating the extreme strictures of Le Bossu and his followers, retains a good deal of his eighteenth-century literary heritage. In many instances, he uses images of roughness and disarray as a neoclassical critic would use them, to derogate incomplete artistic execution. His caustic dismissal of William Taylor in "Historic Survey of German Poetry" portrays Taylor's three-volume literary history as a "huge, anomalous, heterogeneous mass, no section of it like another, oriel-window alternating with rabbit-hole, wrought capital on pillar of dried mud; heaped together out of marble, loose earth, rude boulder-stone; hastily roofed-in with shingles: . . . which nothing but a continued suspension of the laws of gravity can keep from rushing ere long into a chaos of stone and dust" (*CW* 27: 369). His critique of Heinrich Döring's life of Richter castigates the author for agglomerating his biography out of randomly collected materials rather than composing it according to a predetermined and coherent conception. "Stone is laid on top of stone," Carlyle writes, "just as it comes to hand; a trowel or two of biographic mortar, if perfectly convenient, being spread in here and there, by way of cement; and so the strangest pile suddenly arises; amorphous, pointing every way but to the zenith, here a block of granite, there a mass of pipeclay; till the whole finishes, when the materials are finished;—and you leave it standing to posterity, like some miniature Stonehenge, a perfect architectural enigma" (*CW* 26: 3). Carlyle, the author of the "perfect architectural enigma" of *Sartor Resartus*, recognizes in his criticism the complex relation of the new aesthetic to the old; he argues, for example, against the lax assumption by some commentators that the Schlegels are exclusively "the patrons and generalissimos" of the romanticists in their war against the classicists (*CW* 26: 53). And he demonstrates in his own art the complex interaction of a classical and a nonclassical aesthetic: like Goethe, who consciously synthesizes the Greek or classical with the Northern or romantic in his *Helena*, Carlyle combines in *The French Revolution* the architectonic clarity of his three symmetrical volumes with the phantasmagoric disarray of an anarchic modern vision.

Fixed notions of form and structure are undermined by the simultaneous presence of opposed aesthetic principles in Carlyle's writings. Take the passage from *Sartor Resartus* where the Editor (Carlyle) takes Diogenes Teufelsdröckh (also Carlyle) to task for his "almost total want of arrangement." In Diogenes' tome on the history and significance of clothes, the Editor contends,

> his adherence to the mere course of Time produces, through the Narrative portions, a certain show of outward method; but of true logical method and sequence there is too little. Apart from its multifarious sections and subdivisions, the Work naturally falls into two Parts; a Historical-Descriptive, and a Philosophical-Speculative: but falls, unhappily, by no firm line of demarcation; in that labyrinthic combination, each Part overlaps, and indents, and indeed runs quite through the other. Many sections are of a debatable rubric, or even quite nondescript and unnameable; whereby the Book not only loses in accessibility, but too often distresses us like some mad banquet, wherein all courses had been confounded, and fish and flesh, soup and solid, oyster-sauce, lettuces, Rhine-wine and French mustard, were hurled into one huge tureen or trough, and the hungry Public invited to help itself. To bring what order we can out of this Chaos shall be part of our endeavour. (*SR* 34)

The textual chaos of which the Editor complains derives from an aesthetic conflict between the Editor's desire for a homogeneous pattern and Diogenes' preference for mixed and ironic forms; the former recalls Carlyle's castigation of irregularity in William Taylor and Heinrich Döring, the latter Carlyle's celebrations of Richter, whose genial presence looms over *Sartor Resartus*. Carlyle's mad aesthetic banquet, an emblem of his inclusive, ironic texts, forces the reader to work actively to reconstruct the work's shape, and aesthetic, and kind.

Because of Carlyle's refusal to honor the borders of literary and extraliterary discourse, of discrete literary kinds, or even of particular models of artistic unity, a principal distinguishing feature of his works is generic transgression coupled with sustained and conscious stylistic perversity. With Carlyle, as with any consciously modern author, the question of genre is a vexed one. On the one hand, the illusion of fixed and discrete genres remains for him a residual inheritance from an eighteenth-century worldview incompatible with the disturbed nineteenth century. As a critic, Carlyle sees that the great poetic genres of the past must be radically altered to the prose forms of the modern era: thus, for him Rousseau's *Confessions* and Goethe's modern *Märchen* are poems, the *Vicar of Wakefield* an idyll, and the *Life of Johnson* an epic.[17] As an artist attempting to imitate the variegated texture of modern life, he adopts "Farce-Tragedy," "True Fiction," and other mixed forms threatening to generic decorum. On the other hand, Carlyle's art and criticism depend heavily on the canonical genres of epic, tragedy, and comedy, even when he is fighting them. And his examinations of the less canonical forms of fragment, *Märchen*, and *Kunstroman* increase rather than dissipate his interest in generic criticism; despite the stridently antitheoretical vein into which he sometimes lapses, genre remains for him an indispensable way of reading human experience. An accurate estimation of Carlyle and genre must therefore encompass both his dependence on and his resistance to established kinds. Carlyle hints at many genres, but rests with none; he makes the manipulation, displacement, and combination of received forms reflect the modern world whose complexity he embodies.[18]

THREE

Experiments in Genre

Carlyle's complex critical use of generic terms anticipates an equally problematic manipulation of literary forms in his writings of the 1830s, for both the particular genres that he encounters in his early essays and the inclusive mode of composition by which they are combined in an ironic larger structure reappear in his artistic and artistic-historical works. The question of how a modern work might embrace within itself both the multifariousness of modern life and the harmony traditionally deemed necessary for a successful artwork, which Carlyle confronts in his critical treatments of Goethe and his contemporaries, remains central to his artistic practice. Indeed, to separate the critical and the artistic impulses in Carlyle's works becomes impossible, because both concern themselves with the artist's conception of unity and the reader's problem in reconstructing it. Carlyle's concurrent handling of criticism and art, together with his idiosyncratic refashioning of received forms, has been acknowledged in studies of *Sartor Resartus*. But the deserved success of *Sartor*, and its position of prominence in Victorian studies, have caused it to be seen in unnatural isolation as a unique Carlylean fiction. The experimental features that characterize *Sartor* equally typify the historical works that immediately follow it in Carlyle's canon, but in a more complex manner; for in them, the insistent concern with the nature of fictions remains, while the question of what precisely is "made up" becomes increasingly vexed. By focusing on the mutual affinity of Carlyle's experiments in genre during the 1830s, we shall be able to view continuously a decade of his literary activity ostensibly sundered by the gulf between the autobiographical fictions and German philosophy of *Sartor* and the protracted struggle with documentary form in the ensuing French histories. Carlyle's persistent concern with genre is evidenced in the complex designations which he offers, whether in his external commentaries or within the texts themselves, for his novel *Sartor Resartus*, his satire (or "pasquil") "Count Cagliostro," his romance "The Diamond Necklace," and his epic *The French Revolution*. These designations reveal his continuing fascination with the uncertain status of genres in a world where the pandects of Blair and Bossu have been abrogated and new codes are sought.

I

Carlyle's designation of *Sartor Resartus* as a novel appears in a letter of 1833 recommending the work to James Fraser, its eventual publisher. "It is put together in the fashion of a kind of Didactic Novel," he writes, "but indeed properly *like* nothing yet extant. I used to characterize it briefly as a kind of 'Satirical Extravaganza on Things in General' " (*Letters* 6: 396). The uncertain nature of Carlyle's statement appears in its tone of qualification ("in the fashion of a kind of"), in its juxtaposition of a tentative generic identification with an assertion, apparently antipathetic to the idea of genre, that the work is "*like* nothing yet extant," and its subsequent offering of an alternative generic label ("Satirical Extravaganza") that is itself a mixed designation, which raises far more questions than it settles. Furthermore, the meaning of the single word "Novel" in Carlyle's statement is itself problematic. Does Carlyle intend a minimal definition of the novel as a modern prose fiction, or a more exalted conception of the novel as *Kunstroman* (as, for example, in *Wilhelm Meister*, which he translated)? Does Carlyle have in mind the novel form of Richter, who "seldom writes without a meaning far beyond the sphere of common romancers" (*CW* 26: 9)?

This problem of definition surfaces repeatedly in modern criticism of *Sartor Resartus*. G. B. Tennyson calls it "an unorthodox novel by an inventive and original mind," and "a novel that is also an anti-novel." He elliptically acknowledges Carlyle's own description of the work in stating "that *Sartor* is a novel but, of course, not *like* any other."[1] Most important, Tennyson recognizes that any understanding of Carlyle's text must be based on an awareness of genres current when he wrote it: fragment, *Märchen*, and *Roman*. George Levine argues that *Sartor* "can only be regarded as a novel in a very special sense," and substitutes for any simple label the mixed designation of "confession-anatomy-romance," which is, like Carlyle's "Didactic Novel" and "Satirical Extravaganza," complex and multifaceted.[2] Gerry H. Brookes insists that "*Sartor* is not a novel because its narrative is not consistent, because its characters and other fictions do not have the intrinsic and sustained interest that fictions have in a novel," and maintains instead that *Sartor* "is a form of persuasive essay."[3] Lionel Stevenson calls *Sartor* a "semi-fiction," "plotless novel," and "crypto-autobiography," while Alastair Fowler classes it as a "*poioumenon* or work-in-progress novel."[4] For Carlyle, the use of a single generic term, inadequate in itself to comprehend a modern idiosyncratic work, is an invitation to examine that work's complexity. It initiates, rather than concludes, generic exploration, and far from rewarding the indolent reader who wants to affix a dead label on a living text, it encourages a search for a new and elastic designation. Even to the sophisticated reader, *Sartor Resartus* remains what George Saintsbury found it to be on first prematurely encountering it in his youth, an "abracadabra" or textual riddle.[5]

Certainly, its title page offers little in the way of generic clues to the reader, for while the subtitle, "The Life and Opinions of Herr Teufelsdröckh," suggests biography, the title—"The Tailor Retailored"—indicates a more complex form, in which a double layer of metaphorical clothing reveals and conceals the work's central vision. Carlyle does offer hints at the genres he is using in such chapter titles as "Idyllic" and "Romance," but these are characteristically elusive and fragmentary. He revels in proposing generic terms which occupy a bewildering intermediate position between life and art: in the context of *Sartor Resartus*, "Idyllic" can describe either an innocent and peaceful state of life or the classical poetic form of idyll, transmuted into a modern prose form in the experimental writings of the Germans, while "Romance" can denote either the love affair between Teufelsdröckh and Blumine or an idealized narrative characterized by overpowering emotions, by enchantment, and by the polarization of good and evil. Carlyle deliberately teases the reader's sense of ambiguity in offering these uncertain designations. But even more ambiguous is the relation of these embedded passages of idyll and romance to the entire text. More often than not, embedded passages are consistent in kind with the works in which they appear: in epic, for instance, embedded narratives customarily repeat in miniature the features of the larger work, imitating its inclusive framework and reinforcing its heroic ethos. Here, the fragments of idyll and romance have a role adversarial to the overall movement of the text: the sexual focus of "Romance," in particular, contends with the broader philosophical concerns of the *Roman*, and though the terms are cognate, they remain largely antithetical. In *Sartor Resartus*, Carlyle experiments with the insertion in his text of designations which arouse generic expectations that he subsequently examines, manipulates and, occasionally, frustrates. This technique of internally identifying the form of his text becomes central in "Count Cagliostro" and "The Diamond Necklace," which lead to *The French Revolution*.

II

To find the same spirit of generic innovation in two works as apparently diverse as *Sartor Resartus* and "Count Cagliostro" may seem, at first glance, rather incongruous.[6] The one is an acknowledged masterwork, the other what Carlyle called a *parergon*, or "by-work" (*Letters* 6: 316). The one represents the high water mark of Carlyle's interest in German philosophy and aesthetics, the other indicates his growing preoccupation with French history. Yet both, despite their unpretentious first appearances in installments of *Fraser's Magazine*, have a carefully articulated structure and concern with form. Both use a fictional German persona, Teufelsdröckh in *Sartor* and Herr Gottfried Sauerteig in "Count Cagliostro," whose consciousness governs our reception of the text. On a deeper level, both are concerned with reading; both are fictions about fictions; both include accounts of their own creation and a theoretical analysis of the assumptions underlying their forms. Just as *Sartor Resartus* is simultaneously about natural supernaturalism and about the forms in which natural supernaturalism clothes itself, so too "Count Cagliostro" is both about history and about the writing of history: the discovery of a source, the search for a form, and the transmutation of chronicle into art.

Since the story of "Count Cagliostro" is, unlike that of *Sartor Resartus*, a matter of prior knowledge for Carlyle's audience, its overall pattern, "the rise, progress, grandeur and decadence of the Quack of Quacks" (*CW* 28: 317), is largely preestablished. Giuseppe Balsamo, a scamp and trickster raised in the filth of mid-eighteenth-century Palermo, enters most incongruously into monastic orders, from which he is quickly and forcibly expelled after he substitutes the names of local prostitutes for saints' names during a reading of the martyrology. He marries Lorenza Feliciani, whose sexual services he sells, becoming jealous only when she strays beyond the accepted boundaries of copulation to the forbidden territories of love. He travels across Europe as a painter, healer, confidence man, clairvoyant, and Grand Cophta, founder of his own exalted order of Egyptian masonry. Giuseppe Balsamo becomes Count Cagliostro, while his wife—now, because of her new eminence, unavailable for sexual procurement—becomes Countess Seraphina. Having attained European celebrity, Cagliostro meets a sad reversal when he is dragged into the scandalous affair of the Diamond Necklace, stands trial, is banished, and returns, fatefully, to Rome. There, disappointed in his expectation that the Pope might endorse his masonic order, and betrayed by his wife, he falls prey to the Inquisition, which incarcerates him until his death.

Cagliostro's story generates two predominant responses in Carlyle: the first, a moral response, concerns Cagliostro's insistent transgression of the ethical norm of truth, while the second, a formal response, concerns the tropes of imposture and reversal which characterize his career. The interplay of these responses makes "Count Cagliostro," insofar as it is amenable to a purely literary categorization, a satire. Carlyle explicitly identifies it as such in the ironic disquisition on genres, excerpted from Sauerteig's collection of *Aesthetic Lock-picks*, that begins the narrative. Every human life, Sauerteig announces, is a "small strophe, or occasional verse" taken from the "grand sacred Epos, or Bible of World-History," which encompasses the heroic, idyllic, comic, "farcic-tragic," melodramatic, and pasquillic aspects of existence (*CW* 28: 250). The life of Cagliostro, which falls under Sauerteig's category of the "human Pasquil" (*CW* 28: 255), represents consummate falsehood, and therefore stands most completely removed from the heroic spirit of consummate truth it travesties.[7] The inveterately pasquillic nature of Cagliostro's life stands, in Carlyle's conception, "wondrously and even indispensably connected with the Heroic portions" of the epic of world-history (*CW* 28: 318). Following satiric tradition, Carlyle applies heroic devices and conventions to an unworthy pasquillic subject. In taking the "unattainable ideal and type-specimen" of quackery as his hero, Carlyle follows the inverted decorum of satire: the style of his historical miniature, he coyly remarks, "shall if possible be equal to the subject" (*CW* 28: 260).

The satiric discordance between style and subject features prominently in Carlyle's application of the ennobling patterns of epic, myth, romance, and tragedy to the unworthy Cagliostro. Carlyle's halfhearted attempt to give Cagliostro a distinguished progeny and an impressive accumulation of epic epithets ends only in disparagement, when he hails the Count as the "Pupil of the Sage Althotas, Foster-child of the Scherif of Mecca, probable Son of the last King of Trebisond; named also Acharat, and Unfortunate Child of Nature; by profession healer of diseases, abolisher of wrinkles, friend of the poor and impotent, grand-master of the Egyptian Mason-lodge of High Science, Spirit-summoner, Gold-cook, Grand Cophta, Prophet, Priest, and thaumaturgic moralist and swindler; really a Liar of the first magnitude, thorough-paced in all provinces of lying, what one may call the King of Liars" (*CW* 28: 254–255). The cycle of inflation and deflation ("abolisher of wrinkles," "moralist and swindler," "King of Liars") progressively exalts and diminishes Cagliostro's stature. The epic catalogue, which should magnify the hero by linking him to other exemplars of greatness and to a heroic worldview, serves only to link Cagliostro to other quacks. "It was the very age of impostors," Carlyle chants, "cut-purses, swindlers, double-goers, enthusiasts, ambiguous persons; quacks simple, quacks compound; crackbrained, or with deceit prepense; quacks and quackeries of all colours and kinds. How many Mesmerists, Magicians, Cabalists, Swedenborgians, Illuminati, Crucified Nuns, and Devils of Loudun! . . . Consider your Schröpfers, Cagliostros, Casanovas, Saint-Germains, Dr. Grahams; the Chevalier d'Eon, Psalmanazar, Abbé Paris and the Ghost of Cock-lane!"(*CW* 28: 271). Carlyle uses the mythic pattern of apotheosis with a reductive effect when he repeatedly characterizes Cagliostro as a sun, a star, or a comet. The Count "careers onward as a Comet," he writes in a passage whose effect is far from prodigious, "his nucleus, of paying and praising Dupes, embraces, in long radius, what city and province he rests over; his thinner tail, of wondering and curious Dupes, stretches into remotest lands" (*CW* 28: 296–297). Carlyle uses a similarly ennobling pattern from romance, the quest and arming of the hero, to give a similarly reductive picture of Cagliostro's travels throughout Europe: Cagliostro, he writes, "dived deep down into the lugubrious-obscure regions of Rascaldom; like a Knight to the palace of his Fairy; remained unseen there, and returned thence armed at all points" (*CW* 28: 276). Carlyle repeatedly depicts Cagliostro in the inappropriate role of tragic hero, separating the stages of his career with the five-act divisions of high tragedy, and charting his progress through catastrophe and apotheosis to a final decline when "the red coppery splendour" of the hero "darkens more and more into final gloom" (*CW* 28: 315). The satiric intent of Carlyle's recurrent allusions to tragedy is felt during his account of Cagliostro's long and painful final imprisonment, when "the curtain lazily falls" on the hero, offering a conspicuously lame conclusion to his career.

Carlyle further reduces Cagliostro's stature with ironic analogues from Judeo-Christian and classical mythology. Since Cagliostro is a complete apostate from truth, the most appropriate analogue for him is Satan: "if Satan himself has in these days become a poetic hero," Carlyle observes, "why should not Cagliostro, for some short hour, be a prose one?"(*CW* 28: 255). Just as the romantic conception of Satan as hero is an inversion of the Bible and *Paradise Lost*, "Count Cagliostro" is an inverted reading of the bible or epic of world-history from the ironic standpoint of Cagliostro, "the unattainable ideal and type-specimen" of charlatanism. In a perverse way, Cagliostro becomes for the degenerate eighteenth century what Christ was for his age. Indeed, Carlyle uses the explicitly Christian adjuration "I would thou wert either cold or hot" to justify Cagliostro's existence: rather than being the lukewarm supporter of half-truths whom Christ's utterance condemns, Cagliostro is a committed and "decided Liar" (*CW* 28: 254). Elsewhere, Carlyle casts the corpulent Cagliostro in the most incongruous role of Psyche. By forcing the monks to expel him from their company, Cagliostro demonstrates "that he had now outgrown their monk-discipline; as the Psyche does its chrysalis-shell, and bursts it" (*CW* 28: 265). Elsewhere, Carlyle depicts Cagliostro as a blithe Panourgos lolling in "a wide plastic ocean of sham and foam" (*CW* 28: 291).

At other times, Carlyle resorts to animal caricature to calumniate Cagliostro and his friends as the type-specimens of the degraded eighteenth century. The Cardinal de Rohan, the dupe in the Diamond Necklace affair of "Circe de la Motte-Valois," becomes in one image a pig to be fattened for slaughter (*CW* 28: 307), and in another a beached whale devoured by jackals (*CW* 28: 306). Cagliostro manifests "vulpine astucity," "pig-like defensive-ferocity," and "dog-faithfulness, . . . either of the mastiff or of the cur species" (*CW* 28: 267). His ability to shake lesser men "from him like dewdrops from the lion's mane" offers an ironic counterpoint to his canine and porcine attributes (*CW* 28: 268). Carlyle's bestial caricatures reinforce his low but crudely effective use of invective and physical abuse, which appears in his ungracious harping on the Count's obesity and greasiness (the most readily available and immediately rewarding of the satirist's targets). The infant Giuseppe is described, without the sense of wonder that accompanies the nativity of his antithesis, Christ, as a "fat, red, globular kind of fellow" (*CW* 28: 260). The maturing Balsamo remains "stupid" and "pudding-faced," yet he does, Carlyle concedes, have "a kind of blubbery impetuosity, an oiliness so plausible-looking: give him only length of life, he will rise to the top of his profession" (*CW* 28: 267). In his fully developed state, Balsamo is not "anything of an Adonis," as Carlyle notes in an unkind use of litotes, but "a most dusky, bull-necked, mastiff-faced, sinister-looking individual" (*CW* 28: 277). Cagliostro, at the height of his fame, presents "a fat, snub, abominable face; dew-lapped, flat-nosed, greasy, full of greediness, sensuality, oxlike obstinacy; . . . on the whole, perhaps the most perfect quack-face produced by the eighteenth century" (*CW* 28: 301).

A collation of the satiric techniques in "Count Cagliostro" reveals nothing incompatible with a neoclassical aesthetic, for the inverted congruity between style and subject that Carlyle promises stands clearly within the satiric and mock-heroic tradition of eighteenth-century poetry, and he here performs with less deliberate polish what Pope triumphantly executes in his *Dunciad*, devastating a degenerate age's prominent representatives by giving them exalted literary descriptions they do not merit. If Carlyle pillories the eighteenth century in "Count Cagliostro," he nevertheless leans heavily on its literary practice. To discover what is novel and seminal in "Count Cagliostro," we must consider two related aspects of its form: the creation of a deliberate and irresolvable tension between literary and extraliterary discourse, which becomes Carlyle's dominant mode of composition in the 1830s, and the self-conscious examination of its own creation. The conscious antagonism of literature and history is anticipated at the outset by Sauerteig's perverse catalogue of the genres which, despite its obligatory gesture to the venerable *Poetics*, subverts Aristotle's distinction between the generalizing, idealizing faculty of poetry and the particular, factual concerns of history, at the same time as it disregards his fundamental distinction between art, the imitation of life, and life itself. After Sauerteig ends his pseudo-Aristotelian discourse, Carlyle indicates that his depiction of the charlatan Cagliostro will take the form of "human Pasquil," or historical satire, suggested by Sauerteig as one of the kinds embraced by the epic of world-history. This mixed form (permeated, as Carlyle notes, by Germanic, or inclusive, "world-irony") yokes "historical

Fact" with "dramatic Fiction" and "Stern Accuracy" with "bold Imagination." Like Goethe's earlier dramatic treatment of Cagliostro's story in *Der Gross-Coptha*, or like Schiller's fragmentary novel on the subject, the *Geisterseher*, which Carlyle cites as analogues for his own treatment, it combines the documentary and the poetical. Carlyle's metaphoric description of Schiller's practice is particularly telling, since in it Schiller attempts, as Carlyle later does, to use the "poetic" aspects of his historical subject "to burst (since unlocking was impossible) the secrets" of "the scientific phases of the matter" (*CW* 28: 256). The image of the lock anticipates Carlyle's later conception of history as an imprisoned epic which cannot be liberated solely by the discontinuous labors of the artisan historian, while the metaphor of explosion and violent rescue reflects the mental excitement that must accompany the imaginative fusion of artistic history. The historical aspect of Carlyle's mixed form appears in its attention to the verifiable facts of modern history; its fictive aspect appears in its satiric application of the ennobling patterns of epic, romance, and tragedy to an unworthy subject.

The implantation in his text of the contending needs of poetry and history provides Carlyle with tensions that he can exploit to stunning creative effect. But in "Count Cagliostro" the distance between the two is not as great as it later becomes, for both his poetry and his history are less thoroughly experimental than they are in *The French Revolution*, and both are consistent with a rather staid view of the author as one who exerts substantial control over the significance of the phenomena he depicts or documents. His use of satire as a dominant mode presupposes not only his ability to establish a single acknowledged ethical norm, but also his competence to pronounce judgment on those who transgress it. Carlyle comes to find satire, by itself, a limited and ultimately negative form which, when unaccompanied by an admission of the writer's limitations and epistemological uncertainty, presupposes too full an authorial control over meaning. The satiric subtext of *The French Revolution* therefore becomes more furtive and discontinuous than "Count Cagliostro," resembling a human pasquil chopped into pieces and then mixed up with elements of tragedy, elegy, and phantasmagory. Similarly, his didactic applications of Cagliostro's life entail a conception of history as philosophy teaching by experience, which he rejects in his essays on history as inadequate.[8] The magisterial metaphor for history rests on the assumption that the historian can clearly discern the latent meanings of human experience, and that he can in turn relate those meanings in a rational and measured discourse to his pupils. In the mature historical vision of *The French Revolution*, Carlyle is uncertain about the production of discrete meanings from history, and replaces magisterial certainty with the fragmentary evocation of innumerable lives. "Count Cagliostro," then, remains an intermediate experiment in poetic-historical form, but an important one for its author and an instructive one to us.

Carlyle further contributes to the formal complexity of "Count Cagliostro" by undermining the traditional boundary between process and product—by having his text direct the reader's attention to its own genre and to the process of its own creation. The prologue to the work begins not with moral reflections or with the establishment of a historical background but with a consideration, however perverse, of form in general and of the specific form that this experimental piece will take. The discussion of Cagliostro's career begins with a physical and intellectual examination of the texts in which his life appears. The "foolish Inquisition-Biographer" (*CW* 28: 275), who wrote the biased account that Carlyle accepts through default as his most promising source, becomes a character in the piece, existing on the same level of reality in the text with Cagliostro and offering, like Cagliostro, a target for repeated mockery and invective. The author too becomes a character in the drama and a prominent agent in the reader's experience of history:

> The present inquirer, in obstinate investigation of a phenomenon so noteworthy, has searched through the whole not inconsiderable circle which his tether (of circumstances, geographical position, trade, health, extent of money-capital) enables him to describe: and, sad to say, with the most imperfect results. He has read Books in various languages and jargons; feared not to soil his fingers, hunting through ancient dusty Magazines, to sicken his heart in any labyrinth of iniquity and imbecility; nay, he had not grudged to dive even into the infectious *Mémoires de Casanova*, for a hint or two,—could he have found that work, which, however, most British Librarians make a point of denying that they possess. (*CW* 28: 257–258)

That Carlyle records his encounters with squeamish librarians and tells his readers the size and price of the books he rejects as sources for Cagliostro's life places the act of discovery in the foreground of the text and links his *parergon* with a series of prominent nineteenth-century writings that include within themselves their own seminal documents: *Sartor Resartus*, where the editor must stitch together the fragments of Teufelsdröckh's biography; *The Scarlet Letter*, where Hawthorne represents himself in the Custom House reading old documents concerning Hester Prynne; and *The Ring and the Book*, where Browning begins his tale from Roman history with his discovery of the little yellow book hidden away in a bookseller's stall.

What we are finally to make of "Count Cagliostro," with its abrogation of the boundaries between history and poetry, and between process and product, remains a problem. Certainly the work was intended as an unassuming piece of journalism, not, like *Sartor Resartus*, as a central encyclopedic volume. Yet despite its modest aims, "Count Cagliostro" offers Carlyle a vital artistic transition between *Sartor Resartus*, which he was still in the throes of marketing, and his subsequent treatments of modern French history. Carlyle himself certainly had ambivalent reactions to the work, calling it, in his habitual mode of self-deprecation, "a kind of scribblement," "a foolish extravagant piece," and "one of the most distorted bad things . . . I ever wrote" (*Letters* 6: 344, 352n., 388). Yet he demonstrates a genuine desire for its favorable reception and a hearty respect for its vigorous experimental spirit. He provides a telling assessment of "Count Cagliostro" in recommending it to John Stuart Mill as a "half-mad production . . . (with some attempt at half-method in it)" (*Letters* 6: 415). For Carlyle, as for Hamlet, method and madness are inextricable, and when Mill responds by suggesting that he be less insistently ironic and express himself "in a more direct way," he responds politely but unrepentantly (*Letters* 6: 448–449, 449n.). In its formal complexity and perversity, "Count Cagliostro" contains the germ of "The Diamond Necklace," just as that work holds within itself the seeds of *The French Revolution*.

III

"The Diamond Necklace," like "Count Cagliostro," begins neither with a moral reflection nor with historical background, but with an identification and discussion of its own genre.[9] By opening his text with a chapter entitled "Age of Romance," which begins with the statement that the "Age of Romance has not ceased" and contains the contentious assertion that romance exists "in Reality alone"

(*CW* 28: 329), Carlyle places his work within the context of a particular genre while at the same time rendering the meaning of that genre thoroughly problematic. We read, for example, that "no age ever seemed the Age of Romance to *itself*":

> Charlemagne, let the Poets talk as they will, had his own provocations in the world: what with selling of his poultry and pot-herbs, what with wanton daughters carrying secretaries through the snow; . . . it seems to me that the Great Charles had his temper ruffled at times. Roland of Roncesvalles too . . . found rainy weather as well as sunny; knew what it was to have hose need darning; got tough beef to chew, or even went dinnerless; was saddle-sick, calumniated, constipated (as his madness too clearly indicates). . . . Only in long subsequent days, when the tough beef, the constipation and the calumny had clean vanished, did it all begin to seem Romantic, and your Turpins and Ariostos found music in it. (*CW* 28: 327)

Here, unromantic facts such as illness and constipation are incongruously juxtaposed with a discussion of what is "Romantic" in life. Because the opening chapter of "The Diamond Necklace" both identifies and radically redefines its genre, Carlyle's designation of the work as a "small Romance" (*CW* 28: 330) cannot be regarded as casual or haphazard. At its least definitive level, the term "romance" is synonymous with prose fiction, cognate with the French *roman* and the German *Roman* (as used, presumably, in the inclusive rubric *German Romance*). But Carlyle's references to Charlemagne and Roland, as well as his important phrase "the Romance of Life" (*CW* 28: 325), show that he is thinking of romance in a broader, pre-generic sense, as a principle of beautiful, ideal, and desirable life, commonly understood (though not by him) to exist primarily in the past fictions of the chivalric romance, or *Ritterroman*.

Since Carlyle's initial chapter opposes the belief that romance can exist in fantastic narratives alone, a definition of his view of the form should take into account the romantic conventions he is resisting. For example, in Musäus's "Dumb Love," a *Märchen* translated by Carlyle in *German Romance*, there appear many of the features that occur in a standard modern definition of romance. A wealthy young man loses his riches; he desires a beautiful young woman, but encounters resistance from her unwilling mother; he sets out on a journey, from which he subsequently returns; on his way he faces tests, first from an eccentric knight, then from a Goblin Barber; following instructions by the latter, he awaits a mysterious benefactor on a bridge at the autumn equinox; learning from this benefactor the location of some treasure, buried all the time in his father's garden, he returns triumphantly to his home town and marries the young woman. Whereas Musäus's tale is characterized by freedom from the restrictions of probability, the "Romance" of "The Diamond Necklace" is committed to a presentation of modern historical fact, which will demonstrate that "this our poor old Real world" is "Hypermagical" (*CW* 28: 385). And whereas Musäus's tale is characterized by a largely unobtrusive narrator and by a willingness that its blatant conventions appear baldly and without comment, Carlyle's "small Romance" is marked from its opening sentence by the intrusions of its narrator and by a self-conscious analysis of its own literary techniques. Indeed, Carlyle emphasizes his own part in the work by making dramaturgy, or controlled illusion, the dominant metaphor of his text. The further complication in Carlyle's artistry is the reacceptance into his "idiosyncratic history" of elements which the polemic of his opening chapter would seem, at first glance, to exclude. The complexity of Carlyle's treatment of romance results not from a wish to abolish the strange and the wondrous, but from a desire to exhibit the "Hypermagical" nature of life in a radically displaced, historical setting, where the commonplace surfaces and textures of everyday existence give way to their underlying phantasmal realities.

Carlyle's artistic manipulation of romance derives from his ambivalent critical responses toward it, recorded in his miscellanies. In his studies of medieval German literature, he pays tribute to chivalric romance as a naive and unencumbered form of utterance, the thesis in the dialectical development of the genres from fancy to understanding to reason. Yet he denigrates some of the chief delights of "that George-and-Dragon species of composition," with its "Ass-eared Giants, Fiery Dragons, Dwarfs and Hairy Women" (*CW* 27: 221). Certainly in this respect he appears to place himself in the age of understanding, which reveres *sentence* and proscribes the solace of the marvelous, rather than in the age of reason, which advocates precisely the marriage of fact and fancy that he eventually attempts in "The Diamond Necklace." Carlyle's prejudices against chivalric romance resurface in his squibs on its modern inheritor, the Gothic romance. Throughout his critical essays, Carlyle derogates popular fiction, which instead of representing "the actual passions, the hopes, sorrows, joys of living men" comes to reside "in a remote conventional world, in *Castles of Otranto*, . . . among clear, metallic heroes, and white, high, stainless beauties, in whom the drapery and elocution [are] nowise the least important qualities" (*CW* 26: 213). He deprecrates *The Monk, The Mysteries of Udolpho, Frankenstein,* and their German counterparts, which "dwell with peculiar complacency among wizards and ruined towers, with mailed knights, secret tribunals, monks, spectres and banditti," and which demonstrate "an undue love of moonlight, and mossy fountains, and the moral sublime" (*CW* 26: 37–38). His repugnance for the first of these novels, a lurid potboiler, is registered in a letter of 1817. "The other night I sat up till four o'clock, reading Matthew Lewis's Monk," he writes to a friend: "It is the most stupid & villanous novel that I have read for a great while. Considerable portions of it are grossly indecent[,] not to say brutish—one does not care a straw about one of the characters—and tho' 'little Mat' has legions of ghosts & devils at his bidding—one views their movements with profound indifference" (*Letters* 1: 109–110). Although this letter amply reveals Carlyle's contempt for the excesses of romance, it inevitably reflects his attraction to the form, and we would not be unkind to enquire why Carlyle, given his "profound indifference," should have stayed up until midnight, let alone four in the morning. For Carlyle, the roles of myopic rationalist and unyielding moralist are not comfortable ones: his desire is less to banish the specters, the ass-eared giants, and the goblin barbers—they do reappear for him, at the most incongruous times, in the persons of kings, *philosophes,* and revolutionaries—than to accommodate them in some form consistent with his fact-centered aesthetic. But *form* is the key word here. The form must be sufficiently elastic and complex to embrace both the romantic impulse toward the marvelous and the historical respect for the tangible; it must make a virtue of its own perplexity and internal inconsistencies.

To see how Carlyle arrives at such a form we must view in sequence "Wotton Reinfred," *Sartor Resartus,* and "The Diamond Necklace."[10] In the first of these, subtitled "A Romance," Carlyle atypically proposes a genre that he intends to follow without a strong sense of irony or perversity. Unlike his later experiments in the use of romance tradition, the uncompleted "Wotton Reinfred" is structured entirely by the initial separation and subsequent union of a man, named in the title, and a woman, Jane Montagu: after "Wotton," Carlyle rejects the fulfillment of romantic love as the basis for an entire work. It is a bizarre vestige of the sentimental tradition whose popularity had begun to wane long before its composition and whose apotheosis in Goethe's *Werther* Carlyle welcomed as the end of an age of overblown passion. The language of the romance's final encounter, in particular, is characterized by extreme passions and a stylistic hyperventilation that recalls the great sentimental novels of the eighteenth century. Consider, for example, the following passage, in which Jane tells of first meeting her nemesis Edmund Walter, the false suitor whom she must reject before she can be united with Wotton; note the inflated diction, the obtrusive alliteration, and the conventional imploring of destiny:

> It was here that I first saw the being whom I may justly call my evil genius; for since that hour his influence has pursued me only to my hurt, and still hangs like a baleful shadow over my whole life. Oh, my friend! This man, this demon! Why did he ever behold me? Why must the black, wasting whirlwind of his life snatch [me] into its course?

Or consider the following scene, preceded by the sentimental heroine's mandatory bout of insomnia, in which Jane informs her aunt that she intends to reject Walter's proposal:

> After two sleepless nights, and days exposed to a thousand influences of intreaty, menace, and persuasion, I rose with a decidedness of purpose such as I had never before felt; briefly, in words as distinct as were consistent with politeness, I penned my refusal, and, without speaking a word, laid the note before my aunt. Contrary to expectation she showed no anger, but only sorrow; she wept and kissed me; said that my happiness was hers; that if I so wished it, so it should be. Such tenderness melted me; I burst into tears and expressed in passionate language my unhappiness at distressing her.[11]

Given our knowledge of what Carlyle later does with such hyperbolic language, we might readily suspect him of parody. But for the moment he is making a serious effort to write within the confines of a genre he only conditionally accepts. "Wotton Reinfred" stems from an abortive period of fancy in Carlyle's career, and fancy gives way to understanding when he moves from this romance, which crumbles into a fragment, to *Sartor Resartus*, with its embedded fragment of romance.

The "Romance" chapter of *Sartor* presents the Edenic encounter of the amorous Teufelsdröckh with his flower-goddess Blumine. Dominated as it is by the young lover's unbridled fancy, it depicts women as "holy" and "heavenly" beings, "flitting past, in their many-coloured angel-plumage" (*SR* 133), and portrays the lovers' union with far more passion and sexuality than "Wotton Reinfred" manifests:

> Herself also he had seen in public places; that light yet so stately form; those dark tresses, shading a face where smiles and sunlight played over earnest deeps: but all this he had seen only as a magic vision, for him inaccessible, almost without reality. Her sphere was too far from his; how should she ever think of him; O Heaven! how should they so much as once meet together? And now that Rose-goddess sits in the same circle with him; the light of *her* eyes has smiled on him; if he speak, she will hear it! Nay, who knows, since the heavenly Sun looks into lowest valleys, but Blumine herself might have aforetime noted the so unnotable; perhaps, from his very gainsayers, as he had from hers, gathered wonder, gathered favour for him? Was the attraction, the agitation mutual, then; pole and pole trembling towards contact, when once brought into neighbourhood? (*SR* 138–139)

But the "magic vision" of romance, with its deification of women, its apostrophes to heaven, its incessant rhetorical questions, and its trembling passion, finds itself in a hostile setting in *Sartor*: "the sacred air-cities of Hope" are but one abortive step in Teufelsdröckh's progress toward "the mean clay-hamlets of Reality" (*SR* 133); he must abandon sexual passion directed towards an unfaithful woman for a philosophic apprehension of life's less ephemeral aspects. The romance is truncated and fragmentary, because it cannot avail as a structure for the entire work in which it resides. Consequently, despite the eager anticipation of sentimental love, its most affecting moments are cursorily dismissed. "We omit the passionate expostulations, entreaties, indignations" of the lovers' last meeting, Carlyle remarks, "since all was vain" (*SR* 145), and since the hero must leave his earthly paradise to cross the barrens that lead to the Everlasting Yea and to Natural Supernaturalism.

Carlyle's repudiation of romance in *Sartor Resartus* aligns him with a well-established movement in early nineteenth-century fiction. Jane Austen declares in a letter of 1816: "I could not sit seriously down to write a serious romance under any other motive than to save my life; and if it were indispensable for me to keep it up and never relax into laughing at myself or other people, I am sure I should be hung before I had finished the first chapter."[12] Walter Scott, in a review of Austen, defines the movement of the modern novelist away from excessive forms of romance, with their "splendid scenes of an imaginary world," toward "a correct and striking representation of that which is daily taking place around him."[13] Of course novelists like Austen and Scott, while combating the extravagances of romance, find some way to incorporate its central principles into their texts. If Austen pillories the sentimental heroine, with her insomnia, her tear-drenched garments, and her deliberate cultivation of moroseness, she nevertheless finds a man for her by the end of the final chapter. And if Scott admonishes us not to place too much trust in the romantic beauties of Highland glens, chasms, and waterfalls, he does afford us ample opportunity to visit them. Carlyle faces the similar artistic problem of how to shape a text which both opposes and accommodates romance: if the Carlyle who finds *The Monk* immoral and silly must be placated, the Carlyle who stays up until four in the morning to read it must be engaged. In the "Romance" chapter of *Sartor Resartus*, Carlyle is the man of understanding purging himself of the spurious fancy of "Wotton Reinfred." With the unproductive liaison between Teufelsdröckh and Blumine he rejects the theme of sexual and romantic love he addressed in the fragmentary story of Wotton and Jane, and he does not return in any sustained way to a male-female relationship until much later in *Reminiscences*, when he attempts to come to terms with his own love for Jane Welsh Carlyle. In "The Diamond Necklace," Carlyle appears in his more characteristic role as the man of reason who seeks a union between fancy and understanding, between romance and history.

Carlyle introduces to his problematic small romance the very elements that he elsewhere decries as maudlin conventional fictions. Despite his reservations about the "white, high, stainless beauties" of popular novels, he apotheosizes Marie Antoinette as a goddess who "issues, like the Moon . . . , down the Eastern steeps" (*CW* 28: 383). And despite his censure of Monk Lewis's ghosts, he repeatedly portrays his characters as "spectres" surrounded by mysterious threats:

> Walk warily, Countess de Lamotte; for now, with thickening breath, thou approachest the moment of moments! Principalities and Powers, *Parlement, Grand Chambre* and *Tournelle,* with all their whips and gibbet-wheels; the very Crack of Doom hangs over thee, if thou trip. Forward, with nerve of iron, on shoes of felt, *like* a Treasure-digger, in silence, looking neither to the right nor left,—where yawn abysses deep as the Pool, and all Pandemonium hovers, eager to rend thee into rags! (*CW* 28: 368)

Furthermore, for all his apparent dislike of nocturnal settings in popular fiction, Carlyle makes the night scene in the "Park of Versailles" chapter, with its deception, disguise, and mystery, one of the most striking in the whole work. First he goes to great lengths to establish the silence and magical aura of the night, as Paris succumbs to sleep:

> The night is of the darkest for the season; no Moon; warm, slumbering July, in motionless clouds, drops fatness over the Earth. The very stars from the Zenith see not Monseigneur; see only his and the world's cloud-covering, fringed with twilight in the far North. Midnight, telling itself forth from these shadowy Palace Domes? All the steeples of Versailles, the villages around, with metal tongue, and huge Paris itself dull-droning, answer drowsily, Yes! Sleep rules this Hemisphere of the World. (*CW* 28: 369)

Then he intensifies the enchantment of the scene, as the duped Cardinal de Rohan, whom we have already encountered in "Count Cagliostro," approaches the disguised woman whom he wrongly believes to be the queen and to whom he will foolishly give the necklace:

> The flowers are all asleep in Little Trianon, the roses folded-in for the night; but the Rose of Roses still wakes. O wondrous Earth! O doubly wondrous Park of Versailles, with Little and Great Trianon,—and a scarce-breathing Monseigneur! Ye Hydraulics of Lenôtre, that also slumber, with stop-cocks, in your deep leaden chambers, babble not of *him,* when ye arise. Ye odorous balm-shrubs, huge spectral Cedars, thou sacred Boscage of Hornbeam, ye dim Pavilions of the Peerless, whisper not! Moon, lie silent, hidden in thy vacant cave; no

> star look down: let neither Heaven nor Hell peep through the blanket of the Night, to cry, Hold, hold!—The Black Domino? Ha! Yes!—with stouter step than might have been expected, Monseigneur is under way; the Black Domino had only to whisper, low and eager: "In the Hornbeam Arbour!" And now, Cardinal, O now!—Yes, there hovers the white Celestial. (*CW* 28: 370)

Certainly the language here is not without its satiric overtones. The passage just quoted seems half-conscious of its apostrophes and its inflated diction. The glancing squib on Lenôtre's fountains recalls Carlyle's disdain for the symmetry and contrivance of French architecture. And if this episode enchants us with its evocation of "the world's cloud-covering, fringed with twilight in the far North," it equally disenchants us with its description of the "Concierge resupine," who, "with open mouth, audibly drinks-in nepenthe" (*CW* 28: 369). But for Carlyle, satire is the necessary complement to romance and not its inveterate antagonist. His text uses the machinery of romance at the same time as it makes us aware, in the manner of Goethe's *Faust*, that it relies upon machinery. "The Diamond Necklace" is both a work of fancy, which causes us to marvel at the world, and a work of understanding, which seeks to liberate us from spurious enchantments. In its combination of fancy and understanding it is, according to Carlyle's terms, a work of reason.

The grand model for Carlyle's repudiation of romance is *Don Quixote*: Carlyle, like Cervantes, implores us to purge our mind of inherited fictions, which cloud our perception of actualities and which lead us, like Don Quixote, to tilt at windmills. Yet *Don Quixote* is simultaneously the model for Carlyle's experiments in romance, since that work, like Carlyle's French histories, depends ultimately on the rhetorical trope of *apophasis*, which sanctions the continued existence of the very modes of thought it ostensibly opposes. In his *Lectures on the History of Literature*, delivered one year after the appearance of "The Diamond Necklace" and *The French Revolution*, Carlyle states:

> At the outset Cervantes seems to have contemplated not much more than a satire on chivalry—a burlesque. But, as he proceeds, the spirit soon grows on him. One may say that in his Don Quixote he pourtrays [*sic*] his own character, representing himself with good-natured irony, mistaking the illusions of his

> own heart for realities; but he proceeds ever more and more harmoniously. The first time where he appears to have gone deeply into his subject is the scene with the goatherds, where Don Quixote breaks out into an eulogy on the Golden Age, full of the finest poetry, although strangely introduced in the middle of the mockery which appears before. Throughout the delineation of the Don's character and the incidents of the story, there is the vesture of mockery, parody, with a seam of poetry shining through all. . . .
>
> We have the hard facts of this world's existence, and the ideal scheme struggling with these in a high enthusiastic manner delineated there; and for this there is no more wholesome vehicle anywhere than irony, the best way in which these ideas can live. If he had given us only a high-flown panegyric of the Age of Gold he would have found no ear for him, it is the self-mockery in which he envelopes [*sic*] it which reconciles us to the high bursts of enthusiasm, and which will keep the matter alive in the heart as long as there are men to read it![14]

Cervantes is both the satirist of Don Quixote and Don Quixote himself, both the ironist and the romantic. So, too, Carlyle indulges in the proscriptive irony of the eighteenth century at the same time as he incorporates it within the more comprehensive world-irony of modern literature. The initial repudiation of fiction becomes the means of subsequent reacceptance, when Carlyle allows the illusory phantoms of past literary conventions to coexist with the characters of modern history in his small romance. The mixed, ironic form that he shapes in "The Diamond Necklace" is recreated on a larger scale in *The French Revolution*, his greatest experiment in genre; for just as the former embodies features of the Gothic and sentimental fictions that it is partially intended to combat, the latter admits within its company many of the gods and heroes that Carlyle denigrates for having too long tyrannized the European epic imagination.

FOUR

History and Epic

Like the works preceding it in Carlyle's canon, *The French Revolution* depends on the fundamental principle of generic transgression, because it recognizes the laws of genre but does not obey them. The work announces itself in its subtitle as "A History" but then encourages its readers to assert, as John Stuart Mill does, that it "is not so much a history, as an epic poem."[1] It consequently resembles René Magritte's twentieth-century etching of a pipe, absurdly labeled *ceci n'est pas une pipe*: it arouses, and subsequently frustrates, the reader's generic expectations. The principal transgression of Carlyle's text stems from his refusal to accept Aristotle's doctrine that the particular interests of history are distinct from the universal concerns of poetry. This distinction was a commonplace among neoclassical epic theorists and, despite Aristotle's disclaimer that he could see no theoretical objection to a historical epic, it was repeatedly used to derogate such previous historical epics as the *Pharsalia* of Lucan, the *Lusiad* of Camoëns, and the *Henriade* of Voltaire. Sir William Davenant, in his preface to *Gondibert* (1650), criticized Lucan for attempting "to record the truth of Actions" instead of seeking "truth in the Passions," and for giving "a selected Diary of Fortune" rather than "the general History of Nature." He distinguished "Truth narrative and past," which is the concern of historians, from "truth operative," which is the goal of poets. Sir Richard Blackmore maintained, in an essay written the same year, that the epic should treat "a devis'd Probability of Actions and Circumstances, and not a relation of real Events; for otherwise it would not be an imitation of Nature, but Nature it self [*sic*]."[2] Even Edward Gibbon, who with his combined interests in history and epic might presumably have been interested in some theoretical accommodation of the two to each other, wrote that the epicist renders history "rather as it ought to have been, than as it actually was." He observed of the *Aeneid*, for instance, that its historical basis is the "flight of a band of refugees; their squabbles with a few villagers, and the settling of a paltry town."[3]

Carlyle's response to the traditional distinction between history and poetry is to argue that general truths are to be found in particular facts, and that in every object there is a latent poem, waiting to be liberated by a faithful rendering of it. In his conception of history as an imprisoned epic, he stands not with the strict Aristotelians, but with Novalis, who writes that "the whole of history is an Evangel," and Friedrich Schelling, who declares that "History is an epic composed in the mind of God."[4] In "Biography," through the voice of Sauerteig, Carlyle counters the commonplace conception of an epic as a contrived fiction containing supernatural machinery by defining it as a factual, historical narrative. Our interest in epic lies not, he insists, in derivative fictions—"frosty, artifical, heterogeneous things; more of gum-flowers than of roses" (*CW* 28: 51)—but in the germ of historical truth that generated them. Carlyle would counter Gibbon by perversely suggesting that the squabble of a few villagers is more important than the decorous fictions of Virgil, inasmuch as it is a fact and no mere vision. And he would argue against Blackmore that, as much as possible, it is nature itself, and not an imitation of it, that we want. By confounding nature and imitation in his art, Carlyle violates and opens to reexamination his contemporaries' conceptions of both history and epic as kinds of discourse.

I

In form and rhythm, Carlyle's history differs markedly from standard historical writing. "He is neither the descendent of Gibbon nor the ancestor of the Oxford History of England," writes the historian Alfred Cobban. "The examiners of a modern doctoral thesis, confronted with a history on Carlyle's pattern, would greet the phenomenon with consternation; while Gibbon, if he could have read it, might have recanted his faith that the days of the Goths and Vandals could not come back again."[5] Compare his account of the meeting of Charlotte Corday and Jean Paul Marat, for instance, with that offered by Christopher Hibbert in his recent one-volume narrative of the Revolution. I choose Hibbert, from the many nineteenth- and twentieth-century historians I might have selected, because he is in no danger of being taken for the unimaginative Dryasdust historian whom Carlyle deplored and,

hence, for a straw man in my argument; indeed, in his efforts to present a concise, lively, emphatic narrative, Hibbert stands very much in the tradition of Carlyle. Yet whereas Hibbert employs a conventional chronological sequence, underscored by the conventional rhythm of cause and effect, Carlyle violates chronology, and subsumes causation in a broader, less definable wonder. Hibbert introduces Charlotte as

> a tall, strong, mystical yet practical woman from a noble but poor Norman family, a descendant of the dramatist, Corneille. She had been educated at a convent at Caen and had then gone to live with an aunt in whose house she studied Voltaire and Plutarch and those other authors whose works had exercised so profound an influence on the young Manon Roland. When, after the fall of the Girondins, several of their leaders fled to Normandy to advocate *fédéralisme,* she attended their meetings, fell under their influence, undertook to work for them in Paris and, without their knowledge, took it into her head to assassinate the man she held principally responsible for their fall, Jean Paul Marat.[6]

Hibbert's introduction of Charlotte is spare and factual. The enticing detail of her descent from Corneille is unelaborated, and its possible emblematic significance—the irony that the champion of the three unities should contribute through his descendant to a historical event that defies unity and coherence—is left unstated. The causal sequence is clear and orderly. Charlotte reads Voltaire and Plutarch, then she attends the meetings of the Girondins, and then, "under their influence," she decides to murder Marat. Compare Carlyle's introduction of Charlotte:

> She is of stately Norman figure; in her twenty-fifth year; of beautiful still countenance: her name is Charlotte Corday, heretofore styled D'Armans, while Nobility still was. . . . What if she, this fair young Charlotte, had emerged from her secluded stillness, suddenly like a Star; cruel-lovely, with half-angelic, half-daemonic splendour; to gleam for a moment, and in a moment be extinguished: to be held in memory, so bright-complete was she, through long centuries!—Quitting Cimmerian Coalitions without, and the dim-simmering Twenty-five millions within, History will look fixedly at this one fair Apparition of a Charlotte Corday; will note

> whither Charlotte moves, how the little Life burns forth so radiant, then vanishes swallowed of the Night. (*FR* 3: 166–167)

The elevated language ("stately Norman figure," as opposed to "tall," or "heretofore styled D'Armans, while Nobility still was," for "from a noble but poor Norman family") immediately begins Charlotte's transformation into a mythic figure. Her apotheosis as a star propels her into the midst of a potent Zoroastrian myth of the conflict of light with darkness. Her sudden appearance and disappearance hint at countless myths of loss and transformation, serve the function of a *memento mori,* and underscore the universal human condition which links the readers of the history to its actors.

The differences between Hibbert's and Carlyle's accounts of Marat's death scene are equally telling. Hibbert writes:

> She found Marat lying in a high-walled copper bath wrapped in towels, for he could now only thus find relief from the pain and irritation of the skin disease which was slowly putrefying his flesh. She told him what was happening at Caen, giving him the names of men she said were working there against the Jacobins. He picked up a pen from the board upon which he had been writing and copied the names down, commenting, 'They shall soon all be guillotined.' At these words, Charlotte Corday took out her knife and plunged it into his chest, piercing the left lung and the aorta. At his cry of '*À moi, ma chère amie!*' his distraught mistress, Simone Évrard, rushed into the room and seeing the blood pouring from the wound, put her hand over it in an attempt to stop the flow. But Marat was already dead . . .
>
> To the jealous Robespierre's disgust, Marat was now the heroic martyr of the extreme Left.[7]

Note the simple, direct sentences, the tough expression, stripped of adjectives, the preference of factual, clinical language ("piercing the left lung and the aorta") to any expressions of emotion. Then compare Carlyle's account of the same scene:

> Hapless beautiful Charlotte; hapless squalid Marat! From Caen in the utmost West, from Neuchâtel in the utmost East, they two are drawing nigh each other; they two have, very strangely, business together. . . .

> It is yellow [*sic*] July evening, we say, the thirteenth of the month; eve of the Bastille day,—when 'M. Marat,' four years ago, in the crowd of the Pont Neuf, shrewdly required of that Besenval Hussar-party, which had such friendly dispositions, 'to dismount, and give up their arms, then'; and became notable among Patriot men. Four years: what a road he has travelled;—and sits now, about half-past seven of the clock, stewing in slipper-bath; sore afflicted; ill of Revolution Fever,—of what other malady this History had rather not name. . . .
>
> Citoyen Marat, I am from Caen the seat of rebellion, and wished to speak with you.—Be seated, *mon enfant.* Now what are the Traitors doing at Caen? What Deputies are at Caen?—Charlotte names some Deputies. 'Their heads shall fall within a fortnight,' croaks the eager People's-friend, clutching his tablets to write: *Barbaroux, Pétion,* writes he with bare shrunk arm, turning aside in the bath; *Pétion,* and *Louvet,* and—Charlotte has drawn her knife from the sheath; plunges it, with one sure stroke, into the writer's heart. '*À moi, chère amie,* Help, dear!' no more could the Death-choked say or shriek. The helpful Washerwoman running in, there is no Friend of the People, or Friend of the Washerwoman left; but his life with a groan gushes out, indignant, to the shades below.
>
> And so Marat People's-friend is ended; the lone Stylites has got hurled down suddenly from his Pillar,—*witherward* He that made him knows. (*FR* 3: 168–169)

In the first of the quoted paragraphs, Carlyle uses his dualistic portrayal of Corday and Marat, derived partly from the folktale motif of the beauty and the beast, to transform document into myth. Whereas Hibbert's account demonstrates that their meeting was plausible and, in retrospect, explicable, Carlyle's suggests that it was, in a mythic sense, inevitable; as in Thomas Hardy's poem "The Convergence of the Twain," where the Titanic and the iceberg that destroys it are destined to meet, Charlotte and Marat are drawn together by some inexplicable immanent will. In the second paragraph, Carlyle subverts chronology and reverses traditional historical practice by allowing his reflections on events to precede the occurrence of the events themselves. He points up the significance of the date of Marat's murder by contrasting the elevated aims of the Revolution with its bloody consequences; the ironic authorial meditation on Marat's death precedes the narration of that death. At the same time, he allows the metaphorical significance of fact to take precedence over fact itself. Whereas Hibbert introduces Marat's "skin disease" as a reason for his being in the bath, Carlyle first speaks of Marat's ailment as "Revolution Fever," and only subsequently discusses, in a circuitous and dismissive manner, its physical counterpart. In the third paragraph, Carlyle arrestingly dramatizes, rather than factually narrates, Marat's stabbing. Unlike Hibbert, who aims primarily at denotation, he creates a dense and richly connotative account. The epithet "Friend of the People" conjures up the revolutionaries' absurd pretensions, which Carlyle has treated satirically throughout, while the contending epithet "Friend of the Washerwoman" suggests Marat's essential humanity, his capacity to love and to be loved. His departure "to the shades below"—compare the more prosaic "Marat was already dead"—places him in the rank of epic heroes and fittingly perpetuates the passage's mythic thrust. At the beginning of the final paragraph Carlyle moves, as Hibbert does (and with a similar kind of paragraph division), from the death to its historical significance. But whereas Hibbert's concern is with Robespierre's jealousy and the relative strengths of various factions after Marat's death, Carlyle's focus is on a universal moral embodied in the satiric emblem of Marat as Saint Simeon Stylites.

Of course Carlyle, like most other historians, would concede that his concern is with facts. But his artistic conception of history and his transcendentalist philosophy render entirely problematic the crucial question of what a fact is. For Carlyle, every event occurs at the conflux of two eternities, the past and the present, and every object is an emblem of the entire universe. Consequently, no fact exists except in its relation to all other facts. The stylistic implications of this perception can again be illustrated by reference to Hibbert's more conventional narrative. The implied understanding in Hibbert's text is that a fact is something which can be reasonably established and accepted by a variety of observers using the most reliable documents. Although he does not cite his evidence, we can assume, for example, that his description of Charlotte Corday's knife penetrating "the left lung and the aorta" is reasonably based on the available medical documents concerning Marat's death. And his account of what Marat was doing when he died accords well with the accounts of other reliable historians: "He picked up a pen from the board upon which he had been writing and copied the names down, commenting, 'They shall soon all be guillotined.'" Yet, from Carlyle's perspective, Hibbert's facts are correct only insofar as they do not assert anything which cannot be proven; they do not have the depth and amplitude capable of linking events to their context in universal history. Carlyle's account of the same events, no doubt based upon some of the same sources, addresses questions Hibbert does not attempt to answer. In place of a staid description of Marat reaching for a pen, we have him "clutching his tablets to write . . . with bare shrunk arm, turning aside in the bath." Where Hibbert has Marat "commenting," apparently in a detached and unsuspecting manner, Carlyle has him croaking, in a way that reiterates his bestial and demonic nature. And where Hibbert notes, using a weak copula verb, that Marat was already dead when his lover entered the room, Carlyle exclaims forcefully that his life "gushes out, indignant, to the shades below." Carlyle's imaginative reconstructions take him beyond what can be substantiated. There may be no acceptable evidence that Marat clutched his writing tablets or turned aside in the bath, but his physical demeanor during his final minutes is crucial from Carlyle's perspective (as it is from Jacques Louis David's) to the graphic reproduction of his death. There may be no way of knowing whether Marat's spirit was "indignant" or not, but his state of mind at facing unexpected death is an inevitable part of the story of the Revolution. Given Carlyle's conception of history as the imaginative reconstruction of fragmentary evidence into a more complete whole, error and misapprehension are inevitable products of its creation.

The ways in which Carlyle's literary and mythic techniques transmute and complicate the presentation of fact are further exemplified in the following remarkable passage from the first volume, which depicts the strange early morning visitation of a young revolutionary to the besieged royalist general the Baron de Besenval. This nameless revolutionary takes it upon himself to inform the Baron that Paris will inevitably fall into the hands of the Revolution and that, by implication, the *ancien régime* is dead:

> At five o'clock this morning, as [Besenval] lay dreaming, oblivious in the *Ecole Militaire*, a 'figure' stood suddenly at his bedside; 'with face rather handsome; eyes inflamed, speech rapid and curt, air audacious': such a figure drew Priam's curtains! The message and monition of the figure was, that resistance would be hopeless; that if blood flowed, wo [*sic*] to him who shed it. Thus spoke the figure: and vanished. 'Withal there was a kind of eloquence that struck one.' Besenval admits

> that he should have arrested him, but did not. Who this figure with inflamed eyes, with speech rapid and curt, might be? Besenval knows, but mentions not. Camille Desmoulins? Pythagorean Marquis Valadi, inflamed with 'violent motions all night at the Palais Royal'? Fame names him 'Young M. Meillar'; then shuts her lips about him for ever. (*FR* 1: 187)

Here, Carlyle characteristically moves from chronicle, the serial presentation of events, toward art, the synthetic picture of what those events mean. He takes the heroic subtext of history, imprisoned within our limited notions of time and space, and liberates it by transforming the natural into the naturally supernatural. His presentation of the visitor as a mysterious "figure with inflamed eyes" gives the scene a mythic texture that is only latent in his principal source for the passage, the *Mémoires* of Besenval:

> Le 14, à cinq heures du matin, un homme entra chez moi. Cet homme (dont j'ai su le nom) avait les yeux enflammés, la parole rapide et courte, le maintien audacieux, et d'ailleurs la figure assez belle, et je ne sais quoi d'éloquent qui me frappa. "Monsieur le baron, me dit-il, il faut que vous soyez averti, pour prévenir une résistance inutile. Au-jourd'hui les barrières de Paris seront brûlées; j'en suis sûr, et j'y peux rien, ni vous non plus. N'essayez pas de l'empêcher. Vous sacrifieriez des hommes sans éteindre un flambeau." Je ne me rappelle pas ce que je lui répondis, mais il pâlit de rage, et sortit précipitamment. J'aurais dû le faire arrêter: je n'en fis rien.
>
> (On the 14th [of July], at 5 o'clock in the morning, a man entered my lodgings [at the École Militaire]. This man (whose name I have since found out) had flashing eyes, breathless speech, a bold bearing, and besides a rather handsome appearance and a certain eloquence which struck me. "Monsieur le Baron," he said to me, "you must be warned in order to prevent a futile resistance. Today the *barrières* of Paris will be burned. I am certain of it. I cannot do anything about it, nor can you. Don't try to prevent it. You would sacrifice lives without extinguishing a single torch." I do not recall how I answered him, but he paled with rage, and left in a hurry. I should have had him arrested: I did not.)[8]

That Besenval's uninvited guest should be given an otherworldly appearance in Carlyle's narrative is fitting, inasmuch as the reference to Priam's mysterious visitor links the passage with the long-standing epic convention of "the descent of an emissary god or angel from heaven bearing a message to earth."[9]

At the same time as Carlyle's passage refers by means of a footnote (in the manner of a conventional history) to Besenval's memoirs, it points in epic fashion, by this mythic analogue, to the final book of the *Iliad* where the messenger Iris conveys the will of Zeus to Priam:

> Before the King *Jove*'s Messenger appears,
> And thus in Whispers greets his trembling Ears.
> Fear not, oh Father! no ill News I bear;
> From *Jove* I come, *Jove* makes thee still his Care:
> For *Hector*'s sake these Walls he bids thee leave,
> And bear what stern *Achilles* may receive. . . .
> Fierce as he is, *Achilles*' self shall spare
> Thy Age, nor touch one venerable Hair. . . .
> She spoke, and vanish'd.[10]

Carlyle's substitution of "Thus spoke the figure: and vanished" for "il . . . sortit précipitamment" recalls the very wording of Pope's translation of the passage from Homer. Yet this single literary analogue for the historical event is inexact. Young M. Meillar does not bring the kind of consolation to Besenval that Iris brings to Priam: in the burning rubble of Paris there is little solace for a monarchist, no divine intervention, and no second Troy. Consequently, another, and even more overt, analogue must be brought into play. Carlyle's "such a figure drew Priam's curtains" comes almost verbatim from the second part of *Henry the Fourth*, where Northumberland upbraids Morton for hesitating to deliver the news of his son's death:

> Thou tremblest, and the whiteness in thy cheek
> Is apter than thy tongue to tell thy errand.
> Even such a man, so faint, so spiritless,
> So dull, so dead in look, so woe-begone,
> Drew Priam's curtain in the dead of night,
> And would have told him half his Troy was burnt.[11]

This passage better reflects the mood of the Besenval episode: the message is devoid of hope, while the image of fire suggests the inevitable conflagration of Paris and the demise of the *ancien régime*. Yet even here the analogue is not perfect, for Besenval's visitor is by no means regretful, faint, or spiritless. The phrase "such a figure drew Priam's curtains" has the inclusive reference of the epic simile, without its expansiveness and clarity; rather than being a leisurely introduction of analogous matter from an earlier literature into the foreground of the text, it becomes the agent through which meaning escapes from language.[12] By pitting various inadequate analogues against each other, Carlyle establishes a self-conscious and resolutely dialogic text, which leads us to question knowledge itself, as the issue of what can be known, or even named, comes to the fore. The anonymity of the visitor, glancingly suggested in the account of Besenval (who admits to knowing the intruder's name, but refuses to reveal it), figures prominently in Carlyle's recreation. Various possible names, spectral and uncertain, are offered by Carlyle; the one with which he rests, "Young M. Meillar," appears briefly, inexplicably, and fades into silence. As the names advance and recede in the text, fixed identities dissolve; the human "figure" becomes a symbolical "figure," or historical hieroglyph, subject to contending interpretations; and the nature of the symbol itself, both as the historical event and as the verbal reconstitution of it, is called into question.

The extreme density of Carlyle's account becomes apparent when we compare it with a more conventional treatment of the same incident. Using identical details, Jules Michelet writes in his celebrated nineteenth-century history of the Revolution:

> At five o'clock that same morning, [Besenval] had received a strange visit;—a man rushed in; his countenance was livid, his eyes flashed fire, his language was impetuous and brief, and his manner audacious. The old coxcomb, who was the most frivolous officer of the *ancien régime*, but brave and collected, gazed at the man, and was struck with admiration. "Baron," said the man, "I come to advise you to make no resistance; the barriers will be burnt to-day; I am sure of it, but cannot prevent it; neither can you—do not try."
>
> Besenval was not afraid; but he had, nevertheless, felt the shock, and suffered its moral effect. "There was something eloquent in that man," says he, "that struck me; I ought to have had him arrested, and yet I did not." It was the *ancien régime* and the Revolution meeting face to face, and the latter left the former lost in astonishment.[13]

Michelet, like Carlyle, recognizes the power of words to influence historical perception: here as throughout his history a terse, athletic style governs his popular, rousing narrative. And, like Carlyle, he values the symbolic underpinnings of facts, as the nicely turned final sentence attests. Yet the way in which Michelet conveys meaning starkly contrasts with Carlyle's approach to the same data. In Michelet, meaning is given vigorously in well-chiseled words; the sentences are bold and assertive, the judgments swift and sure. In Carlyle, meaning appears furtively, expressions are interrogative or evasive, and a definitive single interpretation of the events is unavailable.

Given his penchant for the mythic transformation of fact, it is hardly surprising that Carlyle was disaffected from nineteenth-century efforts to establish history as a science. He would not have agreed with J. B. Bury's famous assertion that "history is a science, no less and no more."[14] On occasion, Carlyle appeals to scientific rigor in the handling of evidence, as when he complains that "Thiers's *History*, in ten volumes foolscap-octavo, contains, if we remember rightly, one reference; and that to a book, not to the page or chapter of a book" (*CW* 29: 3). Yet for him, the scientific or documentary historian is at best an artisan compiling the discontinuous materials from which a more complete history could be shaped by the artist. Of Leopold von Ranke, the influential early proponent of scientific history, he characteristically remarked that he "was a diligent man," who "gave much about diplomacies useful in his way," but "no picture of men or things."[15] And Carlyle unequivocally admits personal bias as an inevitable part of the historical enterprise: "Each individual takes up the Phenomenon according to his own point of vision, to the structure of his optic organs;—gives, consciously, some poor crotchety picture of several things; unconsciously some picture of himself at least. And the Phenomenon, for its part, subsists there, all the while, unaltered; waiting to be pictured as often as you like, its entire meaning not to be compressed into any picture drawn by man" (*CW* 29: 2).[16]

While Carlyle rejects an exclusively scientific history, he does not go so far as to attempt historical fiction in the tradition of Sir Walter Scott.[17] He adopts Scott's fictitious historian Dryasdust as the rhetorical enemy of his artistry, and he comes close to identifying Scott's artistic purposes with his own when he lauds his perception—the perception missing in Ranke—"that the bygone ages of the world were actually filled by living men, not by protocols, state-papers, controversies and abstractions of men"

(*CW* 29: 77). As Marat's death scene shows, he engages in the graphic reconstruction of facts which has become a staple of the historical novel. Yet Carlyle tends to regard the historical novel as an attempt to portray modern sentiments in an inappropriate dress. In *The Life of Schiller* he dismisses "that half-illicit species of composition, the historic novel" (*CW* 25: 61), while he elsewhere likens it to "a pasteboard Tree, cobbled together out of size and waste-paper and water-colours; altogether unconnected with the soil of Thought, except by mere juxtaposition" (*CW* 26: 253–254). Despite his perception that imaginative reconstruction is necessary to historical completeness, he refuses to enter into the creation of explicitly fictional characters. Carlyle is, as Charles Dickens effusively acknowledges in his dedication, instrumental to the inception and success of *A Tale of Two Cities*, yet he does not create the characters for whom a mid-Victorian audience would laugh and weep.[18] Carlyle parallels Tolstoy in his efforts to relate grand historical events and general principles of causation to the lives of individuals, yet he is unwilling to create the endearing but fictional Andrei, Natasha, and Pierre, the counterparts to Dickens' Charles, Lucy, and Sidney.

Carlyle, then, avoids scientific history on the one hand and the historical novel on the other. In his attempt to depict the French Revolution as one chapter from universal history, he does approximate the theocratic form of history whose grand exemplar is the Bible's demonstration of divine providence in time, from Genesis to Revelations, from Eden to the New Jerusalem. Carlyle insistently charges the historian with the task of demonstrating the ultimate reality underlying disparate phenomena, and he uses the myth of fall and redemption in his account of the Revolution. But for him Eden and the New Jerusalem are imaginative constructs, rather than fixed realities; the cycle from cosmos to chaos to cosmos which the Revolution exemplifies is endlessly recurrent, not unique.[19] Carlyle, obsessed with the idea of change, seems uneasy with any version of history which suggests that progress is inevitable and ultimate. Although he uses the form of dialectic to explain the development of cultures, he does not share Hegel's sense that the movement of history from thesis to antithesis to synthesis will necessarily lead to final progress.[20] Neither is his perspective sympathetic to Thomas Babington Macaulay and the Whig interpretation of history, which shows the past marching progressively toward the wonders of the present.

Finally, because Carlyle is radically uncertain about the meaning of history, he rejects any restrictively didactic conception of the historian's task. Despite his undeniable moral bent, he refuses to accept that history can be, in any simple sense, "Philosophy teaching by experience." If he had recourse to a narrow didacticism, many of his formal problems would be alleviated, for there are traditions of fable and allegory on which he could readily draw. But given his conception of history as "the essence of innumerable biographies," he must create a mixed and plastic form for its representation. He takes from the work of scientific or documentary historians (for they must provide the basis for the innumerable biographies), but moves beyond their limitations to an error-prone but necessary imaginative reconstruction. He attempts, as the historical novelists do, to infuse his characters with life, but does not create fictional personages. He employs the patterns of theocratic history, but does not locate his Eden or his heaven in time. He elucidates the meanings of events (for how can history, properly told, fail to be instructive?), but does not suggest that they can ever be fully defined or exhausted. In short, he creates a radically multifarious form of history: as his style changes, as his "point of vision" (*FR* 1: 214) changes, his sympathies, interpretations, and principles of interpretation alter.

II

If Carlyle's text violates the traditions of history, it equally transgresses the inherited codes of epic. Granted, in his desire to write the "grand Poem" of his time in *The French Revolution* (*Letters* 6: 446), Carlyle does reflect some of the central principles of neoclassical epic theory: its belief in the predominance of epic among literary forms, its desire for one comprehensive action, and its faith in the centrality to epic of moral truth. Nevertheless, his theory of epic (given its fullest expression in a critical fragment of an essay on "Biography" rather than in a sustained treatise) does not accord well with the systematic, prescriptive treatments of epic characteristic of the rigorous neoclassicists. His attempt to locate an epic theme in the "Bible of World-History" (*CW* 28: 250) is, moreover, profoundly unsympathetic to the neoclassical notion of epic as a closed, coherent fiction. Carlyle's revolutionary history runs foul, in particular, of Le Bossu's influential pronouncement that the epic is a fictitious narrative constructed by the author to inculcate a particular moral. According to Le Bossu's theory, an epic is fabricated in much the same way as a fable is, since its characters and incidents are subservient to the already formulated ideas of its author. Carlyle's idea of historical epic makes the conceptual implications of history subservient to events; as an artistic historian, he must liberate the moral significance of actual events rather than fabricate events to depict morals.

Carlyle's abjuration of Le Bossu does not in itself place him in the vanguard of literary thought, for even in the eighteenth century Le Bossu was something of a straw man, whom it was customary to derogate. When Blair dismisses Le Bossu's notion of the priority of moral to fable as "one of the most frigid and absurd ideas, that ever entered into the mind of a Critic,"[21] he expresses a feeling shared by Alexander Pope, Joseph Addison, Blackmore, Voltaire, and William Hayley. Carlyle violates a far more fundamental principle of neoclassical epic theory, the very notion that the epicist is detached from his material and in control of it. Many of the famous epic conventions are predicated on this principle. The epic statement of theme presupposes the author's conceptual control over his material and the possibility of extricating meaning from sign, while such characteristic delaying features as the epic simile and the invocation to a muse demonstrate the author's dominion over the pace of his narrative. The tradition of opening the epic *in medias res* presupposes that the author has already conceived its beginning, middle, and end. Whereas traditional epic knows its end didactically, and can therefore anticipate its end structurally, Carlyle's epic history is deliberately indeterminate, unaware both of its termination and of its final intention. And whereas traditional epic offers its meaning with clarity and composure in its opening lines, Carlyle's text gives its contending meanings furtively and unpredictably, calling the possibility of historical knowledge severely into question. As Albert J. LaValley nicely states, Carlyle "intended to write an epic for the modern age, one that would be both ultimate and full in its recognition of man's deepest drives but would also be different from all previous epics, unresolved and problematic, like the process of history itself."[22]

Much of the calculated uncertainty of Carlyle's text arises from its presentation of an action not yet closed—the revolutionary specter of 1789 continues to haunt Britain in 1837—and therefore not capable of being contained within a hermetically confined epic structure. The lack of detachment which poses a challenge to the text as history renders equally problematic its status as epic. Critics such as Friedrich Schlegel and Richter, whom Carlyle respects far more than he does Le Bossu, are adamant in their assertions that the proper theme of epic lies in the remote past. Madame de Staël, a confidante of the German aestheticians and an important interpreter of their work for Carlyle and other English speakers, similarly insists that the epic is an accomplishment of a nation in its primitive state, and that it is therefore denied to modern societies.[23] Hegel, whose investigations into the relation of historical period and genre offer interesting comparisons with Carlyle's less sustained comments on the same topic, contends that the epic forms shaped by a previous state of society are incongruous with a modern vision. Even in such an early poem as the *Aeneid*, which Sauerteig lists as the first of the "artificial, heterogeneous" modern epics, Hegel finds a disparity between the cultivated author and the heroic world he portrays. Virgil's epic gods, which Sauerteig includes in the company of unbelieved phantasms, "float before our vision as so many invented wonders, as members of an artificial system," according to Hegel. Modern society, he concludes, is incompatible with epic. "The general condition of the world to-day has assumed a form, which, in its prosaic character, is diametrically opposed to everything which we found indispensable to the genuine Epos," Hegel argues, "while the revolutions, which have been imposed upon the actual social conditions of states and nations, are still too strongly riveted in our memory as actual experiences that they should be able to receive an epic type of art."[24] While modern German criticism sees the epic as the integrated, harmonious poem of a nation in its youth, and insists that it be set in the past, Carlyle voluntarily encompasses within his revolutionary text all of the internal contradictions that Schlegel and de Staël and Hegel see as hindrances to a modern epic: the heterogeneous, dialogic body of his history becomes the formal counterpart of Europe in revolution.

To read *The French Revolution* as an epic is necessarily to engage in a process of generic redefinition, for many of the characteristic features of traditional epic are either missing or severely displaced in Carlyle's text.[25] It does not commence with an epic statement of theme, and can only in a strongly qualified sense be said to begin *in medias res*. Its opening sentence, rather than suggesting the universal reference of an "*Arma virumque cano*" or an "Of Man's First Disobedience," begins with the unexplained and unadorned surname of a person almost inconsequential in the remainder of the text; as John D. Rosenberg suggests, this disclosure is immediate almost to the point of incomprehensibility.[26] *The French Revolution* does not have, as most previous epics do, a single principal protagonist to represent the fortunes and ethos of his nation, but a variety of contending and fragmentary heroes. Neither does it present protracted battles and repeated instances of physical valor, since much of the struggle depicted in the work is of "the modern *lingual* or Parliamentary-logical kind" rather than of "the ancient or *manual* kind in the steel battlefield" (*FR* 2: 15). Furthermore, while *The French Revolution* has at its center an epic struggle between dying royalty and nascent revolution, it does not champion the cause of one party against another as traditional epics do, but rather treats the action of the French Revolution from the perspective of modern European humanity in general. Carlyle's history is written in prose rather than in verse, and is characterized by rapid changes in tone and point of view rather than by a detached epic voice.[27] While Carlyle uses or travesties such specific conventions as the epic simile, the catalogue, the invocation, and epic debates and festivals, the paucity of their appearances in the text serves more often to counter than to foster any sense that he is making a concerted effort to follow epic convention.

The French Revolution's relation to epic tradition is further complicated by its explicit references to epic forms and practices. Before narrating an important revolutionary procession, Carlyle apostrophizes: "suppose we too, good Reader, should, as now without miracle Muse Clio enables us,—take *our* station also on some coign of vantage; and glance momentarily over this Procession, and this Life-sea; with far other eyes than the rest do, namely with prophetic? We can mount, and stand there, without fear of falling" (*FR* 1: 134–135). Here the muse of history is credited with the functions proper to the epic muse, the relation of the specific to the universal and of the past to the future. Nevertheless, the special perspective that she offers is removed from any suggestion of heavenly insight, and derives instead from powers of retrospection naturally given by the inevitable passage of time. Her function is performed "without miracle," since Carlyle's modern epic must be founded "on Belief and provable Fact, or have no foundation at all" (*FR* 3: 31). Elsewhere, Carlyle manifests an equally ironic stance toward epic tradition when he depicts as epic machinery a band of brigands,

> an actual existing quotity of persons; who, long reflected and reverberated through so many millions of heads, as in concave multiplying mirrors, become a whole Brigand World; and, like a kind of Supernatural Machinery, wondrously move the Epos of the Revolution. The Brigands are here; the Brigands are

> there; the Brigands are coming! Not otherwise sounded the clang of Phoebus Apollo's silver bow, scattering pestilence and pale terror: for this clang too was of the imagination; preternatural; and it too walked in formless immeasurability, *having made itself like to the Night*. . . . (*FR* 1: 126)

Carlyle's suggestion that this band operates as a kind of epic machinery is seemingly reinforced by the Homeric allusion, since the "pestilence and pale terror" aroused by the sound of the invisible Apollo's bow (in the vehicle of the epic simile) images the agitation of the French people over the anticipated arrival of the brigands (in the simile's tenor). But while the Homeric analogue suggests the equal stature of the two phenomena compared, their equality stems from their both being "of the imagination," and the epic simile undercuts rather than supports the grandeur of the contemporary incident. As Carlyle's subsequent suggestion that the somewhat gullible French nation "will see Shapes enough of Immortals . . . and never want for Epical Machinery" (*FR* 1: 127) implies, the power of the brigands is perhaps better imaged by the human delusions of *Don Quixote* than by the divine enchantments of the *Iliad*. In yet another instance, Carlyle writes of Marie Antoinette's new wardrobe, needlessly prepared for the imminent flight to Varennes, as a sort of epic new clothes:

> New Clothes are needed; as usual, in all Epic transactions, were it in the grimmest iron ages; consider 'Queen Crimhilde, with her sixty sempstresses,' in that iron *Nibelungen Song*! No Queen can stir without new clothes. Therefore, now, Dame Campan whisks assiduous to this mantua-maker and to that: and there is clipping of frocks and gowns, upper clothes and under, great and small; such a clipping and sewing as—might have been dispensed with. (*FR* 2: 157)

Whatever elevation is achieved by Carlyle's allusion to the *Nibelungenlied* and by the stately doublets "frocks and gowns, upper clothes and under, great and small" is destroyed by the triviality of the subject discussed, underclothing, and by the deflationary final phrase "might have been dispensed with."

The complex relation of Carlyle's history to epic tradition is further evidenced by its treatment of war. Discussing the insurrection of women, Carlyle asserts, in epic fashion, the superiority of his own subject over those treated by earlier epicists; like Milton, he shows disaffection with war as "the only Argument / Heroic deem'd":[28]

> Battles, in these ages, are transacted by mechanism; with the slightest possible development of human individuality or spontaneity: men now even die, and kill one another, in an artificial manner. Battles ever since Homer's time, when they were Fighting Mobs, have mostly ceased to be worth looking at, worth reading of or remembering. How many wearisome bloody Battles does History strive to represent; or even, in a husky way, to sing:—and she would omit or carelessly slur-over this one Insurrection of Women? (*FR* 1: 251)

Elsewhere, in describing the superiority of the fall of the Bastille to the fall of Troy, Carlyle nevertheless appears to be celebrating military struggle. "The Siege of the Bastille," he writes,

> weighed with which, in the Historical balance, most other sieges, including that of Troy Town, are gossamer, cost, as we find, in killed and mortally wounded, on the part of the Besiegers, some Eighty-three persons: on the part of the Besieged, after all that straw-burning, fire-pumping, and deluge of musketry, One poor solitary Invalid, shot stone-dead . . . on the battlements! The Bastille Fortress, like the City of Jericho, was overturned by miraculous *sound*. (*FR* 1: 210)

But what most amazes Carlyle about the siege of the Bastille is the remarkably unmilitary nature of its success. Hence, the Homeric struggle that he likens to this "anomalous" siege is no heroic human battle, but rather the war of the pygmies and the cranes (*FR* 1: 191) from the third book of the *Iliad*.

The epic status of *The French Revolution* is further complicated by the absence of a single hero on whose character a coherent action can be based. Commentators have repeatedly looked at Mirabeau as the hero who might possibly have given order to the efforts of the Revolution, regretting that he departs the historical stage in the middle of the second volume; but Carlyle explicitly identifies him as a "Tragic" rather than "Epic" hero (*FR* 2: 147). Others point to Napoleon, noting his brief but recurrent appearances throughout the text and citing his ability to act where others become lost in language and legislation. J. A. Heraud reflects the complexity of this issue in his various suggestions on heroism in Carlyle's text; he notes how Napoleon's appearances lend coherence to the text's structure, suggests that Carlyle might have chosen a single hero for each division of the work (as Spenser does in *The Faerie Queene*), and concludes that Carlyle is the only hero of *The French Revolution*. Most recently, John D. Rosenberg has identified the Paris mob as hero, and John Clubbe has compellingly argued for the importance of Goethe as hero in Carlyle's text.[29] Our ultimate identification of Carlyle's hero in *The French Revolution* must be an elastic and all-encompassing one: his hero is the human being as symbolmaker, the shaper of "Realised Ideals" by which to live. This identification of the hero subsumes the others: Louis XVI and Marie Antoinette as representatives of a dead but once divine monarchy, Mirabeau as political leader, Napoleon as military leader, the people as the destroyers of bankrupt institutions, Goethe as thinker, and Carlyle as maker. But while Carlyle's fragmentary revelations of heroism are challenging and exciting, they hardly offer the kind of focus given by the wrath of Achilles or the wanderings of Aeneas or man's first disobedience.

The question of heroism is one to which Carlyle obstinately refuses us a clear and fixed answer; another is the relation of epic and drama in his text. Carlyle scholars have debated the issue of whether *The French Revolution* is an epic or a drama since the nineteenth century, and continue to do so.[30] While we must certainly acknowledge that generic labels become useless if they become too broad, too much rigor in their application can be misplaced. To state definitively that Carlyle's text is an epic or a drama runs counter to its mixed form and deliberate inconclusiveness: the work is, in a fragmentary, displaced, and perverse sense, both. Carlyle has good cause to know the differences between epic and drama from Aristotle, from the correspondence of Goethe and Schiller, and from Richter's treatise on aesthetics. But he is intrigued by the possibilities of an inclusive form which suggests both: in his essay on the *Nibelungenlied*, he examines it simultaneously as a northern *Iliad* and as an Aristotelian tragedy (*CW* 27: 216–273). Carlyle does not want us to answer our generic questions about his text; but he does not want us to stop asking them, for it is only through our effort to find unity in his multi-axial form that we engage in the virtuosic reading that the text demands.

We might with good reason argue that *The French Revolution* is not an epic but, as the work's own subtitle suggests, a history, which uses scattered features of traditional epic in an inconsistent though occasionally brilliant manner. At the most, we might accord Carlyle's work the position of a "tertiary epic," as Richard Jenkyns terms *Don Juan,*[31] a work that, rather than faithfully following the conventions of primary epic as secondary epic does, makes those conventions the object of self-conscious examination and burlesque. Or we might with equally good reason argue that *The French Revolution* is, despite its deviation from tradition in accidental features, epic in essence. In defense of this last position, it might be suggested that Carlyle's text clearly manifests the predominant features of epic as defined, for example, by Thomas Greene: expansiveness, wonder, and a theme of political struggle. According to Greene, epic centers on "the two-fold concern of politics—the establishment of control through violence and the right use of control in government." Its action "is most fully realized through changes of institutions or regimes," he writes, "changes which extend its consequences throughout society and throughout time. Thus the epic is the great poem of beginnings and endings. The *Aeneid* is typical, beginning with an ending and ending with a beginning."[32] Carlyle presents a cataclysmic struggle of cosmic importance and, like Virgil (in Dryden's summary of the *Aeneid*), portrays "one empire destroyed, and another raised from the ruins of it."[33] The expansiveness of Carlyle's treatment, the gravity of his presentation, and the importance of his theme all suggest the designation "epic."

These contrasting critical positions, argued from quite different assumptions about the nature of genre, must both be taken into account in a generic consideration of *The French Revolution,* for they broadly reflect the field of interpretation available to Carlyle, from Le Bossu's tightly defined notion of epics as extended fables to Hugh Blair's global definition of them as "poetical recitals of great adventures."[34] The former view, which resists the injudicious application of one generic label to works widely divergent in form, asserts the priority of previous epics in defining the epic genre. The latter, which shares Friedrich Schlegel's aversion to obsolete categories, allows the right of a modern work to modify inherited forms according to the inherent principles of a particular generic tradition. The provocative form of *The French Revolution,* in which Carlyle approaches epic tradition with the same perversity that marks his handling of romance in "The Diamond Necklace," affords room for both responses. The most valuable formal approach to Carlyle's history is, therefore, neither to affirm nor to reject the work's epic status—either of which would be a valid conclusion of a generic study—but to acknowledge how his text challenges its readers to reconsider the principles of genre. The fierce internal warfare of Carlyle's text plays out a struggle between innovation and conservation like the political struggle he aims to describe. As we shall see in the following chapter, this warfare appears most compellingly in his juxtaposition of modern themes with inherited epic machinery.

FIVE

New and Antiquated Myths

Nicholas Boileau began a fierce debate in the late seventeenth century by advocating the exclusive use of classical mythology in epic. The champion of the ancients in their quarrel with the moderns, Boileau insisted that proper models for epic machinery were to be found in them, and not in Christianity, which should be reserved for higher uses than the provision of ornamental literary fictions. Boileau's antagonists, the authors and advocates of Christian epics, countered by positing the virtue of employing the agents of a living faith, rather than unbelieved pagan gods, to perform the will of heaven. For the duration of this skirmish, which spread into Britain and lasted well into the eighteenth century, the two parties launched arguments and counterarguments at each other, agreeing only in their censure of Camoëns, who, in his epic of Portuguese exploration, uses both kinds of machinery.[1] In "Biography," Carlyle rakes the embers of this fading dispute, and dismisses all forms of myth—"the dead Pagan gods of an *Epigoniad,*" "the dead-living Pagan-Christian gods of a *Lusiad,*" and "the concrete-abstract, evangelical-metaphysical gods of a *Paradise Lost*"—as "Superannuated lumber," machinery that has become too overtly mechanical (*CW* 28: 51). Having chosen a modern argument for his epic history, he faces the artistic problem of finding an appropriate myth to present its universal significance. Throughout his works, Carlyle identifies this problem of finding a credible myth as one of the central difficulties of modern life. In *Sartor Resartus*, Teufelsdröckh acknowledges Voltaire's demonstration that "the Mythus of the Christian Religion looks not in the eighteenth century as it did in the eighth." After granting Voltaire the correctness of his views on the obsolescence of Christianity, he proposes a new effort "to embody the divine Spirit of that Religion in a new Mythus" and bravely declares: "what are antiquated Mythuses to me?" (*SR* 194). A desire to have done with "antiquated

Mythuses" is fundamental to Carlyle's writings, for much as he approves of the lost age of faith (and writes about it most eloquently in the medieval passages of *Past and Present*), he deprecates any turning to obsolete beliefs, whether "in the divine right of Game-destroyers" or "in consecrated dough-wafers, and the godhood of a poor old Italian Man" (*FR* 1: 149). By rejecting outmoded tales, Carlyle makes unavailable to himself the trappings of previous classical and Christian epics and forces himself to find a new myth capable of sustaining his argument.

I

Carlyle's myth of modern life, as developed in the critical miscellanies and *Sartor Resartus*, presents three consecutive stages of human relation to the universe, roughly corresponding to Johann Gottlieb Fichte's alternating periods of belief and unbelief in human history. In the initial age of faith, represented by Abbot Samson in *Past and Present*, humans live harmoniously with the external world, which for them reflects transcendent realities. In the age of cant and doubt, represented by the Arch-Quack Cagliostro, Voltaire the demythologizer, the Wertherean Byron, and the young Goethe, some ally themselves with obsolete symbols and formulas separated from the reality they originally signified; others recognize the vacancy of their inherited symbols and either ridicule or mourn their vacancy. Finally, in the age of renewed faith, typified by the mature Goethe, in whose works we see a "mind working itself into clearer and clearer freedom" (*CW* 27: 430), humans rediscover in the temporal and conditional world symbols of transcendent reality. This cyclical movement from faith through doubt to a renewed faith underlies all of Carlyle's periodical essays on French and German subjects. It is clearly reflected in *Sartor* where Diogenes moves from an idyllic childhood, through a stage of doubt and wandering, to an eventual realization that the universe is alive and beneficent.

The version of Carlyle's tripartite schema that most clearly prepares us for the informing myth of *The French Revolution* appears in the crucial and often cited essay "Characteristics" (1831). The mythic cosmology of "Characteristics" pictures human consciousness as being precariously poised over a deeper and more powerful unconsciousness: Nature, Carlyle writes, "will have us rest on her beautiful and awful bosom as if it were our secure home; on the bottomless boundless Deep, whereon all human things fearfully and wonderfully swim, she will have us walk and build, as if the film which supported us there . . . were no film, but a solid rock-foundation" (*CW* 28: 3). Humanity begins in a state of "paradisaic Unconsciousness," which is later destroyed by ratiocination, just as Eden is lost through the Fall (*CW* 28: 2–3). Self-consciousness becomes the besetting evil of modern life, as humans become alienated from their universe: whereas previously the eternal and the infinite revealed themselves in earthly symbols, now "the Divinity has withdrawn from the Earth" and abandoned humankind (*CW* 28: 29–30). The regeneration of the modern spirit occurs when "the eternal fact begins again to be recognised, . . . that God not only made us and beholds us, but is in us and around us; that the Age of Miracles, as it ever was, now is" (*CW* 28: 42). With that regeneration, the cycle of "paradisaic Unconsciousness," doubt, and redemption is completed.

The French Revolution, like "Characteristics," uses a variety of deeply rooted mythic patterns, divorced from their traditional classical and Judeo-Christian contexts. The first of these is the presentation of a mythic cosmology, in which the temporal and the spatial realms are evidences of a transcendent power. Carlyle exhorts his reader to picture the Revolution as a particular manifestation in time and space of the "Shoreless Fountain-Ocean of Force" which makes up the universe (*FR* 2: 103). As in "Characteristics," he portrays the known world as hovering precariously over a vast mystery: "all Knowledge and all Practice," he writes, "hang wondrous over infinite abysses of the Unknown, Impracticable; and our whole being is an infinite abyss, *over-arched* by Habit, as by a thin Earth-rind, laboriously built together" (*FR* 1: 38). But, also as in "Characteristics," the world portrayed is a symbolic one, where the known images the unknown; thus, the principal theme of *The French Revolution* is the making and unmaking of symbols, or "Realised Ideals," that "grow; and, after long stormy growth, bloom out mature, supreme; then quickly (for the blossom is brief) fall into decay; sorrowfully dwindle; and crumble down, or rush down, noisily or noiselessly disappearing" (*FR* 1: 10).

The mythic patterns of *The French Revolution* are all predicated on this symbolic universe, where persons, places, and times become endowed with special significance. In *The French Revolution*, as in "The Diamond Necklace," historical characters are transformed into gods and heroes. Carlyle's portrayal of Marie Antoinette, for example, adopts the mythic pattern of apotheosis. Early in Volume

I, "the fair young Queen, in her halls of state, walks like a goddess of Beauty, the cynosure of all eyes" (*FR* 1: 32), while later, during the *Parlement* of Paris, she appears as a deity of light caught in eclipse. "Her dwelling-place is so bright to the eye, and confusion and black care darkens it all" (*FR* 1: 93–94). During the insurrection of women, she enters the banqueting hall of Versailles, "issuing from her State-rooms, like the Moon from clouds, this fairest unhappy Queen of Hearts; royal Husband by her side, young Dauphin in her arms" (*FR* 1: 247). And later she again appears with the Dauphin, "like a bright Sky-wanderer or Planet with her little Moon" (*FR* 2: 61). In his apotheosis of Marie Antoinette, Carlyle follows closely the model of Edmund Burke's *Reflections on the Revolution in France*, where she is similarly exalted in almost identical language.[2] Carlyle, reflecting his mixed reaction to the revolution in his form, offers these fragments of a conservative, monarchical myth which regards the fall of the Bourbons as a tragedy. These fragments contend with others that celebrate the powers of the revolutionaries.

If the divine attributes of Marie Antoinette are beauty and light, the heroic attributes of the revolutionists are power and fire. When first introduced, the "world-compeller" Mirabeau "steps proudly along, . . . and shakes his black *chevelure*, or lion's-mane; as if prophetic of great deeds." Through his "shaggy beetle-brows, and rough-hewn, seamed carbuncled face," Carlyle writes, "there look natural ugliness, small-pox, incontinence, bankruptcy,—and burning fire of genius; like comet-fire glaring fuliginous through murkiest confusions" (*FR* 1: 137). Here, the annalist's facts are irradiated by the volcanic power of the mythographer. A similar diabolic power is evident in Carlyle's Miltonic portrait of Camille Desmoulins as a fallen angel, or "Son of the Morning," who shines "with a fallen, rebellious, yet still semi-celestial light," like "starlight on the brow of Lucifer" (*FR* 1: 236). Mirabeau and Desmoulins are intermediate figures, caught between the resplendent godliness accorded to Marie Antoinette and the grotesque ghastliness accorded to many of the other actors in the drama. Louis XV's minister Maupeou is one of the "subterranean Apparitions" that "vanish utterly,—leaving only a smell of sulphur" (*FR* 1: 4). Madame Dubarry is called variously "the scarlet Enchantress," "Witch Dubarry," and a "false Sorceress" (*FR* 1: 3, 15, 22), while Marat is an "obscene Spectrum" and a "swart unearthly Visual-Appearance" (*FR* 3: 65). Doctor Guillotin, notorious for his "cunningly devised Beheading Machine," becomes a wandering shade.

"For two-and-twenty years," Carlyle writes, "he, unguillotined, shall hear nothing but guillotine, see nothing but guillotine; then dying, shall through long centuries wander, as it were, a disconsolate ghost, on the wrong side of Styx and Lethe" (*FR* 1: 143–144). The various patrols, *parlements*, and tribunals of the Revolution are peopled by specters, a resigning government ministry is a ministry of ghosts, and a crazed band of revolutionaries becomes a group of anonymous phantasms, wandering "through a paralytic France," which is "all enchanted, spellbound by unmarching Constitution, into frightful conscious and unconscious Magnetic-sleep" (*FR* 2: 268–270).

Carlyle's portrayal of persons as gods, heroes, and specters renders an unpredictable mythic texture to his narrative, especially in scenes depicting the encounters of the Revolution's principal figures. These encounters are written in the form of phantasmagories, where mysterious beings arrive, confer, and mysteriously depart. The meeting of Mirabeau and Marie Antoinette, which signifies to Carlyle the vain hope for a sane accommodation leading to just reform, is depicted as a fortunate nocturnal encounter of the gods:

> Mirabeau and the Queen of France have met; have parted with mutual trust! It is strange; secret as the Mysteries; but it is indubitable. Mirabeau took horse, one evening; and rode westward, unattended,—to see Friend Clavière in that country-house of his? Before getting to Clavière's, the much-musing horseman struck aside to a back gate of the Garden of Saint-Cloud: some Duke d'Aremberg, or the like, was there to introduce him; the Queen was not far; on a 'round knoll, *rond point*, the highest of the Garden of Saint-Cloud,' he beheld the Queen's face; spake with her, alone, under the void canopy of Night. What an interview; fateful, secret for us, after all searching; like the colloquies of the gods! (*FR* 2: 123)

The mythic wonder of this passage is derived from the unexpected manner in which facts are presented: from the unanticipated interrogative in "to see Friend Clavière in that country-house of his?," the vague suggestiveness of "some Duke D'Aremberg," the evocative naming and reiteration of "the Garden of Saint-Cloud," and the setting of this divine colloquy "under the void canopy of Night." The spectral mythic encounter that infuses the meeting of the historical characters establishes the symbolic importance of an otherwise inconsequential event. The meeting of General Dumouriez and Marat at a Paris soiree is shaped, in a contrasting manner, by the motif of the unwelcome spectral visitor:

> Dumouriez is in Paris; lauded and feasted; paraded in glittering saloons, floods of beautifulest blonde-dresses and broadcloth-coats flowing past him, endless, in admiring joy. One night, nevertheless, in the splendour of one such scene, he sees himself suddenly apostrophised by a squalid unjoyful Figure, who has come in *un*invited, nay despite of all lackeys; an unjoyful Figure! The Figure is come 'in express mission from the Jacobins,' to inquire sharply, better then than later, touching certain things: 'Shaven eyebrows of Volunteer Patriots, for instance?' Also, 'your threats of shivering in pieces?' Also, 'why you have not chased Brunswick hotly enough?' Thus, with sharp croak, inquires the Figure.—'*Ah, c'est vous qu'on appelle Marat,* You are he they call Marat!' answers the General, and turns coldly on his heel.—'Marat!' The blonde-gowns quiver like aspens; the dress-coats gather round; Actor Talma . . . and almost the very chandelier-lights, are blue: till this obscene Spectrum, swart unearthly Visual-Appearance, vanish, back into its native Night. (*FR* 3: 64–65)

The prodigious appearance of a loathsome and at first anonymous specter in a secure place recalls any number of myths and folktales, and superimposes the enchantment of magic on the documentation of fact. The portrayal of Marat as a deformed child of night anticipates his final fateful encounter with the starlike Charlotte Corday.

These phantasmagories occur in a mythic universe, where the infinite irradiates the finite, and the eternal penetrates time. As Mircea Eliade has it, in a useful pun, a mythic cosmology has its *templum* and its *tempus*: the sacred place (or its antithesis, haunted ground) and the sacred time (or its opposite, the witching hour).[3] Just as prior myths characteristically designate certain locations as holy and protected and others as enchanted and dangerous, Carlyle's history depicts a series of places that appear to be havens, but prove to be haunted and subject to destruction. At the beginning of the work, Madame Dubarry and other parasites on royalty make Versailles a sanctuary for Louis XV. They have, Carlyle writes, "(verily by black-art) built them a Domdaniel, or enchanted Dubarrydom; call it an Armida-Palace, where they dwell pleasantly; Chancellor Maupeou 'playing blind-man's-buff' with the scarlet Enchantress; or gallantly presenting her with dwarf Negroes;—and a Most Christian King has unspeakable peace within doors, whatever he may have without" (*FR* 1: 3–4). But the sense of "unspeakable peace" that this sanctuary affords is severely undercut by the image of the "Armida-Palace, where the inmates live enchanted lives; lapped in soft music of adulation; waited on by the splendours of the world;—which nevertheless hangs wondrously as by a single hair" (*FR* 1: 4). With the cutting of that single hair—with the imminent death of Louis—"the wonderfullest talisman" of Versailles is destroyed, and "all Dubarrydom rushes off, with tumult, into infinite Space" (*FR* 1: 4). The "Versailles Galaxy" with its "new ever-shifting Constellations" becomes haunted by "the pale grinning Shadow of Death, ceremoniously ushered along by another grinning Shadow, of Etiquette" (*FR* 1: 18). The motif of the Dance of Death, which traditionally represents the unwelcome intrusion of a personified Death into the lives of even the wealthiest and most prosperous, reflects the tenuousness of Louis' sanctuary:

> Yes, poor Louis, Death has found thee. No palace walls or life-guards, gorgeous tapestries or gilt buckram of stiffest ceremonial could keep him out; but he is here, here at thy very life-breath, and will extinguish it. Thou, whose whole existence hitherto was a chimera and scenic show, at length becomest a reality: sumptuous Versailles bursts asunder, like a dream, into void Immensity; Time is done, and all the scaffolding of Time falls wrecked with hideous clangour round thy soul: the pale Kingdoms yawn open; there must thou enter, naked, all unking'd, and await what is appointed thee! . . . Wert thou a fabulous Griffin, *devouring* the works of men; daily dragging virgins to thy cave;—clad also in scales that no spear would pierce: no spear but Death's? A Griffin not fabulous but real! (*FR* 1: 20)

Images of wondrous palaces and constellations give way to demonic figures of grinning shadows and griffins, and in the horrific reversal of the Revolution the monarchy's palace and shelter becomes its prison; at the end of Volume I, Versailles is a diving bell surrounded by an ocean of insurrection.

At the beginning of Volume II, when the royal family has been forced to relocate to Paris, another *locus amoenus* is found in the Tuileries, as a much different nautical image indicates: "the

Château of the Tuileries is repainted, regarnished into a golden Royal Residence; and Lafayette with his blue National Guards lies encompassing it, as blue Neptune (in the language of poets) does an island, wooingly" (*FR* 2: 2). This new sanctuary offers the protection of a *hortus conclusus*, for the royal family can walk "unattended in the Tuileries Gardens," without fearing the attentive crowds. "Simple ducks, in those royal waters, quackle for crumbs from young royal fingers: the little Dauphin has a little railed garden, where he is seen delving, with ruddy cheeks and flaxen curled hair; also a little hutch to put his tools in, and screen himself against showers. What peaceable simplicity!" (*FR* 2: 3). But the pastoral images of the gardens, the ducks, and the beautiful youth, as well as the images of protection offered by the "little railed garden" and the "little hutch," are deceptive; just as Versailles is an "Armida-Palace" tenuously suspended by a single hair, the Tuileries is "an Atreus' Palace" (*FR* 2: 5) whose associations of cannibalism, murder, revenge, and dynastic dissolution will threaten the pastoral simplicity of the Tuileries Gardens.

As with the *templum*, so too with the *tempus*: times, like places, are beneficent or menacing in Carlyle's mythography. The upheaval of the Revolution, the victory of subterranean darkness over terrestrial and celestial light, is represented by a comprehensive mythology of Night. Carlyle repeatedly refers to the Revolution as a manifestation of the powers of "Chaos and Nox" (*FR* 2: 112) or "Atropos . . . and Nox" (*FR* 2: 291) and describes it as the time when "Night and Orcus . . . have burst forth . . . from their subterranean imprisonment: hideous, dim-confused" (*FR* 3: 27). Indeed, he peoples his history with an entire progeny of Night, constantly calling to mind Hesiod's *Theogony*, where "destructive Night" spawns Death, Sleep, "the brood of Dreams," the Fates, Nemesis, "cheating Deception," and "overbearing Discord."[4] Carlyle designates revolutionaries as "Sons of Night" and "Sons of Darkness" (*FR* 2: 114; 3: 40, 237), and calls Marat "a living fraction of Chaos and Old Night" (*FR* 3: 74). Of the revolutionary lawyers he states: "Such figures shall Night, from her wonder-bearing bosom, emit; swarm after swarm" (*FR* 2: 19). And the Revolution itself he terms "the newest Birth of Nature's waste inorganic Deep, which men name Orcus, Chaos, primeval night" (*FR* 3: 223).

Appropriately, many of the most mysterious and important scenes of the Revolution have a nocturnal setting. Of the night of 13 July 1789, the eve of the taking of the Bastille, Carlyle writes:

"Let Paris court a little fever-sleep; confused by such fever-dreams, of 'violent motions at the Palais Royal';—or from time to time start awake, and look out, palpitating, in its nightcap, at the clash of discordant mutually-unintelligible Patrols; on the gleam of distant Barriers, going up all-too ruddy towards the vault of Night" (*FR* 1: 179). The poetic evocation of night provides a striking backdrop for the imminent violence of the following day, while its troubled fever-dreams and incomprehension mysteriously anticipate the full madness of the Revolution. During the insurrection of women, when "Insurrectionary Chaos lies slumbering round the Palace" of Versailles, we read how the "troublous Day has brawled itself to rest." "Deep sleep has fallen promiscuously on the high and on the low; suspending most things, even wrath and famine. Darkness covers the Earth. But, far on the North-east, Paris flings-up her great yellow gleam; far into the wet black Night" (*FR* 1: 276). In each of these instances, a nocturnal setting, evoked in conspicuously poetic and rhythmical language, is used as the backdrop for a not-yet-comprehended transaction. The portrayal of sleep as leveler, falling "on the high and on the low," contradicts the severe division of the state and underscores Carlyle's resistance to partisan affiliation, while the sense of peace and silence that night brings is strangely at odds with the violence of revolutionary France. The presence of night, which in Carlyle's symbolic cosmology often represents communion with the unconscious and with the power of nature, serves as a reminder of the universal stage on which the historical drama is being played.

Carlyle again employs the dreamy mystery of night to render the aftermath of the Bastille's fall. As the disturbed city of Paris manages to "brawl itself finally into a kind of sleep," the defeated general Besenval "marches, with faint-growing tread, down the left bank of the Seine, all night—towards infinite space." Meanwhile, at the Palace of Versailles, the court wakes slowly and uneasily from its illusions of power to the unsettling reality of the Revolution. "The Versailles Ball and lemonade is done," writes Carlyle:

> the Orangerie is silent except for nightbirds. Over in the Salle des Menus Vice-President Lafayette, with unsnuffed lights, 'with some Hundred or so of Members, stretched on tables round him,' sits erect; outwatching the Bear. This day, a second solemn Deputation went to his Majesty; a second, and then a third: with no effect. What will the end of these things be?

> In the Court, all is mystery, not without whisperings of terror; though ye dream of lemonade and epaulettes, ye foolish women! His Majesty, kept in happy ignorance, perhaps dreams of double-barrels and the Woods of Meudon. Late at night, the Duke de Liancourt, having official right of entrance, gains access to the Royal Apartments; unfolds, with earnest clearness, in his constitutional way, the Job's-news. '*Mais,*' said poor Louis, '*c'est une révolte*, Why, that is a revolt!'—'Sire,' answered Liancourt, 'it is not a revolt,—it is a revolution.' (*FR* 1: 199–200)

This passage subsumes its satire on the trivial dreams of the French aristocracy in an elegiac prose lyric, signaled by the narcotic first sentence, which creates an aura of silence and serenity antithetical to the day's revolutionary events. The nocturnal setting lends a mythic cast to the scene appropriate for Carlyle's desire to create a modern myth from historical facts, as does the astronomical reference to the constellation of the Bear, which raises the activities of limited mortals to a cosmic plane. The entire scene, rooted though it is in recorded history, becomes transformed by myth: at the moment when Louis, like Saturn, for the first time conceives the implications of his dynastic overthrow, the received fragments of historically documented conversation become imaginatively fused with their underlying mystery.

In these night scenes and elsewhere, Carlyle adopts a mythic use of time borrowed from traditional epic, the fusion of solar and astronomical cycles with human activity. Examples from previous epics include Homer's celebrated epithet of the rosy-fingered dawn, Dante's meticulous references to astronomy and the signs of the zodiac, and Milton's solar setting for Book IX of *Paradise Lost*:

> The Sun was sunk, and after him the Star
> Of *Hesperus*, whose Office is to bring
> Twilight upon the Earth, short Arbiter
> Twixt Day and Night, and now from end to end
> Night's Hemisphere has veil'd the Horizon round. (9: 48–52)

A comparable example from *The French Revolution* is the following quite beautiful passage from the closing pages of the final volume: "Meek continual Twilight streaming up, which will be Dawn and a Tomorrow, silvers the Northern hem of Night; it wends and wends there, that meek brightness, like a silent prophecy, along the great ring-dial of the Heaven" (*FR* 3: 283).

This mythic use of time figures significantly in the episode of the flight to Varennes, where Carlyle presents the fateful inability of the royal family to escape from France against the backdrop of a complete solar revolution from night to day to night. Louis and his family set out from Paris when "Midnight clangs from all the City-steeples" and "most mortals are asleep" (*FR* 2: 161). This is an "ambrosial night," when Paris is "silent except for some snoring hum" (*FR* 2: 162), but it is also, as we are ominously reminded, a "precious night, the shortest of the year" (*FR* 3: 163). As night fades, the royal family rides on, surrounded by "the great slumbering Earth" and regarded by "the great watchful Heaven." "All slumbers save the multiplex rustle of our new Berline," writes Carlyle. "Loose-skirted scarecrow of an Herb-merchant, with his ass and early greens, toilsomely plodding, seems the only creature we meet. But right ahead the great Northeast sends up evermore his grey brindled dawn: from dewy branch, birds here and there, with short deep warble, salute the coming Sun. Stars fade out, and Galaxies; Street-lamps of the City of God" (*FR* 2: 163–164). While the dawn holds promise for the royal family, little progress is made as "the day bends ever more westward" (*FR* 2: 170), and another night approaches:

> Wearied mortals are creeping home from their field-labour; the village-artisan eats with relish his supper of herbs, or has strolled forth to the village-street for a sweet mouthful of air and human news. Still summer-eventide everywhere! The great Sun hangs flaming on the utmost Northwest; for it is his longest day this year. The hill-tops rejoicing will ere long be at their ruddiest, and blush Good-night. The thrush, in green dells, on long-shadowed leafy spray, pours gushing his glad serenade, to the babble of brooks grown audibler; silence is stealing over the Earth. (*FR* 2: 172–173)

As this night (also the "shortest of the year"!) descends, as "the ruddy evening light" gives way to the "thick shades of Night" (*FR* 2: 174, 176–177), the royal family moves forward to its imminent capture. "Thus they go plunging," Carlyle writes: "rustle the owlet from his branchy nest; champ the sweet-scented forest-herb, queen-of-the-meadows *spilling* her spikenard; and frighten the ear of Night. But hark! towards twelve o'clock, as one guesses, for the very stars are gone out: sound of the tocsin from Varennes? Checking bridle, the Hussar Officer listens: 'Some fire undoubtedly!'—yet rides on, with double breathlessness, to verify"

(*FR* 2: 178). Meanwhile, Varennes "lies dark and slumberous," "the rushing of the River Aire singing lullaby to it" (*FR* 2: 179).

It is not surprising that Carlyle's historical methods in the Varennes episode and others have unsettled some professional historians, for his facts are thoroughly infused by myth.[5] Quite apart from the question of whether he misconstrues basic events or introduces erroneous details, his use of even indisputable facts remains problematic. We know that Carlyle resists the kind of overt fabrication found in Musäus's tale of "Dumb Love," where a young hero faces a Goblin Barber and meets a mysterious benefactor on a bridge at the autumn equinox. Yet in his text a historical figure like Jean Paul Marat can become a goblin barber, a mythic or fabulous figure, while a Charlotte Corday can become his angelic demon and nemesis. And the apparently random fact that the flight to Varennes takes place at the summer solstice conveys, as much as the autumn equinox does in Musäus's story, a magical sense of time, and a wonderful correspondence between the heavens and earth. Sunrise and sunset are removed from the accidental to the symbolic level, as they mirror the rising and falling fortunes of the French monarchy.

II

The recurrent mythic patterns of *The French Revolution* are complemented by specific allusions to established literary mythologies.[6] Carlyle is a highly allusive author, and his "new Mythus" of the Revolution contains an epic range of allusions to "antiquated Mythuses." The divergent origins of his references to classical and vernacular epic, to Judeo-Christian religion, and to Carolingian and Teutonic legend suggest the scope of his epic topic, the making and unmaking of "Realised Ideals." The Christian mythus, assaulted in the eighteenth century by Voltaire and the *philosophes*, offers a fitting analogue to the "new Church of Jean Jacques Rousseau" (*FR* 1: 219) that replaced it. Classical mythology, so intimately associated with classical epic, provides a multiplicity of analogues by which a modern scene can be succinctly portrayed as a part of universal history.

Carlyle's mythical allusions fall into three main patterns: images of death, night, and the underworld; images of cataclysm, dismemberment, and fated destruction; and images of deities and heroes. Since Carlyle's mythic universe describes revolution as coming from subterranean forces, *The French Revolution* depicts events as occurring in the darkest regions of the classical underworld: the names of Erebus, Tartarus, Orcus, Cimmeria, and Dis echo throughout the text as a spectral refrain. The unleashed mob becomes Cerberus, the three-headed dog of the underworld (*FR* 1: 281), and the Jacobins' Club a "Tartarean Portent, and lurid-burning Prison of Spirits in Pain" (*FR* 2: 32), while Marat finds earth "a penal Tartarus . . . ; his horizon girdled . . . not with golden hope, but with red flames of remorse" (*FR* 3: 25–26). An ineffectual revolutionary assembly becomes a "fuliginous confused Kingdom of Dis," with "Tantalus-Ixion toils," "angry Fire-floods," and "Streams named of Lamentation" (*FR* 2: 242), and the Revolution itself becomes an "Enceladus Revolt," because the giant Enceladus pinned under Mount Aetna is emblematic of the volcanic upheaval of "Innovation" against "Conservation" (*FR* 1: 39). Carlyle's frequent allusions to the "Neptuno-Plutonic Geology" (*FR* 1: 80) of the classical underworld are reinforced by evocations of the analogous infernal figures and regions of the Judeo-Christian tradition (and hence of *Paradise Lost*): Tophet, Moloch, Beelzebub, Satan, and Pandemonium.

The destructive unleashing of these subterranean forces is reflected in a series of mythical images of cataclysm and disintegration. The classical myths of Pandora's Box, Aeolus and the Cave of the Winds, and Deucalion's flood suggest the destructive nature of unharnessed power, while those of the fall of the house of Atreus and the fall of Troy give a prophetic sense of the French monarchy as a doomed institution. The inability of France to produce an Orpheus capable of harnessing the Maenadic power of the Revolution recurs throughout the text as a central image of the incessant war between chaos and cosmos. Analogous biblical references include the story of Babel, Noah's flood, God's planned destruction of Nineveh in Jonah, Ezekiel's visions of the fall of empires, and the Apocalypse. Other references to the enchanted Armida-Palace from Tasso's *Gerusalemme Liberata*, the Roman Saturnalia, the last battle in the Hall of the Nibelungen, and the Islamic Angel of Death Azrael give a further sense of upheaval and destruction.

The final pattern of Carlyle's explicit mythical allusions is the portrayal of historical personages as classical gods and heroes. A central instance of this pattern is Carlyle's much discussed depiction of the royalist party as Olympian deities and the revolutionists as Titans and demigods.[7] Royalist deities such as Mars de Broglie and Mercury de Brézé sit, remote from men, on "cloudy Ida" (*FR* 1: 170), while Lafayette performs the function of Poseidon, who "raises his serene head" and calms "the upper Aeolus blasts" of society, but who may not be able to calm "the *sub*marine Titanic Fire-powers" (*FR* 2: 135). Danton, a prominent leader of those submerged forces in society, is described through a formulaic epithet as the "brawny Titan" (*FR* 3: 24), the "Titan of the Forlorn Hope" (*FR* 3: 46), and "Titan Danton" (*FR* 3: 129), who carries the Revolution "on his giant shoulders; cloudy invisible Atlas of the whole" (*FR* 2: 279). Mirabeau is portrayed as "the Serpent-queller" Hercules, engaged in internecine struggle with "the Typhon of Anarchy" (*FR* 2: 137), but unlike his mythic counterpart, Mirabeau is unable to complete his labors, for "there is a Nessus-Shirt on this Hercules; he must storm and burn there, without rest, till he be consumed" (*FR* 2: 140).

The sheer number of Carlyle's references to antiquated myths prompts the question of what validity mythical allusion has in an avowedly iconoclastic work. In "Biography," Carlyle denigrates the dressing of new human feelings in old pagan garb as "hoydenish masking," criticizes the reliance of modern authors on the "meaningless Deception" of epic machinery, and censures even Homer for using mythical deities as "mere ornamental fringes" (*CW* 28: 50–51). He dismisses ancient borrowings as irrelevant substitutes for modern observation, and depicts slavish reliance on past models as a lack of faith in our ability to shape worthy objects of belief from contemporary life. Yet past myths, when judiciously used by the modern author and not offered as substitutes for observation, are accorded a limited respect by Carlyle. Since "all Mythologies were once . . . *believed*," past myth has significance for modern persons insofar as "we believe it to have been believed, by the Singer or his Hearers; into whose case we now laboriously struggle to transport ourselves; and so, with stinted enough result, catch some reflex of the Reality, which for them was wholly real and visible face to face" (*CW* 28: 50). Myth as embodied in literature is an incomplete reflection of the reality faced by the mythmaker, just as cathedrals in *The French Revolution* represent only the "memory of a Creed," "Smoke-Vapour: *un*extinguished Breath as of a thing living" (*FR* 1: 8). Whereas the poet who "merely make[s] decorative allusions to an established literary mythology" is imitating a reflection, the poet who "actually *sees* the world as mythical"[8] is imitating past mythmakers by creating symbols from immediate experience. The symbol created by the modern mythopoeic poet is, like that of a past mythmaker, a direct rendering of reality. The difference between the two symbols is the immediacy of reality in the former and the remoteness of it in the latter.

The primary function of mythical allusion in Carlyle's history is the creation of an analogy between present and past experience, especially in consideration of the "Inward Sense" that creates "all Phenomena of the spiritual kind" (*FR* 1: 6). Because the old clothes that represent the rejected myths also represent "the unchanging need of every age for clothes," as Robert Langbaum helpfully points out,[9] past mythology naturally coexists with modern mythopoeia. The basis for the analogy between past and present myth, however, lies not in the outworn literary vesture of inherited tales, but in the initial belief that underlies them. While Carlyle, like some of the Victorian mythographers who follow him, traces the development of myth from primal belief to ornate literary mythology, he values the perpetuated written form of myth not as its highest, but as its most degenerate form.[10] The overtly literary nature of Carlyle's own allusions serves to emphasize the difference between past and present symbols. Although both are expressions of reality, the modern symbol is predominant because it expresses what is, not what was. In every juxtaposition of a mythical allusion and a modern incident, Carlyle unites a form that reflects a past reality with a present reality that is acquiring symbolic form; and, all the while, he points the reader to the theme that underlies both, the creation of a world by the inward sense.

The analogy between past and present symbols serves a variety of purposes in *The French Revolution*. Carlyle's mythical allusions fittingly reflect his own mythic universe, where custom, light, and civilization lie poised over the abyss of dark unconscious power, and where all phases of myth—its creation, its death, and its inappropriate perpetuation—are significant. They further parallel the mythopoeic efforts of the French nation as it installs, in an effort to establish its own "Realised Ideals," a variety of inappropriate pagan forms: feasts, altars, pagan prayers, incense, statues of pagan deities, and Roman artworks by David. The symbols of past myths intercede between the untutored reader, conditioned to regard contemporary life as unmythical, and the new myth, while at the same time helping to create the rough splendor of a world in creation. Moreover, their inclusion in the text adds to the modern myth's scope. The retention of themes, characters, and images from the mythologies of previous epics is itself an epic device; Carlyle, having envisaged a continuity between himself as artist historian and the creators of past myths, follows epic tradition in exploring the uniqueness of his new myth through its continuity with the old.[11]

Most important, mythical allusion aids Carlyle, the artist historian with a synthetic conception of disparate events, to link past, present, and future in "the All of Things" (*FR* 2: 103). The downfall of Danton, for example, is made a part of universal history by mythical allusion. The "great Titan," writes Carlyle, avoids "black Arachne-webs," retreating "to native Arcis" to be with his "everlasting Mother" (*FR* 3: 251). Having aided in the overthrow of Olympus (Versailles), he must now extricate himself from the prophetic image of the spider Arachne (France under the Reign of Terror) which, having challenged divinity, kills itself. In Carlyle's mythic epithets, apparently casual parallels between modern and mythical experience take on proleptic and structural functions. Carlyle calls the Versailles banquet of 1 October 1789 "fatal as that of Thyestes" or "that of Job's Sons," as if either the classical or the biblical allusion will serve equally well, but soon the banquet gains the epithet "Thyestes Repast," which introduces a parallel between the fall of the Bourbons and the fall of the house of Atreus (*FR* 1: 247–248). The epithet "Armida-Palace" applied to Versailles creates a precise analogy between Madame Dubarry and the heathen enchantress Armida, and between the "Most Christian King" Louis XV and the Christian knight Rinaldo, imprisoned by Armida in Tasso's epic (*FR* 1: 4). The popular general Lafayette becomes "Poseidon Lafayette," who, as the "Hero of Two Worlds," must calm "the upper Aeolus" and steer between "Sansculotte Scylla" and "Aristocrat Charybdis" (*FR* 2: 130, 133, 135). These epithets express a character's nature in its briefest form by placing the "reflex" or symbol of a past reality in juxtaposition with a modern reality from which, through the medium of artistic history, new symbols are being formed.

Carlyle's mythic epithets show how thoroughly dialogic (in the strictest etymological sense of the word) his text is. The epithet "Poseidon Lafayette" yokes two words from radically disparate realms of experience. "Poseidon" derives from the remote, conventional world of a well-established literary mythology cut off from the context of contemporary life. "Lafayette" comes from the realm of modern history, which cannot easily be dissociated from the wanton daughters, tough beef, constipation, and torn hose that Carlyle itemizes at the beginning of "The Diamond Necklace." By conjoining these two words Carlyle demonstrates his unwillingness to submit to a univocal literary language and acknowledges its problematic relation to contemporary life. The fact that he includes "Poseidon" at all shows, however, that he does not intend to dismiss literary language out of hand. When Carlyle writes that Lafayette and his "blue National Guards" surround the Tuileries "as blue Neptune (in the language of poets) does an island" (*FR* 2: 2), he points up, but does not alter, the essentially literary nature of his figure. Carlyle's practice, here as elsewhere, is inveterately paradoxical, for his unwillingness to allow the claim of past poetic mythology to be a unique voice for poetic expression is accompanied by his admittance into his history of traditional mythological themes, images, and characters. Just as "The Diamond Necklace" embodies features of the Gothic fictions that it is partially intended to combat, *The French Revolution* incorporates many of the gods and heroes that Sauerteig denigrates for having stultified the epic imagination. Again, Carlyle has recourse to the rhetorical strategy of *apophasis*, the technique of *Don Quixote*, which uses a satire on the idiocies of chivalry as the basis for a resurrection of the chivalric age. Initial repudiation becomes the means of subsequent reacceptance when Carlyle allows the illusory phantoms of past mythologies to coexist, sometimes harmoniously, sometimes incongruously, with the characters of modern history in the text of his disimprisoned epic.

hard to
be sure
what 9C
did!

SIX

Satire, Elegy, and Farce-Tragedy

Despite the radical changes that our formal definitions of epic have undergone during the past five centuries, inclusiveness has remained a distinguishing feature of the form for theorists, from Torquato Tasso in the sixteenth century to Thomas Greene in our own day.[1] The wide compass of *The French Revolution*, which ranges from Don Quixote and Saint Simeon Stylites to Captain Cook's murder and scholarly authorities on cannibalism, exemplifies the kind of inclusiveness, or comprehensive vision, that these theorists write about. Yet to apply the criterion of epic inclusiveness to Carlyle's history remains a tricky proposition. The abiding assumption of European epic theorists—neoclassical and modern—is that the epicist, describing a past and comprehensible action, can subsume various materials within a single vision. By frequently abjuring the advantages of remoteness and retrospection, Carlyle allows the sheer diversity of his material to threaten the coherence of his structure and the unity of his voice. Faced with his hundreds of incongruous mythical allusions, we are forced to ask whether he expands the circumference of epic, as previous epics traditionally do by incorporating the myths used by their predecessors in the genre, or explodes it. Faced with the generic inclusiveness of his text, the subject of the present chapter, we must consider whether he subsumes diverse forms in a predominant epic vision or sets them off against each other in an anarchic contention of multiple texts.

In his 1837 review of *The French Revolution*, John Stuart Mill, who played such a vital role in the writing of the text, praises Carlyle's prose epic for possessing "a theme the most replete with every kind of human interest, epic, tragic, elegiac, even comic and farcical, which history affords."[2] His suggestion, rephrased, is that Carlyle's theme, by encompassing an entire range of human experience, brings within its epic compass the literary modes that correspond to each of those experiences and that exist elsewhere, independently, as the genres of epic, tragedy, elegy, comedy, and farce. This view reflects Mill's earlier thoughts in his 1833 essay on poetry—where he states that epic is "esteemed the greatest effort of poetic genius, because there is no kind whatever of poetry which may not appropriately find a place in it"[3]—and is consistent with the literary aesthetic of Carlyle. We have seen how in the opening paragraphs of "Count Cagliostro" Carlyle describes "the grand sacred Epos, or Bible of World-History" as an inclusive form containing the heroic, the elegiac, the idyllic, the comic, the pastoral, the "farcic-tragic," the melodramatic, and the satiric. He elsewhere announces that the epic theme of the French Revolution contains all these areas of human interest, and hence all these literary modes. In an 1837 review of French histories of the Revolution in Mill's *London and Westminster Review*, Carlyle writes of the *Histoire Parlementaire de la Révolution Française*: "We have scenes of tragedy, of comedy, of farce, of farce-tragedy oftenest of all; there is eloquence, gravity; there is bluster, bombast and absurdity: scenes tender, scenes barbarous, spirit-stirring, and then flatly wearisome: a thing waste, incoherent, wild to look upon; but great with the greatness of reality; for the thing exhibited is no vision, but a fact" (*CW* 29: 9–10). So too in his own account of the Revolution, he describes how "the most variegated of scenes paints itself." "In startling transitions, . . . the sublime, the ludicrous, the horrible succeed one another; or rather, in crowding tumult, accompany one another" (*FR* 3: 206–207). Carlyle's perception of the Revolution's self-contradictory nature resembles, and perhaps derives from, Burke's. "The most wonderful things," Burke writes in his *Reflections on the Revolution in France*, "are brought about in many instances by means the most absurd and ridiculous, in the most ridiculous modes; and, apparently, by the most contemptible instruments. Everything seems out of nature in this strange chaos of levity and ferocity, and of all sorts of crimes jumbled together with all sorts of follies. In viewing this monstrous tragi-comic scene, the most opposite passions necessarily succeed, and sometimes mix with each other in the mind: alternate contempt and indignation, alternate laughter and tears, alternate scorn and horror."[4] In this chapter I shall examine several prominent literary modes as they are integrated into the inclusive structure of *The French Revolution*: satire, elegy, farce, comedy, and tragedy. I shall attempt to show how, in an action framed by "no vision, but a fact," these "variegated" modes are inseparable, with the sphere of satire intersecting that of elegy, and with farce joining tragedy.

I

The satirist, Matthew Hodgart writes, "offers us a travesty" of his subject "which at once directs our attention to actuality and permits an escape from it. All good satire contains an element of aggressive attack and a fantastic vision of the world transformed." Although satire ordinarily "aims at simplification, at a pretence of misunderstanding and at denunciation," Hodgart contends, it can appear episodically in works that aim to understand "the complexities of life," in works "whose overall vision is other than a satirical one."[5] *The French Revolution* offers a complex moral vision that transcends a simply satiric outlook on its subject, yet since human ignorance and folly figure so prominently in Carlyle's conception of the Revolution, satire is one of the dominant literary modes contained within the text's encyclopedic form.[6] Carlyle uses incidental satire, with its temporary unwillingness to understand the complexity of a multifaceted historical phenomenon, alongside the more tolerant perspectives of elegy, comedy, and tragedy. After having established in the "Realised Ideals" chapter his satiric norm of a society existing harmoniously with transcendent Nature, Carlyle satirizes the discrepancy between that norm and modern France, with its diseased monarchy, ineffectual constitutionalism, and anarchic revolution. He presents highly imaginative portraits of all ranks of French society performing grotesque and absurd actions. He combines a profound concern for the human condition and for political institutions with a perverse distancing element of travesty and fantasy. And he repeatedly uses the most common techniques of satire: mimicry and caricature, deflation, and burlesque.

In mimicry and caricature, Hodgart writes, the satirist produces "a ludicrous distortion in which the compulsive gestures and tics of the victim are exaggerated: a newly-created character is built out of them and superimposed on the original likeness."[7] As a mimic and caricaturist, Carlyle isolates a dominant feature of his satiric object and makes it ridiculous through insistent repetition and grotesque distortion. He satirizes French intellectuals by taking their interest in a scientific approach to language and making it into an obsessive concern that prevents them from operating effectively in any other endeavor; he depicts them as endlessly occupied with pursuing a "Theory of Irregular Verbs" (*FR* 1: 215). Elsewhere he castigates them, because of their philosophic zeal, as followers of a new religion, with a new evangelist (Rousseau), a new gospel, and new rituals. And he is scarcely kinder to the more firmly established Roman Catholic church, which he characterizes as a corpse reanimated by electricity. "Remark," he exhorts his reader, "what somersets and contortions a dead Catholicism is making,—skilfully galvanised" (*FR* 2: 155). The indecisive Louis XVI is made "a King Popinjay: with his Maurepas Government, gyrating as the weather-cock does, blown about by every wind" (*FR* 1: 37). More acted upon than acting, Louis is "poor King Log, tumbled hither and thither as thousand-fold chance and other will than his might direct" (*FR* 2: 3–4). Like the *Punch* cartoonists and other masters of Victorian caricature, Carlyle uses grotesque exaggeration to make lethal social comments.

One of Carlyle's most common means of caricature is the depiction of humans as animals, a technique ubiquitous in satire. The satirist, writes Hodgart, "reminds us that homo sapiens despite his vast spiritual aspirations is only a mammal that feeds, defecates, menstruates, ruts, gives birth and catches unpleasant diseases." Animal caricature, he continues, "reduces man's purposeful actions, the ambitious aims of which he is proud and his lusts of which he is ashamed to the level of brute instinct: hog in sloth, fox in stealth." Hodgart asserts that the function of satire is to warn "us that man is a dangerous animal";[8] Carlyle observes in *The French Revolution* that "there is no animal so strange as man" (*FR* 1: 16), and displays man's strangeness by making many of his characters animals. The number of his references to animals gives his history the sense of a beast fable or a mock-epic war of the beasts. As we might anticipate from reading Carlyle's historical satire "Count Cagliostro," dogs and birds predominate in his zoological treatment of French society. The Duc de Richelieu has an "old dissipated mastiff-face" (*FR* 1: 17) and Marat is "left at large; . . . as a sort of bandog whose baying may be useful" (*FR* 2: 25). ("All dogs have their day; even rabid dogs," Carlyle later observes of him [*FR* 3: 8].) A member of the National Assembly "sniffs" a speaker, while "the Galleries . . . bark rabid" (*FR* 2: 14). Phillipe D'Orléans is a "pert scaldheaded crow" who thinks that he is allowed to "alight at pleasure, and peck" on the "mere wooden Scarecrow" of royalty (*FR* 1: 92). Marat flies "to Versailles and back again;—swart bird, not of the halcyon kind" (*FR* 1: 249). Atheist Naigeon naively "crows, in his small difficult way, heralding glad dawn" (*FR* 2: 24). After a military defeat, "Patriotism flies, shrieking, execrating." "Danton with Camille and Fréron [take] wing, for their life," while "Marat burrows deep in the Earth, and is silent" (*FR* 2: 193). Marat, rabid dog, raven, and mole, elsewhere has the voice of a "bullfrog, or bittern by the solitary pools" and, "unseen of men, croaks harsh thunder" (*FR* 2: 107–108). The recurrent visual motif of bestiality undercuts any sense of a realistic or continuous world, and undermines the characters' illusions of human dignity.

Carlyle redoubles his satiric attack on French institutions with deflationary language. The months of the new French calendar, instituted as a sign of the new society's liberation from antiquated myths and monarchies, he translates disparagingly as *Vintageorious, Fogarious, Frostarious, Snowous, Rainous, Windous, Buddal, Flowral, Meadowal, Reapidor, Heatidor,* and *Fruitidor* (*FR* 3: 184). The nicknames given by Louis XV to the elderly princesses of the royal family he likewise translates as Rag, Snip, Pig, and Dud (*FR* 1:16–17). These same princesses Carlyle describes, using the common satirical scheme of *zeugma,* as going "to embroidery, small-scandal, prayers, and vacancy." The first two items in this series of nouns create an impression of extreme triviality, while the final reference to "vacancy" undercuts any sense of importance rendered by "prayers" (*FR* 1: 17). Carlyle dismisses Madame de Buffon as the "light wife of a great Naturalist much too old for her" (*FR* 1: 92) and, in a similar fashion, calls Demoiselle Candeille "a woman fair to look upon, when well rouged" (*FR* 3: 227). The Duc de Richelieu he terms, in epithets which are heroic more in form than in intention, "conquerer of Minorca, companion of Flying-Table orgies, perforator of bedroom walls" (*FR* 1: 24).

Of greater structural importance than his deflationary diction are Carlyle's deflationary metaphors. The most appropriate metaphor of inflation and deflation in Carlyle's history is the hot-air balloon or windbag. In the first instance, the hot-air balloon launched by the brothers Montgolfier in 1783, which rises "like some new daylight Moon" and "descends; welcomed by the universe," becomes the satiric emblem of prerevolutionary France, "which shall mount, specifically-light, majestically in this same manner; and hover,—tumbling whither Fate will." "So," Carlyle concludes, "riding on windbags, will men scale the Empyrean" (*FR* 1: 51). The image of men riding on windbags pictures the initially satiric and ultimately tragic discrepancy between social aspiration and social reality. Near the end of Carlyle's text, when the tragic potentialities of French society have fulfilled themselves, Robespierre becomes the "unhappiest of windbags blown nigh to bursting" (*FR* 3: 267). Another metaphor of unrealized aspiration is the Age of Gold to be instituted by "*Astraea Redux* . . . (in the shape of philosophism)" (*FR* 1: 31). The myth of the returning Saturnian deities suggests regeneration, justice, and social harmony, the very goals of the Revolution. But the faith that an over-optimistic philosophism has in its regenerative powers is sadly at odds with the social and economic problems of France. Because of the nation's severe financial crisis, the dignified, mythic Astraea Redux becomes the prosaic, demythologized "Astraea Redux without Cash" (*FR* 1: 44). The Age of Gold becomes the Age of Paper, since paper, in the form of "Bank-paper" ("wherewith you can still buy when there is no gold left") and "Book-paper" ("splendent with Theories, Philosophies, Sensibilities"), is a more fitting symbol of the age of the *philosophes* (*FR* 1: 29).

Carlyle's inflated metaphors are closely related to his use of burlesque, a form which is often associated with mock-heroic verse and which adopts a deliberately incongruous, elevated literary manner for subjects that are incapable of warranting its elevation. Carlyle employs many of the exalted conventions of epic for historical characters who are not sufficient in will or stature to be epic heroes. During the flight to Varennes, for example, he portrays a dawn which, in keeping with the epic use of mythic time, appears to welcome the arrival of a great leader. "Stars fade out, and Galaxies; Street-lamps of the City of God," Carlyle exclaims. "The Universe, O my brothers, is flinging wide its portals for the Levee of the GREAT HIGH KING." But the reality of Louis XVI and his fleeing family is at variance with the welcome given. "Thou, poor King Louis, farest nevertheless, as mortals do, towards Orient lands of Hope; and the Tuileries with *its* Levees, and France and the Earth itself, is but a larger kind of doghutch,—occasionally going rabid" (*FR* 2: 164). The metaphor of galaxies and a heavenly city, when coupled with the contrasting metaphor of the hutch of rabid dogs, reduces to absurdity the aspirations of French monarchy. Later in the same episode, Carlyle depicts the coach in which the royal family is traveling as the Sun-Chariot of Phaeton and Apollo. "Dawn on our bewilderment, thou new Berline," he apostrophizes, "dawn on us, thou Sun-Chariot of a new Berline, with the destinies of France" (*FR* 2: 170). But this chariot is, according to Carlyle's understanding of the Varennes incident, a needless encumbrance that prevents an undetected escape from France.

Many of the metaphoric identifications of French life with heroic mythology serve the purposes of burlesque rather than of epic elevation. Beaumarchais fighting a lawsuit is "like a lean French Hercules" who "ventured down, driven by destiny into the Nether Kingdoms; and victoriously tamed hell-dogs there" (*FR* 1: 43), while Finance Minister Necker, "Atlas-like, sustains the burden of the Finances" (*FR* 1: 47). The identification of a historical character with Atlas, which in the cases of Danton and Mirabeau creates a metaphoric tension between myth and modern history, here dwindles into a ridiculous discrepancy. The *Parlement* of Paris Carlyle addresses as an artificially constructed ruler of heaven: "Thou too (O heavens!) mayest become a Political Power; and with the shakings of thy horse-hair wig shake principalities and dynasties, like a very Jove with his ambrosial curls" (*FR* 1: 62). And various demagogues become Olympian deities of awesome stature: "Sweet also is the meed of patriotic eloquence, when your D'Espréménil, your Fréteau, or Sabatier, issuing from his Demosthenic Olympus, the thunder being hushed for the day, is welcomed, in the outer courts, with a shout from four thousand throats; is borne home shoulder-high 'with benedictions,' and strikes the stars with his sublime head" (*FR* 1: 83). A feeble attempt at apotheosis founders on an image of inflated self-esteem, appropriated from Horace and Swift.[9]

II

The reductive effect of all these satiric techniques is balanced by the predominantly laudatory effect of Carlyle's passages of elegy, a form which looks at human limitations from a perspective radically different from that of satire. The predominance of the elegiac mode in his history arises immediately from the ubiquity of death in the Revolution and ultimately from his concern with the decay of humans and human institutions. Since *The French Revolution* begins with the death of a king and treats the downfall of kingship, it fittingly elegizes both "Sovereigns" and "Sovereignties" at its outset:

> Sovereigns die and Sovereignties: how all dies, and is for a Time only. . . . The Merovingian Kings, slowly wending on their bullock-carts through the streets of Paris, with their long hair flowing, have all wended slowly on,—into Eternity. Charlemagne sleeps at Salzburg, with truncheon grounded; only Fable expecting that he will awaken. Charles the Hammer, Pepin Bow-legged, where now is their eye of menace, their voice of command? Rollo and his shaggy Northmen cover not the Seine with ships; but have sailed off on a longer voyage.

> The hair of Towhead . . . now needs no combing; Iron-cutter . . . cannot cut a cobweb; shrill Fredegonda, shrill Brunhilda have had out their hot life-scold, and lie silent, their hot life-frenzy cooled. Neither from that black Tower de Nesle descends now darkling the doomed gallant, in his sack, to the Seine waters; plunging into Night: for Dame de Nesle now cares not for this world's gallantry, heeds not this world's scandal; Dame de Nesle is herself gone into Night. They are all gone; sunk,—down, down, with the tumult they made; and the rolling and the trampling of ever new generations passes over them; and they hear it not any more for ever. (*FR* 1: 7–8)

This beautiful and heavily conventional prose poem adopts many of the traditional images and motifs of elegy: deafness, darkness, cold, immersion, the lament for dead heroes, *ubi sunt,* Death the Leveler, and the Fall of Princes. With its delightfully awkward assertion of the finality of death—"and they hear it not any more for ever"—it establishes the elegiac mode that repeatedly irradiates the text.[10]

Carlyle's prose elegies in *The French Revolution* are brief, impassioned, formal in structure, and elevated in style and diction. They appear as separate lyrics, embedded within a suspended narrative, which attempt to comprehend loss by reference to a universal meaning. They reflect the traditional elegy's concern with what Carlyle calls, in a different context, "eulogy and dyslogy, and summing-up of character" (*CW* 28: 478), by pointing out their subjects' closeness to or remoteness from the ideal of true humanity. Whereas Louis XV is dismissed with regret as a "Solecism incarnate," which a beneficent oblivion cannot yet swallow up (*FR* 1: 22), the Royalist Marquis de Bouillé is eulogized as a rare embodiment of bravery and truth in an age of cant. Here again the scheme of *zeugma* is used but to quite different effect—for exaltation and not for reduction:

> With little of speech, Bouillé rides; with thoughts that do not brook speech. Northward, towards uncertainty, and the Cimmerian Night: towards West-Indian Isles . . . ; towards England, towards premature Stoical death; not towards France any more. Honour to the Brave; who, be it in this quarrel or in that, *is* a substance and articulate-speaking piece of human Valour, not a fanfaronading hollow Spectrum and squeaking and gibbering Shadow! (*FR* 2: 184–185)

Carlyle's elegies relate the nature of their particular subjects to the general condition of France and to the universal human condition. The following elegy for the dead and the absent, with its traditional elegiac images and motifs (the extinction of light, the sympathetic grieving of nature, *ubi sunt*, Time the Reaper, and Death the Leveler), moves from a consideration of individuals to a lament for the state of revolutionary France and to an evocation of universal mutability:

> Théroigne will not escort here; neither does Mirabeau now 'sit in one of the accompanying carriages.' Mirabeau lies dead, in the Pantheon of Great Men. Théroigne lies living, in dark Austrian Prison; having gone to Liége [*sic*], professionally, and been seized there. Bemurmured now by the hoarse-flowing Danube: the light of her Patriot Supper-parties gone quite out; so lies Théroigne: she shall speak with the Kaiser face to face, and return. And France lies—how! Fleeting Time sheers down the great and the little; and in two years alters many things. (*FR* 2: 186)[11]

Finally, Carlyle's elegies link the present state of their subjects to both the past and the future, thereby creating an image of "the All of Things" and uniting disparate facts with their transcendent significance. Of Madame Dubarry, for example, Carlyle writes:

> She is gone: and her place knows her no more. Vanish, false Sorceress; into Space! Needless to hover at neighbouring Ruel; for thy day is done. Shut are the royal palace-gates for evermore; hardly in coming years shalt thou, under cloud of night, descend once, in black domino, like a black night-bird, and disturb the fair Antoinette's music-party in the Park; all Birds of Paradise flying from thee, and musical windpipes growing mute. Thou unclean, yet unmalignant, not unpitiable thing! What a course was thine: from that first trucklebed (in Joan of Arc's country) where thy mother bore thee, with tears, to an unnamed father: forward, through lowest subterranean depths, and over highest sunlit heights, of Harlotdom and Rascaldom—to the guillotine-axe, which shears away thy vainly whimpering head! Rest there uncursed; only buried and abolished: what else befitted thee? (*FR* 1: 22–23)

In this passage, Carlyle unites the retrospective aspects of Dubarry's birth and court intrigues with the prospective aspects of the "guillotine-axe" and her "vainly whimpering head."

All of Carlyle's elegiac techniques come into play in his farewells to the Revolution's principal actors: Mirabeau, Danton, Marat, and Robespierre. The longest and most important of these farewells treats Mirabeau as "a gigantic Heathen and Titan; stumbling blindly, undismayed, down to his rest." It embraces the traditional elegiac pattern of universal mourning for the loss of a revered individual:

> Even so, ye silent Patriot multitudes, all ye men of France; this man is rapt away from you. He has fallen suddenly, without bending till he broke; as a tower falls, smitten by sudden lightning. His word ye shall hear no more, his guidance follow no more.—The multitudes depart, heart-struck; spread the sad tidings. . . . The gloom is universal; never in this City was such sorrow for one death; never since that old night when Louis XII. departed. . . . King Mirabeau is now the lost King; and one may say with little exaggeration, all the People mourns for him. (*FR* 2: 142–143)

Mirabeau is praised as one who allies himself with nature rather than formulas, "a Reality and no Simulacrum; a living Son of Nature our general Mother; not a hollow Artifice, and mechanism of Conventionalities, son of nothing, *brother* to nothing" (*FR* 2: 145). Finally, the elegy depicts his individual nature in its general significance for the history of the French nation. The pyre on which Mirabeau's life "blazes out . . . and becomes ashes" is the "World-Pyre, which we name French Revolution" (*FR* 2: 145), and the loss of that life is the loss of France itself: "The chosen Last of the Mirabeaus is gone; the chosen man of France is gone," Carlyle laments. "It was he who shook old France from its basis; and, as if with his single hand, has held it toppling there, still unfallen. What things depended on that one man! He is as a ship suddenly shivered on sunk rocks: much swims on the waste waters, far from help" (*FR* 2: 148). In a similar manner, Carlyle portrays the death of Danton as the loss of one of France's few fully truthful men:

> So passes, like a gigantic mass of valour, ostentation, fury, affection and wild revolutionary force and manhood, this Danton, to his unknown home. He was of Arcis-sur-Aube; born of 'good farmer-people' there. He had many sins; but

> one worst sin he had not, that of Cant. No hollow Formalist, deceptive and self-deceptive, *ghastly* to the natural sense, was this; but a very Man: with all his dross he was a Man; fiery-real, from the great fire-bosom of Nature herself. He saved France from Brunswick; he walked straight his own wild road, whither it led him. He may live for some generations in the memory of men. (*FR* 3: 259–260)

The dignity and gravity of expression, the stately parallel structures, and the final, conditional assertion of immortality through human memory all serve to elevate this farewell to a departing hero.

Carlyle's elegies for Marat and Robespierre, tinged as they are with disapprobation, serve less readily than his elegies for Mirabeau and Danton to identify their subjects with ideal humanity. Marat is portrayed at his death not as a Titan stumbling undismayed to his rest, but as a "lone Stylites" who "has got hurled down suddenly from his Pillar" (*FR* 3: 169). His loss is received not, as Mirabeau's, by genuine mourning, but by a series of artificial and ineffectual attempts at deification: the comparison of Marat to Christ by republican orators, the state funeral and burial in the Pantheon, the painting of his death scene by David, "and such other Apotheosis . . . as the human genius . . . can devise" (*FR* 3: 169–170). Carlyle adopts the tone of true elegy only when he ceases to consider Marat in his somewhat regrettable public role and considers him instead for his private worth. He records the "sole circumstance" which he can "read with clear sympathy, in the old *Moniteur* Newspaper: how Marat's Brother comes from Neuchâtel to ask of the Convention, 'that the deceased Jean-Paul Marat's musket be given him.' " "For Marat too had a brother and natural affections," Carlyle writes, "and was wrapped once in swaddling-clothes, and slept safe in a cradle like the rest of us. Ye children of men!—A sister of his, they say, lives still to this day in Paris" (*FR* 3: 170). Having already questioned the extravagant comparison of Marat to Christ, Carlyle allows the unmistakable allusion to a child "wrapped once in swaddling-clothes" to stand for Marat's common humanity. In the case of Robespierre, too, Carlyle turns to private friends rather than public allies for testimonials to his subject's worth:

> O unhappiest Advocate of Arras, wert thou worse than other Advocates? Stricter man, according to his Formula, to his Credo and his Cant, of probities, benevolences, pleasures-of-

> virtue, and suchlike, lived not in that age. A man fitted, in some luckier settled age, to have become one of those incorruptible barren Pattern-Figures and have had marble-tablets and funeral-sermons. His poor landlord, the Cabinet-maker in the Rue Saint-Honoré, loved him; his Brother died for him. May God be merciful to him and to us! (*FR* 3: 285–286)

Elegy shifts the focus of Carlyle's text from the accidental to the universal: it dissipates the fixities of partisan allegiance and particular historical function in the light of universal human nature and of the sense that we are all "children of men."

Because of Carlyle's emphasis on the common humanity of all participants in the Revolution, the minor characters elegized become as important as the major characters. The royalist Princess de Lamballe, brutally killed during the infamous September of 1792, is elegized with grave and indignant lament:

> That fair hind head is cleft with the axe; the neck is severed. That fair body is cut in fragments; with indignities, and obscene horrors of mustachio *grands-lèvres*. . . . She was beautiful, she was good, she had known no happiness. Young hearts, generation after generation, will think with themselves: O worthy of worship, thou king-descended, god-descended, and poor sister-woman! why was not I there; and some Sword Balmung or Thor's Hammer in my hand? (*FR* 3: 29–30)

Of the Duke de la Rochefoucault, Carlyle states succinctly that he "dies lamented of Europe; his blood spattering the cheeks of his old Mother, ninety-three years old" (*FR* 3: 44). Jeanne-Marie Phlipon, the wife of the revolutionary minister Roland, who demonstrates extreme courage and composure at her execution, is elegized as a rare example of truth and loyalty in an age of untruth:

> Noble white Vision, with its high queenly face, its soft proud eyes, long black hair flowing down to the girdle; and as brave a heart as ever beat in woman's bosom! Like a white Grecian Statue, serenely complete, she shines in that black wreck of things;—long memorable. Honour to great Nature who, in Paris City, in the Era of Noble-Sentiment and Pompadourism, can make a Jeanne Phlipon, and nourish her to clear perennial Womanhood, though but on Logics, *Encyclopédies*, and the Gospel according to Jean-Jacques! (*FR* 3: 211)

Carlyle's concern with common humanity makes the political allegiance of the person elegized, royalist or revolutionary, Princess de Lamballe or Jeanne Phlipon, secondary in importance to her dedication to, or apostasy from, nature.

This concern further leads to communal elegies for groups of anonymous soldiers and for political parties. Carlyle elegizes the Swiss Guards, who place duty before self-interest by remaining loyal to Louis XVI, as an "ineffaceable red streak" of soldiers "dispersing, into blackness and death." With the elegy's characteristic imagistic transitions from light to darkness, from motion to stillness, and from sound to silence, Carlyle commemorates their dedication:

> Not martyrs were ye; and yet almost more. He was no King of yours, this Louis; and he forsook you like a King of shreds and patches: ye were but sold to him for some poor sixpence a-day; yet would ye work for your wages, keep your plighted word. The work was now to die; and ye did it. . . . Not bastards; true-born were these men: sons of the men of Sempach, of Murten, who knelt, but not to thee, O Burgundy!—Let the traveller, as he passes through Lucerne, turn aside to look a little at their monumental Lion; not for Thorwaldsen's sake alone. Hewn out of living rock, the Figure rests there, by the still Lake-waters, in lullaby of distant-tinkling *ranche-des-vaches*, the granite Mountains dumbly keeping watch all round; and, though inanimate, speaks. (*FR* 2: 302)

In assessing the fall of the Girondins, Carlyle gives not the unqualified praise he accords to the Swiss Guards, but a mixture of eulogy and dyslogy. He observes antithetically that the Girondins "wanted a Republic of the Virtues" but "could only get a Republic of the Strengths" (*FR* 3: 163). Yet while he remains cognizant of the disparity between their aspirations and their performance, he does depict their downfall as a part of the regrettable departure of all humanity. "The chorus is wearing weak; the chorus is worn *out*;—farewell for evermore, ye Girondins. Te-Deum Fauchet has become silent; Valazé's dead head is lopped: the sickle of the Guillotine has reaped the Girondins all away. 'The eloquent, the young, the beautiful and brave!' exclaims Riouffe. O Death, what feast is toward in thy ghastly Halls!" (*FR* 3: 199). The sickle of Time the Reaper, which becomes in a deliberately forced metaphor the blade of the guillotine, serves, together with the personified Death, as a reminder of the fate common to humankind. Carlyle tempers his final judgment on the Girondins with a recognition of their intrinsic humanity and worth. "Such was the end of Girondism. They arose to regenerate France, these men; and have accomplished *this*. Alas, whatever quarrel we had with them, has not their cruel fate abolished it? Pity only survives" (*FR* 3: 201).

In Carlyle's farewell to the Girondins, as in the elegies for Marat and Robespierre, we can perceive the disparity between aim and achievement that characteristically lends itself to satire. Whereas elegy emphasizes eulogy and praise, satire emphasizes dyslogy and vituperation; and whereas elegy works towards a consolation that identifies the elegized subject with the truthful and effectual power of the universe, satire aims to ridicule the satirized subject's separation from reason and truth. Within the encyclopedic framework of *The French Revolution*, Carlyle presents elegiac passages that become largely, though not entirely, satiric elegies. In a chapter of the first volume unsympathetically titled "Loménie's Death-Throes," Carlyle describes how Loménie de Brienne is retired from power, protected only by "huge featherbeds of Promotion," and eulogizes him in a heavily ironic manner: "Flimsier mortal was seldom fated to do as weighty a mischief." He replaces the elegy's traditional request that its subject be remembered with a plea that this ineffectual minister be forgotten: "Let us pity the hapless Loménie; and forgive him; and, as soon as possible, forget him" (*FR* 1: 109–110). De Brienne suffers not the martyr's physical death, but the undignified figurative death of patronage and superannuation. In portraying the downfall of Prince Philippe D'Orléans, satirically dubbed "Prince of the Power of Air," Carlyle uses his favorite image of the windbag in conjunction with a satiric rhythm of inflation and deflation, stating that Philippe "starts aloft, or is flung aloft, even into clearness and a kind of memorability,—to sink then for evermore" (*FR* 2: 114–115). On another occasion, Carlyle commemorates the Marquis de Brézé, a man governed by a bizarre devotion to nobility and decorum, with a mixture of satire and pathos:

> Hapless De Brézé; doomed to survive long ages, in men's memory, in this faint way, with tremulent white rod! He was true to Etiquette, which was his Faith here below; a martyr to respect of persons. Short woollen cloaks could not kiss Majesty's hand as long velvet ones did. Nay lately, when the poor little Dauphin lay dead, and some ceremonial Visitation came,

> was he not punctual to announce it even to the Dauphin's *dead body*: 'Monseigneur, a Deputation of the States-General!' *Sunt lachrymae rerum.* (*FR* 1: 165)

The satiric effect of this passage's deflationary language ("true to Etiquette," "a martyr to respect of persons") is tempered by the pathos of its anecdote and its terse final observation on the tears of things.

III

Carlyle's mingling of the epideictic mode of elegy with the dyslogistic mode of satire has a dramatic analogy in his mixed form of farce-tragedy. His insistent preoccupation with the proximity of the farcical and the tragic in life and art is evidenced by the frequent use of "farce-tragedy" and related designations throughout his works. In his 1830 essay on Richter he writes of "the rugged grim farce-tragedy often manifested in Hogarth's pictures" (*CW* 27: 151). In "Count Cagliostro" he includes the "farcic-tragic" among the literary modes encompassed by the *epos* of universal history. And in his review of the *Histoire Parlementaire* he cites "farce-tragedy" as the form appearing "oftenest of all" within that work. The preponderance of farce-tragedy that Carlyle notes in the *Histoire Parlementaire* appears also in his own account of the Revolution, where the laughable and the lamentable are placed in the closest proximity to each other. The Revolution is a form of "mumming," where the French communally enact their "sorrowful farce-tragedy" (*FR* 2: 197). The procession of the captured royal family to Paris after the abortive flight to Varennes is "comico-tragic," "a Pickleherring Tragedy" moving along "in most *un*gorgeous pall . . . towards its doom, of slow torture, *peine forte et dure*" (*FR* 2: 187).

Farce in *The French Revolution* involves the depiction of futile, self-destructive, and potentially tragic actions which are made risible by the temporary distancing of any tragic sentiment on the part of the reader. A representative instance of farce in Carlyle's history is his amusing depiction of the imprisoned revolutionary soldier Drouet, who had arrested the royal family on the flight to Varennes, escaping his Austrian captors on a kite; this passage is delightful largely because it is, quite atypically, free from the darker and more horrific aspects of the Revolution:

> Representative Drouet as an Old-dragoon, could fight by a kind of second nature: but he was unlucky. Him, in a night-foray at Maubege, the Austrians took alive, in October last. They stript him almost naked, he says; making a show of him, as King-taker of Varennes. They flung him into carts; sent him far into the interior of Cimmeria, to 'a Fortress called Spitzberg' on the Danube River; and left him there, at an elevation of perhaps a hundred and fifty feet, to his own bitter reflections. Reflections; and also devices! For the indomitable Old-dragoon constructs wing machinery, of Paperkite; saws window-bars; determines to fly down. . . . Authentic History, accordingly, looking far into Cimmeria, discerns dimly a phenomenon. In the dead night-watches, the Spitzberg sentry is near fainting with terror:—Is it a huge vague Portent descending through the night-air? It is a huge National Representative Old-dragoon, descending by Paperkite; too rapidly, alas! For Drouet had taken with him 'a small provision-store, twenty pounds weight or thereby'; which proved accelerative: so he fell, fracturing his leg; and lay there, moaning, till day dawned, till you could discern clearly that he was not a Portent but a Representative. (*FR* 3: 239–240)

The subject of this passage suffers military defeat and capture, public humiliation, incarceration, a fall, and painful injury. But however potentially tragic his predicament, the language and tone of the passage determine that its sentiment is farcical: our sense that Drouet might have been wise to anticipate that his twenty pounds of provisions might have "proved accelerative" distances us from the painful aspects of the incident.

Comedy, as used in the designation "comico-tragical," suggests the laughable and the ridiculous, and is therefore almost synonymous with farce. As the modal opposite of tragedy, however, comedy further connotes a pattern of rising fortune and social integration, such as is characteristically found in comic drama. In this sense, comedy represents the rise to power of the new revolutionary society, as it overcomes an obstructive royalty. This new society is represented by the traditional regenerative images of the Age of Gold, dawn, and millennium. When Louis XV is buried, we read that "a New Era is come; the future all the brighter that the past was base." "Man awakes from his long somnambulism," Carlyle exclaims, "chases the Phantasms that beleaguered and bewitched him. Behold the new morning glittering down the eastern steeps; fly, false Phantasms, from its shafts of light; let the Absurd fly utterly, forsaking this lower Earth forever" (*FR* 1: 26, 30–31). Near the conclusion of his history, Carlyle again declares: "Behind us is but the Guillotine; before us is Victory, Apotheosis and Millennium without end" (*FR* 3: 237). Despite the regenerative imagery of the Revolution, the discrepancy between its constructive aspirations and largely destructive reality makes the mode of comedy susceptible to farce, satire, and ultimately tragedy.

Much of *The French Revolution* is consciously written in the mode and language of tragedy: "the nodus of a drama, not untragical," "a poetic Tragedy," "a *catastasis* or heightening," "tragic, almost ghastly," "an uncertain catastrophe," "this natural Greek drama, with its natural unities."[12] In Carlyle's mixed historical-poetic form, the generic terminology of the *Poetics* becomes one means of reading experience. The language of tragedy, concerned with a fall in fortune from eminence and power to destruction and impotence, is applied to royalist and revolutionary alike. Carlyle presents the imminent downfall of Louis XVI, imprisoned in the Tuileries, as the conclusion of a tragic drama. "The victim having once got his stroke-of-grace, the catastrophe can be considered as almost come. There is small interest now in watching his long low moans: notable only are his sharper agonies . . ." (*FR* 2: 1). He exhorts the reader to regard Louis' execution with the tragic emotion of pity, since all mortals have "a whole five-act Tragedy in them." "For Kings and for Beggars," he declares, "for the justly doomed and the unjustly, it is a hard thing to die. Pity them all: thy utmost pity, with all aids and appliances and throne-and-scaffold contrasts, how far short is it of the thing pitied!" (*FR* 3: 107). The tragedy of the royal family, with its fall from throne to scaffold, is imaged, unlike the regenerative dawn of comedy, by autumn and disintegration. During their incarceration in the Tuileries, the royal family spends "Months bleak, ungenial, of rapid vicissitude; yet with a mild pale splendour, here and there: as of an April that were leading to leafiest Summer; as of an October that led only to everlasting Frost" (*FR* 2: 5). When the restorative aspirations of the Revolution begin to fail, it too becomes associated with autumn, as images of comic regeneration give way to those of tragic disintegration: "In the last nights of September, when the autumnal equinox is past, and grey September fades into brown October, why are the Champs Elysées illuminated; why is Paris dancing, and flinging fireworks?" (*FR* 2: 195). In Carlyle's vision of the Revolution, all of France must suffer the tragic movement of a "New

Golden Era going down in leaden dross, and sulphurous black of the Everlasting Darkness" (*FR* 3: 112).

The mixed form of farce-tragedy appears in *The French Revolution* when, because the work is founded on fact rather than on an artifically created vision, its various literary modes cannot be separated from each other. In this form, the ridiculous, grotesque, and often degrading modes of farce, comedy, and satire become inextricably mingled with the ennobling modes of tragedy and elegy. A single compelling example of this mixed form is the book "Regicide" from the third volume. As its title suggests, this book treats the execution of Louis XVI, the "King himself," and the extinction of "Kinghood in his person," a definitively tragic action, deserving the "utmost pity, with all aids and appliances and throne-and-scaffold contrasts" (*FR* 3: 107). Yet "Regicide" is as much as any other book of Carlyle's history characterized by the techniques of farce and satire. The National Convention debating the King's sentence is so overwhelmed by high-pitched, frenetic oratory that it becomes in Carlyle's caricature a full-scale operatic chorus: as the Convention deliberates, "the Tribune drones,—drowned indeed in tenor, and even in treble, from time to time; the whole Hall shrilling up round it into pretty frequent wrath and provocation" (*FR* 3: 95). "Oration, spoken Pamphlet follows spoken Pamphlet, with what eloquence it can: President's List swells ever higher with names claiming to speak; from day to day, all days and all hours, the constant Tribune drones;—shrill Galleries supplying, very variably, the tenor and the treble" (*FR* 3: 96). Meanwhile, the spectators who witness the fatal debate from the galleries act like the audience at an opera:

> Gallant Deputies pass and repass thitherward, treating them with ices, refreshments and small-talk; the high-dizened heads beck responsive; some have their card and pin, pricking down the Ayes and Noes, as at a game of *Rouge-et-Noir*. Farther aloft reigns Mère Duchesse with her unrouged Amazons; she cannot be prevented making long *Hahas*, when the vote is not *La Mort*. . . . Members have fallen asleep; Ushers come and awaken them to vote: other Members calculate whether they shall not have time to run and dine. (*FR* 3: 103)

Members of the Convention who engage themselves in the horrific act of regicide by their votes for death are treated as ridiculous and inconsequential persons. Carlyle dismisses Deputy Thuriot with mock praise, stating that he "can stretch a Formula as heartily as most men," and deflates the "cruel Jean-Bon" by requesting that the reader "write him not, as the Dictionaries too often do, *Jambon*, which signifies mere *Ham*" (*FR* 3: 96). He describes Jacob Dupont, who goes to inappropriate lengths to inform the Convention that he is an atheist, as having a "restless loud-rattling slightly-furnished head" (*FR* 3: 97). Wounded citizens who come to testify against Louis are both pathetic and, at the same time, grotesquely, cruelly humorous. "Crippled Patriots hop on crutches round the Salle de Manége [*sic*], demanding justice. The Wounded of the Tenth of August, the Widows and Orphans of the Killed petition in a body; and hop and defile, eloquently mute, through the Hall: one wounded Patriot, unable to hop, is borne on his bed thither, and passes shoulder-high, in the horizontal posture" (*FR* 3: 98). The execution of Louis carries no suggestion of pathetic fallacy, or universal mourning of nature for a tragic loss; rather, "Pastry-cooks, coffee-sellers, milkmen sing out their trivial quotidian cries: the world wags on, as if this were a common day" (*FR* 3: 111).

The intrusion of comic elements in a predominantly serious epic does not, in itself, place *The French Revolution* outside of the traditional practice or theory of epic. After all, comedy is one of the many aspects of existence to be embraced within the inclusive structure of a cosmic vision. Even so central a neoclassical critic as Joseph Addison, for instance, cites several examples of comedy in heroic literature: Homer's treatment of the Olympian gods, Virgil's depiction of Monoetes "thrown overboard, and drying himself upon a rock," and Milton's presentation of the fallen spirits taunting the angels in a passage that is "nothing else but a string of puns."[13] What is, however, distinctive in Carlyle's history is its unwillingness to establish clear boundaries between the comic and the tragic. When Milton states at the beginning of Book IX of *Paradise Lost* that he must alter his style from the idyllic mode of "God or Angel / With Man" to the "Tragic" mode of "breach / Disloyal on the part of Man, revolt, / And disobedience" (9: 1–8), he signals his ability to separate the diverse types of human behavior and literary form that are included within the encyclopedic compass of his work. But when Carlyle comes to write of a parallel, though morally problematic, revolt and disobedience in "Regicide," he cannot extricate his tragic theme from the "spectral, pandemonial" aspect of the National Convention (*FR* 3: 103), which like Milton's Pandemonium demands dark, infernal comedy. As Albert J. LaValley notes, the "epic of fact will of necessity be rough-edged like fact itself,"[14] and will therefore not allow a detached, elevated perspective from which the epicist can clearly distinguish the divergent human realities and literary modes that arise from his historical theme. Consequently, Carlyle's attention to particular facts and to the multifaceted quality of historical experience challenges, and indeed threatens, the aspiration to clearly demarcated form that the exclusive generic labels of epic, elegy, satire, farce, and tragedy suggest.

SEVEN

Emblems and Fragments

Aristotle looms large in Carlyle's experiments with genre, both as an influential thinker in his own right and as the rhetorical enemy against whom the guerilla warfare of modern criticism is directed. Carlyle depends heavily on the Aristotelian distinctions between history and epic, epic and drama, and tragedy and comedy, even when he violates them; he uses and manipulates Aristotle's assumption that there are clearly defined types of action in literature which lead from weal to woe, or from woe to weal, and which present particular visions of human nature, noble in tragedy, ignoble in comedy. Yet his contention with Aristotle does not in itself account for the impact of his text, for the transgression of Aristotelian dictates was not strikingly new by the 1830s. Carlyle combines with his manipulation of the canonical genres a simultaneous exploration of divergent symbolic modes—emblem and fragment, allegory and phantasmagory—not embraced by the *Poetics*. My investigation of these modes throughout the next two chapters has two principal aims: by returning once more to the critical miscellanies, I hope to trace the origins of these forms in Carlyle's writing; and by showing how they are integrated in his artistic history, I hope to give a more complete account of the structure of *The French Revolution*.

Nowhere more than in its structure does *The French Revolution* manifest its paradoxical relation to the epic genre as defined by earlier critical theorists. The French and English neoclassicists describe epic structure in Aristotelian fashion as the presentation of a single action with a discernible beginning, middle, and end, while the modern German aestheticians, likewise involved in a restatement of Aristotle's genre theory, see epic structure as the composed presentation of a total world view, made possible by the epicist's temporal separation from his subject. Influenced by both the neoclassicists and the modern Germans, Carlyle gives his history a carefully demarcated architectonic stucture, indicated by its neat division into three volumes. To describe only the architectonic scaffolding of his history is, however, to ignore the conflicting formal demands that shape it, for his attempt to delineate a continuous epic structure is opposed by his exploration of disparate facts, which leads to mixed literary modes, to discontinuous form, and to apparent structural confusion.

Le Bossu, the master of literary scales and compasses, writes in his treatise on heroic poetry that an epic contains "the Causes and Designs" of an action (the beginning), "the Effects of these Causes, and the Difficulties that are met with in the Execution of these Designs" (the middle), and "the Unraveling and Resolution of these Difficulties" (the end). In addition, he provides corresponding tripartite schemata of the major classical epics. The *Iliad*, he states, begins with the onset of Achilles' rage, continues with the effects of his passion, and ends with his placation, while the *Odyssey* begins with the departure of Odysseus from Troy, continues with his misfortunes at sea, and ends with his reinstatement as ruler of Ithaca. The action of the *Aeneid*, he contends, arises from the taking of Troy through the strategem of the wooden horse, continues with Aeneas' wanderings and battles, and concludes with the establishment of peace in Italy.[1] Joseph Addison, attempting to reconcile *Paradise Lost* with previous epic criticism and practice, adopts a comparable tripartite interpretation: the action of that poem is, he argues, "contrived in Hell, executed upon Earth, and punished by Heaven."[2]

Carlyle's division of his history into three volumes is roughly consistent with this threefold schema of cause, effect, and resolution. Volume I, "The Bastille," treats the impotence of the established government to restrain the anarchic forces of revolution. It begins with the death of Louis XV (an event emblematic of the death of kingship, the initiating action of *The French Revolution*), continues with a demonstration of the insufficiency of *philosophes* and royal ministers to govern, and ends with the consequent triumph of the Sansculottes in capturing the Bastille and removing the royal family to Paris. Volume II, "The Constitution," presents the impotence of monarchy and depicts the inability of new forms of government to harness the Revolution's power. It begins with the hopeful but fatally insufficient Feast of Pikes, continues with the death of Mirabeau, the single man most capable of fashioning a new order, and ends, as its final chapter title ominously tells us, with a "Constitution Burst in Pieces." Volume III, "The Guillotine," presents the final destruction of royalty, anticipated by the weakness of royalty in the first volume, and the collapse of the Revolution, anticipated by the inefficacy of constitutionalism in the second.

Carlyle's architectonic superstructure is, as we might expect, delusory, for its neatness, its apparent deference to neoclassical clarity and decorum, belies the formal and conceptual complexity of its individual sentences and paragraphs. In particular passages we see various genres, not always harmoniously embraced by the inclusive compass of the epic vision, but contending and threatening to pull the text apart. Furthermore, in the smallest units of expression we encounter divergent modes of symbolic expression. The emblem is a brief discontinuous form which shares the epic's concern for pattern and totality and which is therefore congruent with the sustained vision of an allegory or an allegorical epic. The fragment, however, delights in its deliberate lack of totality and tends to counter the epic drive toward continuity; it corresponds not to a sustained allegory or clearly articulated epic but to the variegated and troubled form of phantasmagory.

I

In his essay "On History" (1830), Carlyle identifies the limitations of narrative form as a crucial problem for the historian, and differentiates between narrative, which must be "successive" and "linear," and action, which is "simultaneous" and "solid" (*CW* 27: 88–89). Despite the dynamic power of Carlyle's style, in which the reader "is hurried, as if by an all-pervading and irresistible violence, from one problem to another,"[3] Carlyle insistently avoids narrative in favor of action: despite the etymological relation of history to story, his histories achieve their maximum effect when they resist chronological or narrative ordering. As George Levine states, the "extraordinary quality of Carlyle's style is that it manages to create so much excitement in the handling of essentially static conceptions."[4] A resistance to narrative can be traced through the course of Carlyle's literary career. G. B. Tennyson notes in his account of Carlyle's early development that the experience of writing novelistic fiction in "Wotton Reinfred" demonstrated to Carlyle the inappropriateness of his attempting to write a *Kunstwerk* in a continuous novelistic style, the comic and antinarrative vein of Sterne and Richter (which was to produce *Sartor Resartus*) being more congenial to his abilities. The bipartite and tripartite structures that Tennyson identifies as characteristic of Carlyle's work from his early journalistic articles through *Sartor Resartus* are non-narrative in their inspiration.[5] And *Sartor Resartus* itself is, like *The Prelude* and the other nineteenth-century autobiographical works with which it keeps company, "radically achronological."[6] Of the major genres that Carlyle incorporates into the fabric of *Sartor*, fragment, *Märchen*, and *Kunstroman*, the only one suited to a long continuous narrative, the *Kunstroman*, is not used continuously. Carlyle uses even his narrative materials in a non-narrative manner, as Levine helpfully intimates: Levine's description of the tripartite structure of *Sartor Resartus* as the text, exemplum, and application of a sermon, like Tennyson's description of it as the vesture, body, and spirit of a vision, is conceptual rather than narrative.[7] *The French Revolution*, in spite of its broadly chronological arrangement, is similarly concerned with overcoming the illusions of temporal succession: it shows how the past tense "is a most lying thing" (*FR* 3: 81) and demonstrates of successive events how the "one lay in the other, the one *was* the other *minus* Time" (*FR* 2: 105). From the desire to manifest relations among temporally disjoined events derives the importance Carlyle places on the prose emblem.[8]

The verbal emblem of the sixteenth and seventeenth centuries is, as Peter M. Daly argues in his comprehensive study of *Literature in the Light of the Emblem*, a continuous verbal development of the visual emblem found in countless Renaissance emblem books. Three distinguishing characteristics of the sixteenth- and seventeenth-century word-emblem have striking similarities to the later form of verbal emblem employed by Carlyle. First, the word-emblem is, like its forerunner the verbal emblem, a static form in which the constituent elements are arranged conceptually rather than narratively. Second, the word-emblem is a visual form, in which language is used to embody both the *pictura* and the *scriptura* of the visual emblem. Third, the word-emblem presupposes a correspondence between the visible world and the unseen. Emblematic thought is, as Daly contends, a kind of "controlled associative thinking"[9] which derives from the largely harmonious world view that the Renaissance inherited from the Middle Ages. "The typological exegesis of the Middle Ages," he writes, "presumed an ordered and meaningful universe, created by God to reveal himself and his plan for the salvation of man. Both the medieval allegorist and the renaissance emblematist held that everything that exists points to meanings beyond the things themselves, or as [Albrecht] Schöne puts it: 'that which exists at the same time carries significance.' "[10]

The first characteristic of the word-emblem, its static form and conceptual arrangement, is compatible with Carlyle's habitual preference for non-narrative modes of writing, and with his desire to transmute linear and successive events into a solid and simultaneous form. In his essays, Carlyle uses the static form of the emblem to embody the inherent significance for modern society of the individual under consideration: Goethe, Novalis, Voltaire, Diderot, Richter, or Johnson. In "Count Cagliostro," "The Diamond Necklace," and *The French Revolution*, he uses the emblem for the static representation of characters caught up in the dynamic movement of historical change. The artistic attraction of the emblem for Carlyle in his histories is its capacity to render in brief compass a movement of epic scope. We can picture this capacity by comparing Andrea Alciati's visual emblem "Ex Bello, Pax" with the action of the *Aeneid*. This emblem depicts a hive of bees inhabiting the abandoned helmet of a soldier; its intended meaning, which derives from the equation of the helmet with war and of the hive with peace, is that war precedes peace and social harmony. Through the juxtaposition of two simple visual motifs, this emblem succinctly embodies a movement comparable to the entire narrative of the *Aeneid*, in which the Italian wars of Aeneas precede and make possible the founding of the new Troy and the establishment of the Roman Empire. In its verbal form—in *The Faerie Queene*, for example—the emblem frequently operates in precisely this manner to encapsulate the significance of the longer work in which it is embedded. The verbal emblems of *The French Revolution* embody narrative movements in static and non-narrative form. Early in Volume I, for example, when the dying Louis XV will not allow death to be mentioned in his presence, Carlyle remonstrates with him: "It is the resource of the Ostrich; who, hard hunted sticks his foolish head in the ground, and would fain forget that his foolish unseeing body is not unseen" (*FR* 1: 19). This verbal emblem, which—after the fashion of traditional bird emblems—uses a fact of nature to represent an inner state, embodies in one static picture the serial events of the "Bastille" volume and the tragic downfall of the Bourbons.

The second feature of the word-emblem, its insistently visual nature, is of paramount importance to Carlyle, for whom the artist's supreme function is to incorporate "the everlasting Reason of man in forms visible to his Sense" (*CW* 26: 255). Carlyle's highest praise of his revered Goethe is reserved for "his singularly emblematic intellect; his perpetual never-failing tendency to transform into *shape*, into *life*, the opinion, the feeling that may dwell in him; which, in its widest sense, we reckon to be essentially the grand problem of the Poet." In Goethe, "Everything has form, everything has visual existence; the poet's imagination *bodies forth* the forms of things unseen, his pen turns them to *shape*" (*CW* 26: 244).[11] Carlyle's attention to "visual existence" in Goethe, like many of his observations on that writer, make a self-reflexive comment on his own literary aims. The writings of Carlyle, like those of Wordsworth and Emerson, repeatedly assert the supremacy of the eye in our apprehension of natural and artistic forms. In "Goethe's Works," Carlyle states through the voice of Teufelsdröckh that "man is by necessity an idol-worshipper (no offence in him *so* long as *idol* means accurately *vision*, clear *symbol*)" (*CW* 27: 391). In *On Heroes*, he writes that all "creeds, liturgies, religious forms" are "eidola" or "things seen" (*CW* 5: 121). And *The French Revolution* is replete with references to vision and the visible world: "Eidolon" or "Thing Seen," "Emblem," "vesture," "Picture," "the Eye above," "the eye of prophecy," "vision (spectral yet real)," "emblematic," "point of vision," "the living emblem," "visual-objects," "dimvisible," "veil," "revelation," "reflex," "faint ineffectual Emblem," "the mere natural eye," "the eye of History," "significant glimpse of things," "idol-worshipper," "*sight*-worshipper," "sensuous imaginative," and "hieroglyphically."[12]

Carlyle's insistence on the visual is intimately linked to his belief in the correspondence of the seen to the unseen and hence to the third characteristic of the word-emblem, its "controlled associative thinking." According to Carlyle's mythic account of the development of human thought, before the modern loss of faith philosophy and religion were characterized by their perception of universal correspondences in nature. For pagans, he states, "all things . . . were an emblem of the Godlike" (*CW* 5: 9–10). Throughout the Middle Ages and the Renaissance "the Godlike stood embodied under many a symbol in men's interests and business; the Finite shadowed forth the Infinite; Eternity looked through Time." After the rationalism of the eighteenth century and the consequent eclipse of faith, when man wanders homeless, "looking up to a Heaven which is dead for him, round to an Earth which is deaf," the interdependence of the seen and the unseen is broken or unrecognized (*CW* 28: 29–30). In the modern period of reforged faith, which Carlyle sees heralded in contemporary German literature, correspondences between the seen and the unseen are reestablished and "new emblems" are made (*CW* 26: 65). Thus Novalis, who like Goethe "speaks in emblems," is praised by Carlyle for his ability to comprehend nature "not analytically and as a divisible Aggregate, but as a self-subsistent universally connected Whole." To Novalis, "Nature is no longer dead, hostile Matter, but the veil and mysterious Garment of the Unseen; as it were, the Voice with which the Deity proclaims himself to man" (*CW* 27: 28–29). Carlyle's sense that "All visible things are emblems" (*SR* 72) links the traditional piety of the seventeenth-century emblematist Francis Quarles ("And, indeed, what are the Heavens, the Earth, nay every Creature, but *Hieroglyphicks* and *Emblemes* of [God's] Glory?") to the transcendentalism of Emerson ("The world is emblematic").[13]

Carlyle's immediate contact with the emblem comes through the later British tradition of Quarles and John Bunyan, whose emblem poems were distributed in numerous editions and were widely used, into the nineteenth century, for the edification of children.[14] In stating that Goethe's "emblematic intellect" is manifested "in the quiet cunning epigram, the allegory, the quaint device, reminding us of some Quarles or Bunyan," Carlyle clearly identifies the basic elements of their emblematic art: the *pictura* (or "device"), the *scriptura* (or "epigram"), and the "allegory" according to which they are combined (*CW* 26: 244). Carlyle, steeped as he is in the Bible and Protestant homiletics, takes readily to Quarles and Bunyan and absorbs their moral bent. And Bunyan's *Pilgrim's Progress*, which he knows intimately and quotes incessantly as a kind of shorthand for moral states and emotions, offers him a crucial model for a verbal counterpart to the visual emblem. Carlyle's writings further reflect the diffuse but pervasive influence of earlier classical emblems. Carlyle repeatedly adopts the figures of Proteus, Janus, Icarus, and the Phoenix, and he occasionally fuses them with their counterparts in the later emblematic tradition, as when he dubs an indecisive revolutionary "Janus Bifrons, or *Mr. Facing-both-ways*, as vernacular Bunyan has it" (*FR* 2: 289).

Carlyle uses the word *emblem* and its associated forms— adjective, adverb, and even verb—insistently, and with a rich variety of meanings: a representative excerpt from an author's works, an object characteristic of all nature, an anecdote or incident exemplary of an entire life or historical process. *The French Revolution* demonstrates Carlyle's profound interest in emblem, not only in its broad sense (as a visual, significant object) and in its heraldic sense (as the identifying mark of a political group or folk), but also in its specific formal sense as an artistic combination of *pictura* and *scriptura.* In the "Procession of the Black Breeches" chapter of Volume II, Carlyle writes that

> this Procession has a character of its own. Tricolor ribands streaming aloft from Pike-heads; ironshod batons; and emblems not a few; among which see specially these two, of the tragic and the untragic sort: a Bull's Heart transfixed with iron, bearing this epigraph, '*Coeur d'Aristocrate,* Aristocrat's heart'; and, more striking still, properly the standard of the host, a pair of old Black Breeches (silk, they say), extended on cross-staff, high overhead, with these memorable words: '*Tremblez, tyrans; voilà les Sansculottes,* Tremble, tyrants; here are the Sans-indispensables!' (*FR* 2: 260)

Carlyle perceives in the emblem an interdependence of the visual object and its written counterpart, the epigraph. By isolating the black breeches as an object for the reader's consideration, he demonstrates his sensitivity to the emblematic significance of historical fact. By commenting on the "tragic" and "untragic" aspects of the emblems, he shows his awareness of the implications that their solid and simultaneous form will have when transposed to the linear and chronological mode of historical narrative. And by incorporating the breeches in his chapter title, he further shows how the emblem-making activity present in the historical events he depicts parallels his own emblematic artistry; just as the writer of epic narrative embeds in his work the heroic narratives of his characters, Carlyle as emblematist places within his history the emblems of the French revolutionaries, thereby identifying himself with them in their common heroic task of refashioning the "Realised Ideals" by which they are to live. Elsewhere, Carlyle writes how "Couthon, borne in a chair, taps on the wall, with emblematic mallet, saying, '*La Loi te frappe*' " (*FR* 3: 217). Yet again, without this time using the term *emblem,* he writes of the siege of Thionville: "The Thionvillers, carrying their insolence to the epigrammatic pitch, have put a Wooden Horse on their walls, with a bundle of Hay hung from him, and this Inscription: 'When I finish my hay, you will take Thionville' " (*FR* 3: 57).

Carlyle uses the traditional form of the emblem in conjunction with the more characteristically modern form of the symbol. Peter

M. Daly distinguishes the "univalent" meaning of the former from the "rich plurisignation" of the latter: "Where the word-emblem does convey a plurality of meanings, these do not interweave, as in the modern poetic symbol, but rather form a list of distinct and separate meanings, deriving from different qualities of the pictured object."[15] Carlyle makes no clear semantic distinction between emblem and symbol, since both are in a broad sense visible manifestations of unseen realities. His practical uses of these forms are continuous, inasmuch as his symbols are highly conceptual and his emblems make an unmistakable, though secondary, appeal to the emotions. Nevertheless, our twentieth-century distinction between univalence and polyvalence is by no means alien to Carlyle, whose crucial distinction between allegory and phantasmagory, to be examined in detail below, is thoroughly grounded in it. And Carlyle's artistic practice deliberately involves the use of contending symbolic modes in constructing a heterogeneous text. The picture of the ostrich cited above is clearly emblematic: by using one fact of the bird's existence, its peculiar feature of burying its head in the sand, Carlyle conveys one aspect of human experience, the refusal by Louis XV to accept the fact of his impending death; secondary associations, such as the suggestion that modern man has degraded himself and taken on bestial characteristics, are designated as such by the emphasis on a central isolated meaning. The emblem of the phoenix renders in a brief, static, and convenient form one clearly demarcated fact: the death of monarchy and the birth of democracy. Yet the imagery of fire which laces the text, and which is associated with the emblem of the phoenix, suggests the multiple meanings of creation and destruction, divine energy and hell.

We can begin to trace Carlyle's experiments with emblematic form in his poems, which contain several moral meditations on man and nature.[16] These poems, with topics such as a moth burned by a candle, a beetle, and a swallow building a nest under the eaves, resemble Robert Burns' meditative poems "To a Mouse" and "To a Louse," as well as Bunyan's emblem poems for children, which derive their simple pictures from birds, fish, stones, and bees. The "Tragedy of the Night-moth" (*CW* 26: 469–470) offers a definitive example of Carlyle's efforts in this form. As the speaker sits at midnight, reading "Goethe's mystic page" by the light of a candle, a "moth-*savante* with rapture gazing" flies mesmerized into the flame and dies. Carlyle moralizes the incident as a demonstration of the danger incurred by too strong a desire for knowledge:

Poor moth! near weeping I lament thee,
  Thy glossy form, thy instant woe;
'Twas zeal for 'things too high' that sent thee
  From cheery earth to shades below.

Short speck of boundless Space was needed
  For home, for kingdom, world to thee!
Where passed unheeding as unheeded
  Thy little life from sorrow free.

But syren hopes from out thy dwelling
  Enticed thee, bade thee earth explore,—
Thy frame, so late with rapture swelling,
  Is swept from earth forevermore!

Then, in characteristic emblematic fashion, he transfers the moral from the natural object to himself:

Poor moth! thy fate my own resembles
  Me too a restless asking mind
Hath sent on far and weary rambles,
  To seek the good I ne'er shall find.

Like thee, with common lot contented,
  With humble joys and vulgar fate,
I might have lived and ne'er lamented,
  Moth of a larger size, a longer date!

But Nature's majesty unveiling
  What seem'd her wildest, grandest charms,
Eternal Truth and Beauty hailing,
  Like thee, I rushed into her arms.

Carlyle's lyric depends on the durable motif of the singed moth or fly, which derives from traditional emblematics and appears frequently in later literature (in Goethe and in Tennyson's *In Memoriam* [54], for instance). It recreates the *pictura* that Bunyan adopts, with a rather different moral, in "Of the Fly at the Candle," where the candle represents Christian truth and the singed fly "a lively Picture is of those / That hate, and do this Gospel light oppose."[17]

Carlyle's prose emblems tend less toward the moral and meditative bent of the poetry than toward satire. A single sentence from a notebook entry of 1826 will serve as an apt example: "The philosophy of Voltaire and his tribe exhilarates and fills us with glorying for a season; the comfort of the Indian who warmed himself at the flames of his—bed" (*Two Note Books* 85). The Carlylean prose emblem is typically contained within a single sentence; unlike the more protracted prose character, which is pleased to adduce many examples of a particular trait, it endeavors to express the significance of a person or event in a restricted compass by presenting a single compelling image. It uses few and simple visual motifs, usually considering one historical character or group of characters in the light of a single fact from natural history or legend. The arrangement of the emblem is spatial and conceptual rather than temporal and narrative and therefore produces the controlled reading of a two-dimensional picture. In the example provided, the dash is used as a means of delay and suspension; what it delays, however, is not a narrative event, but a final part of the picture, which completes the horrific significance of the image. The texture of the picture in Carlyle's prose emblems, accentuated by parenthesis and fragmentation, is grotesque and rough-hewn, following the aesthetic of roughness advocated in the (broadly emblematic) passage of "Voltaire" where he prefers "a cartoon by Raphael" to "a geometrical diagram by Fermat" (*CW* 26: 449). As E. Beresford Chancellor nicely remarks concerning the visual texture of his writing, "Carlyle is the Géricault of literature, Macaulay its David."[18] The subject matter of Carlyle's prose emblems is similarly grotesque. Typically, a figure from modern history is depicted in a limited, futile, or self-destructive activity: the distance between his perception of his own activity (in this instance the light and warmth generated by the enlightened philosophy of Voltaire) and the reality of what he does (the self-destructive nature of that philosophy) suggests the grotesque alienation of sympathy characteristic of satire, at the same time as it suggests the tragic degeneration of modern life.

In his essays, Carlyle uses the emblem to embody in one simple picture a figure representative of an entire *phasis* of modern history. Thus Voltaire, "the paragon and epitome of a whole spiritual period" (*CW* 26: 401–402), appears prominently in a series of emblems which offers an instructive instance of Carlyle's experimentation with the emblem form. In "Goethe," as in the notebook entry cited above, Voltaire is pictured as a misguided incendiary:

> With bold, with skilful hand, Voltaire set his torch to the jungle [of established religion]: it blazed aloft to heaven; and the flame exhilarated and comforted the incendiaries; but, unhappily, such comfort could not continue. Ere long this flame, with its cheerful light and heat, was gone: the jungle, it is true, had been consumed; but, with its entanglements, its shelter and its spots of verdure also; and the black, chill, ashy swamp, left in its stead, seemed for a time a greater evil than the other. (*CW* 26: 216)

Ah!

Here the image of self-destruction is retained from the earlier emblem, while the scope of the emblem is extended to encompass a slight temporal movement and a consequent imagistic contrast between the "flame, with its cheerful light and heat," and "the black, chill, ashy swamp." In his essay on Novalis (the maker of new emblems and, hence, the antithesis of the philosophic iconoclast), Carlyle places Voltaire with David Hume in a boat, trying to "sound the deep-seas of human Inquiry" with "the plummet of French or Scotch logic." These "well-gifted and highly meritorious men," he concludes, "were far wrong in reckoning that when their six-hundred fathoms were out, they had reached the bottom, which, as in the Atlantic, may lie unknown miles lower" (*CW* 27: 54). The sense of futility that this picture offers is repeated in a series of emblems in "Voltaire," which image the ultimate senselessness of his attacks on religion. "Religion cannot pass away," Carlyle writes: "The burning of a little straw may hide the stars of the sky; but the stars are there, and will reappear" (*CW* 26: 468). Voltaire "has not drunk the moon; but only the *reflection* of the moon, in his own poor water-pail," he observes in the final sentence of his essay.

These emblems of human futility, which read like the morals of a fable, are coupled with characteristic Carlylean emblems of aimlessness. Using his recurrent motif of a floating body at the mercy of the currents, he writes that Voltaire "meets [life's] difficulties not with earnest force, but with gay agility; and is found always at the top, less by power in swimming, than by lightness in floating" (*CW* 26: 426). This motif functions in Carlyle's essays and histories, as it later does in the poetic iconography of Matthew Arnold, as a figure of modern man trapped between a dead faith and a faith not yet born. Carlyle's ultimate depiction of the aimlessness of philosophizing is his image of Voltaire as the chief fool in a ship of fools:

"to him it is nowise heartrending that this Planet of ours should be sent sailing through Space, like a miserable aimless Ship-of-Fools, and he himself be a fool among the rest, and only a very little wiser than they" (*CW* 26: 426–427). The grotesquely comic image, reminiscent of Hieronymus Bosch's painting of the ship of fools, comes to take on tragic overtones in *The French Revolution* when France, bereft of the guidance that a more complete philosophy than Voltaire's might have offered, becomes a self-destructive fire ship.

Carlyle's repeated attempts to imprison Voltaire within the confines of the emblem contain a basic formal irony, for the underlying assumptions of the emblem are largely antithetical to the thrust of Voltaire's philosophy. Voltaire is for Carlyle the great iconoclast, the demythologizer of the traditional world of correspondences on which the emblem is based; Carlyle counters his efforts by trying to revive the analogical frame of mind in "new emblems," which use traditional myths and religions but are not inevitably tied to them. Voltaire is both too modern and too obsolete to appreciate the emblem: too modern because he has swept away the antiquated mythuses embodied in traditional figures—for which Teufelsdröckh thanks him in *Sartor Resartus*—and too obsolete because, bound by eighteenth-century rationalism, he is unable to comprehend the modern need for a new mythus. In "Characteristics," a different formal irony is used to depict those who, unlike Voltaire, realize their need for a faith but are not able to find it. Here, the author as emblematist avails himself of the clarity of form, the control of symbolic meaning, and the self-assurance denied to his subjects, the romantic poets and critics:

> Behold a Byron, . . . [who] without heavenly loadstar, rushes madly into the dance of meteoric lights that hover on the mad Mahlstrom; and goes down among its eddies. Hear a Shelley filling the earth with inarticulate wail; like the infinite, inarticulate grief and weeping of forsaken infants. A noble Friedrich Schlegel, stupefied in that fearful loneliness, as of a silenced battle-field, flies back to Catholicism; as a child might to its slain mother's bosom, and cling there. In lower regions, how many a poor Hazlitt must wander on God's verdant earth, like the Unblest on burning deserts; passionately dig wells, and draw up only the dry quicksand; believe that he is seeking

> Truth, yet only wrestle among endless Sophisms, doing desperate battle as with spectre-hosts; and die and make no sign! (*CW* 28: 31–32)

This series of pictures—a descent into the maelstrom, forsaken infants, a child nursed by a dead mother, wells dug in the desert—provides a picture gallery, or perhaps a verbal emblem book, of modern desperation. Although their form is emblematic, their thematic focus is on the stillborn efforts of modern thinkers to revive the emblematic intellect.

Carlyle's French histories demonstrate how the implications of the mental states he describes in his essays on modern thought are worked out in historical time. In the essays, the sentence-long emblem is a fitting unit of expression for the overall conceptual purpose of the work. In the historical writings, for which the essays are a preparation, the emblem functions not just as the embodiment of an idea but also as a truncated, or in Carlyle's terms, simultaneous counterpart to narrative that disregards chronology and renders proleptically or retrospectively the entire story. The satiric emblems of "Count Cagliostro" sum up, in bizarre and grotesque ways, the entire rise and fall of Cagliostro, together with the mechanistic and ultimately futile endeavors of his age. One of these presents the Count and his beloved Countess in a "japanned Chariot, rushing through the world, with dust-clouds and loud noise, at the speed of four swift horses, and topheavy with luggage." This "wonderful machinery, of horses, wheels, top-luggage, beef-eaters"—not an emblematic chariot from Renaissance iconography, though perhaps a travesty of one—holds "a gross, thickset Individual, evincing dulness enough; and by his side a Seraphina, with a look of doubtful reputation." Carlyle, anticipating the end of his narrative and the inevitable outcome of the Count's deceptions, asks how "the whole Engine, like a steam-coach wanting fuel, does not stagnate, go silent, and fall to pieces in the ditch" (*CW* 28: 256). Elsewhere, Carlyle highlights the Count's inveterate impostures and his subsequent exposure in an emblem of Cagliostro as thespian. "Unparalleled Cagliostro!" he declares. "Looking at thy so attractively decorated private theatre, wherein thou actedst and livedst, what hand but itches to draw aside thy curtain; overhaul thy paste-boards, paintpots, paper-mantles, stage-lamps, and turning the whole inside out, find *thee* in the middle thereof!" (*CW* 28: 257). To his pictures of mechanism and imposture, which, strageti-cally placed at the beginning of the piece, govern our perception of the entire narrative, Carlyle adds an image of predation when he portrays the Count as "a Noah's Raven" flying "out upon that watery waste of dissolute, beduped, distracted European Life, to see if there is any carrion there" (*CW* 28: 275). This quasi-biblical emblem later resonates with the classical emblem of the Countess de Lamotte as Circe and the Cardinal de Rohan as her enchanted pig (*CW* 28: 307), and anticipates the conclusion of Cagliostro's career in the affair of the Diamond Necklace, where the Count becomes the prey of the society he has so long preyed upon.

The emblems of "The Diamond Necklace" figure the overweening ambitions of pre-Revolutionary France, and its subsequent disintegration and destruction. Monsieur Boehmer, the jeweller who commits the folly of making the extravagant necklace before he has a buyer for it, is pictured as Icarus, one of the perennially popular subjects for mythic emblems: "Icarus-like, he must mount too high; have his wax-wings melted, and descend prostrate,—amid a cloud of vain goose-quills" (*CW* 28: 331). Madame Dubarry, the mistress of Louis XV, is "a foul worm; hatched by royal heat, on foul composts, into a flaunting butterfly; now diswinged, and again a worm!" (*CW* 28: 336). The Cardinal de Rohan becomes "the shamefulest Mud-volcano, gurgling and sluttishly simmering, amid continual steamy indistinctness . . . ; with occasional terrifico-absurd mud-explosions!" (*CW* 28: 342). The theatrical Countess de Lamotte, who deceives the unwary Cardinal, is in her classical guise Proteus and in a figure from Bunyan "Mrs. Facing-both-ways" (*CW* 28: 384). The dual function that the emblem performs in the experimental histories of "Count Cagliostro" and "The Diamond Necklace," as static delineator of historical character and as a simultaneous rendering of chronologically separated events, is vital in effecting a transition from the essays to *The French Revolution* where a series of emblems, discussed in the next chapter, is used to present a sustained, though discontinuous, allegory.

What, finally, are we to make of Carlyle's reliance on the emblem? We might argue that the form is tired and lifeless, a residual inheritance from his childhood inundation by the Protestant tradition of Bunyan and the Bible; Carlyle's recourse to the stale figures of Janus and Icarus, we might contend, marks him as an author whose literary repertoire is thin. After all, he is himself most caustic about writers who lean on arid, obsolete forms. The emblems can, however, be defended on their own terms, for even where the motif is traditional, the verbal presentation of it is fresh and vigorous. The picture of Boehmer as Icarus mimics with its syntax the jeweller's rise ("he must mount too high"), zenith ("have his wax-wings melted"), and abrupt fall ("and descend prostrate"): its final phrase ("amid a cloud of vain goose-quills") arrests us with its delightfully hyperbolic "cloud" and its substitution of the reductive "goose-quills" for the more standard term "feathers." In addition, Carlyle's emblems mingle recognizably traditional motifs with related figures of his own shaping. The phrase "new emblems" which Carlyle uses to describe the modern Germans and, by extension, himself, suggests both continuity and discontinuity, and therefore offers us a clue to the balance we need in assessing his relation to emblematic tradition. Carlyle is attempting to perpetuate an inheritance from which he feels separated by the iconoclastic rationalism of the eighteenth century. Therefore, his own new emblems are self-conscious attempts to revive an older convention in a society alienated from tradition. Finally, these closed forms, whose meaning is tightly controlled by the author, reside in Carlyle's texts alongside other figures that are more suggestive and open. If Carlyle wrote only in emblems, we might well judge him, according to his own critical standards, to be an anachronism, slavishly adhering to tired, conservative, antiquarian forms; what makes him a fit chronicler of revolution are his attempts to wed such conservative forms to others, such as the fragment, that are more modern, contentious, and subversive.

II

The fragment, as a deliberately chosen and intentional form, appears in a variety of manifestations in late eighteenth-century and early nineteenth-century literature: as the discontinuous unit of expression by which a larger fiction is sustained, as a popular and common kind of periodical article, and as an evocative symbolic form developed by the modern Germans.[19] The first of these manifestations, the novel made up of fragments, is well exemplified in Henry Mackenzie's *The Man of Feeling* (1771). Mackenzie's novel, now remembered principally for its extreme presentations of sentimentality, is based on a delightful contrivance established in its brief introduction by its fictional editor. The editor, we learn, is out hunting one day with a curate when his hunting dog leads them far astray in an abortive chase after gamebirds. They arrive at a remote spot previously inhabited by young Harley, whom we subsequently discover to be the sentimental hero of the novel. The curate remarks that he has in his possession a manuscript which contains Harley's narrative; being a "strenuous logician," however, and not finding a single syllogism in the work, he has begun to use the manuscript for gun-wadding. The more sentimentally disposed editor, who has relegated a book of German philosophy to the same function, makes a trade, obtains the remaining fragments, and attempts to piece them into a coherent narrative. He uses their discontinuous nature as the pretext for a rhetorical diminution of their worth, calling them "a bundle of little episodes, put together without art, and of no importance on the whole, with something of nature, and little else in them." In a note appended to Chapter XI—the first chapter of the novel!—he insists that he "is accountable only for scattered chapters, and fragments of chapters; the curate must answer for the rest."[20] Like Mackenzie and like Richter, his immediate model, Carlyle shapes an inclusive fiction from a series of fragments in *Sartor Resartus*.[21] That didactic novel, like *The Man of Feeling*, is assembled by an editor, who must piece together from the bags of biographical material shipped to him by Hofrath Heuschrecke (Councillor Grasshopper) a coherent life of Teufelsdröckh. The fragmentation of the source materials allows for an aesthetic and philosophical distancing on the part of the narrator: he can express his disapprobation of their contents, using the same trope of rhetorical diminution that Mackenzie employs; he can disavow any ability on his part to shape from them a complete and coherent truth; and he can retailor Teufelsdröckh's tailoring of the universe. At the same time as the fragment is made to seem, for rhetorical purposes, an encumbrance to the editor, it allows the author, freed from speaking in his own person, a certain stylistic and conceptual bravado.

In the decades following *Sartor Resartus* Carlyle uses the second kind of fragment—the fragmentary journal article—in less obviously fictive and imaginative contexts. This widespread form of fragment again allows for artistic distancing (since the fragments themselves and the customary editoral introductions to them are pseudonymous), layering (since their discourse stems from Carlyle, the editorial persona that introduces the fragment, and the authorial persona that writes it), and license (since their views are placed in an ironic context). In "On History Again" (1833) Carlyle, speaking in the person of Oliver Yorke (the fictitious editor of *Fraser's Magazine*, in which the work initially appeared), presents an essay on history as a "singular Fragment" from an "Inaugural Discourse" delivered by Diogenes Teufelsdröckh (*CW* 28: 167–176). By adopting the singular form of the fragment, Oliver Yorke allows the singular ideas of Teufelsdröckh to appear without considerable apology or acquiescence on the part of the journal. Furthermore, by purporting to present only one portion of a larger address, the editor offers the speaker's focused views on a single topic while maintaining the illusion of a more encyclopedic frame of reference. In the notorious "Occasional Discourse on the Nigger Question" (1849) Carlyle uses an even more striking form for more controversial ideas (*CW* 29: 348–383). This fragment of a lecture, conveyed to the publisher by the "respectable unfortunate landlady" of the disreputable Doctor Phelim McQuirk, the "Absconded Reporter" and "last traceable source" for the discourse, arrives with "no speaker named, no time or place assigned, no commentary of any sort given," and ends in mid-sentence with the words "Explicit MS." The progress of the speaker's strange discourse is marred by the dissent, derision, and ultimate departure of his audience. Finally, in "The Opera" (1852) Carlyle uses the fragment as a vehicle for criticizing modern British society (*CW* 29: 397–403). Here the fragment is introduced by Carlyle himself who, apologizing to the editor for his inability to contribute some writing of his own, offers something written by Professor Ezechiel Peasemeal, "a distinguished American" recently honored by the "Phi Beta Kappa Society of Buncombe." As in "On History Again," the speaker is a foreigner, and the fragment given is part of a larger work (Doctor Peasemeal's *Conspectus of England*). The use of a naive foreign observer to criticize native society, as in Montesquieu's *Lettres Persanes* and Goldsmith's *Citizen of the World*, gives Carlyle an alien but telling perspective from which to view Britain. The presentation of the fragment as an excerpt from the encyclopedic *Conspectus*, presumably a systematic examination of all areas of British culture in the light of a central overriding vision, suggests that the particular social activity examined, the opera, is in some sense emblematic of the entire society. The excerpted fragment presents in miniature the meaning of the entire work, since Peasemeal's contention that "Music has, for a long time past, been avowedly mad, divorced from sense and the reality of things," suggests the delusion and folly of modern Britain in general.

The most important manifestation of the fragment form for Carlyle is the third, the poetic and symbolic fragment, developed as a deliberately conceived literary kind by the Schlegels, whose fragments in the *Lyceum* and the *Athenaeum* are important innovations in critical thought and style, and by Novalis, whose experiments with fragment Carlyle quotes and discusses extensively in his 1829 essay on that author. According to Carlyle's view of Novalis, "all that he has left is in the shape of Fragment; detached expositions and combinations, deep, brief glimpses" (*CW* 27: 28), and "fractions" of an unwritten "grand 'encyclopedical work' " (*CW* 27: 38). A single fragment from Novalis, quoted by Carlyle, will serve both as an example of and an apology for the fragment: "Every beloved object is the centre of a Paradise" (*CW* 27: 40). Every fragment contains within it the germ of an epic, or Bible, or encyclopedia, and every object contains within itself the poetic and spiritual sense of the whole universe. This seminal perception of the relation of parts to wholes bears fruit in Carlyle's histories, where isolated events from contemporary French life come to embody the significance of an entire era. As Carlyle writes in "The Diamond Necklace," whatever object the artistic historian chooses to write on, "were it the meanest of the mean, let him but paint it in its actual truth, as it swims there, in such environment; world-old, yet new and never-ending; an indestructible portion of the miraculous All,—his picture of it were a Poem" (*CW* 28: 329). The poet's love of the object—his sense of the interpenetration of the infinite in the finite and the eternal in the temporal—determines its suitability to be the center of a paradise and hence of the Bible of World-History which contains that paradise. The poet's picture of the beloved object will take various forms, depending on the clarity with which the object renders up its spiritual significance. Sometimes, as Carlyle notes, Novalis writes in clear emblems: "Man is a Sun; his Senses are the Planets" (*CW* 27: 39) seems to be emblematic, with its fixed and simple equation of one sign to one thing. At other times, Novalis writes in symbols, where the multiple significations of the object are fluctuating and uncertain. Carlyle carefully notes that in his selection of Novalis's fragments he has inclined toward those that are susceptible to translation and ready comprehension. "Far stranger and deeper things there are, could we hope to make them in the smallest degree understood," he writes. "But in examining and reëxamining many of his *Fragments*, we find ourselves carried into more complex, more subtle regions of thought than any we are elsewhere acquainted with: here we cannot always find our own latitude and longitude, sometimes not even approximate to finding them; much less teach others such a secret" (*CW* 27: 41–42). This elusive, polyvalent form of fragmentary discourse Carlyle pits against the univalent, self-contained emblem throughout his artistic histories.

The emblem and the fragment are linked yet contending modes of writing, used by Carlyle to represent the differing ways in which the objects of nature and the events of history embody universal truths. The emblem is a self-contained form, with clearly demarcated edges; the fragment is incomplete, with jagged edges or none at all to separate it from its context. As G. B. Tennyson notes, the "proverb, the maxim, the apophthegm, the epigram"—forms closely related to the emblem—"all offer some sort of prudential wisdom, polished and pointed by time, use, or wit," yet the fragment is "ultimately ineffable" and "offers a glimpse of the Truth."[22] The emblem fixes the relation between the object and its significance, and rejects plurisignation; the fragment offers various and possibly contradictory significations, opens itself up to diverse commentaries, and demands that its meaning be recreated by its author and reader. In the emblem, the author stands outside the phenomenon depicted; in the fragment, the author remains within the realm of uncertainty created by the phenomenon, where he must actively take part in its reconstruction. In the emblem, human personality is entire, fixed, and discrete, and can therefore be subjected to moral judgment according to unchanging ethical standards; in the fragment, human personality is fluctuating and incomplete, and the very notion of individual identity frequently dissolves. These contending symbolic modes of emblem and fragment, in their extended manifestations as allegory and phantasmagory, become agents in the internal formal conflict of *The French Revolution.*

EIGHT

Allegory and Phantasmagory

We can attain a deeper appreciation of the mixed form of *The French Revolution* by understanding two contrasting literary kinds, allegory and phantasmagory, explored by Carlyle in his critical essays and adopted for creative purposes in his experiments in artistic history. Both allegory and phantasmagory are, for Carlyle, symbolic forms, in which the finite, the visible, and the temporal manifest the infinite, the unseen, and the eternal. Both allegory and phantasmagory are, therefore, appropriate for Carlyle's artistic intention in *The French Revolution*, the depiction of the making and unmaking of symbols, or "Realised Ideals" (*FR* 1: 8), in modern history. Yet despite their common symbolic basis, the two forms differ, because of the contrasting relation in each between the "symbol" and the "thing signified" (*CW* 26: 195). In allegory the relation of symbols to the meanings they represent is simple, fixed, and discrete; in phantasmagory that relation is complex, fluctuating, and uncertain. In allegory symbols have a single meaning or a limited number of clearly discernible meanings; in phantasmagory symbols have multiple and hidden significations. The two forms are consequently used for different ends by Carlyle: allegory represents the reason, order, and cosmos in his historical vision, whereas phantasmagory represents dark, disturbed fantasy, disorder, and chaos.

I

In many ways allegory, by itself, might seem to be the most appropriate literary form for Carlyle's artistic vision. Throughout his writings Carlyle shows a strong predilection for the form as it appears in the Bible, in *Pilgrim's Progress*, and, to a lesser extent, in *Wilhelm Meister* and *The Faerie Queene*. He uses Bunyan's emblematic imagery continually in his works and letters as a shorthand expression for moral states and emotions. He praises *Wilhelm Meisters Wanderjahre* as a kind of modern Spenserian allegory, "an allegory not of the Seventeenth century, but of the Nineteenth; a picture . . . of what men are striving for, and ought to strive for, in these actual days" (*CW* 26: 233). Carlyle appreciates allegory because it perpetuates the biblical patterns of providential guidance, human folly, devotion, and apostasy, which are basic to his thought and work. He functions largely as an allegorist in the episode of Diogenes Teufelsdröckh's conversion in *Sartor Resartus*, which made him famous as a teacher and spiritual guide in the mid-nineteenth-century. There he offers a pattern of salvation which, though divorced from the creeds of the Judeo-Christian tradition, borrows its language, its *mythos*, and its characteristic forms. Consider, for instance, the following paragraph from the "Everlasting No" chapter, where Diogenes bewails the lack of any guiding sign from heaven:

> Thus has the bewildered Wanderer to stand, as so many have done, shouting question after question into the Sibyl-cave of Destiny, and receive no Answer but an Echo. It is all a grim Desert, this once-fair world of his; wherein is heard only the howling of wild-beasts, or the shrieks of despairing, hate-filled men; and no Pillar of Cloud by day, and no Pillar of Fire by night, any longer guides the Pilgrim. To such length has the spirit of Inquiry carried him. 'But what boots it (*was thut's*)?' cries he: 'it is but the common lot in this era. Not having come to spiritual majority prior to the *Siècle de Louis Quinze*, and not being born purely a Loghead (*Dummkopf*), thou hadst no other outlook. The whole world is, like thee, sold to Unbelief; their old Temples of the Godhead, which for long have not been rainproof, crumble down; and men ask now: where is the Godhead; our eyes never saw him?' (*SR* 161)

Although this passage is rich in its allusions and dense in its imagery, it alleviates the reader's burden of interpretation by establishing a clear equivalence between its vision of modern life and received patterns of meaning. The images of the wilderness, the pillar of cloud, and the pillar of fire derive from the familiar Exodus narrative and reiterate its theme of the human quest for divine sanction. The allegorical mode of the passage, with its one-to-one equations of the wilderness to the modern world and of the decaying temples to a dying Christianity, derives from *Pilgrim's Progress* and the Bible. Diogenes himself represents, as a nineteenth-century surrogate for Bunyan's Christian, the modern thinker wandering through the wasteland of modern life. The schematic allegory of the conversion episode, atypical even of *Sartor Resartus*, accounts for its importance as a source of solace to the Victorians and for its continuing popularity as a classic statement of Carlyle's experience. It yields its meaning so readily that it makes an attractive exemplum of his thought and of his importance to the nineteenth century.

Yet, however much Carlyle is drawn towards allegory, he denies that it is, in isolation, an adequate form for the modern age. Like his romantic predecessors, he vigorously asserts the moral function of art, while at the same time castigating forms that are too narrowly didactic. He discounts the fable because it "is in its nature chiefly *prohibitive*" (*Two Note Books* 292). He denigrates the "Apologues, Fables, Satires, Exhortations and all manner of edifying Moralities" that dominated European literature through the eighteenth century, because they appeal too narrowly to the limited faculty of understanding and exclude the complementary imaginative elements which unite with understanding in the best modern literature (*CW* 27: 283). Carlyle's artistic conception of history as "the essence of innumerable Biographies" precludes an exclusive reliance on allegory, which lends itself more readily to the narrowly didactic conception of history as "Philosophy teaching by Experience" that he largely rejects (*CW* 27: 85–86). Finally, allegory by itself is inadequate to embody the historical moment of modern European civilization caught between a dead faith and a faith not yet born, since allegory ("the product of the certainty, not the producer of it") presupposes the existence of the mythus on which it plays.[1] In *The French Revolution*, therefore, Carlyle counters his strong allegorical impetus towards a biblical rendering of modern European history with contending strains of phantasmagory.

Phantasmagory differs from allegory not only in its symbolic method but also in its historical derivation. Whereas allegory has a long artistic and critical tradition, phantasmagory is, from Carlyle's perspective, of quite recent origin. The word "phantasmagoria" was coined in 1802 to describe the shadows produced by a magic lantern show. Its meaning was almost immediately generalized to encompass the phantasms and illusions generated by dreams or illness. Carlyle uses "phantasmagory" in both its original and its generalized sense. Following partly the example of Goethe, who experiments with verbal phantasmagory in *Helena*, he further extends its meaning to identify a literary kind that adopts the fluctuating and uncertain effects of the original phantasmagoria. And extending the application of this form beyond the overtly poetic boundaries of Goethe's treatment, Carlyle uses it, in combination with more traditional forms, in the writing of artistic history. He plays at phantasmagory briefly in "Count Cagliostro," when he portrays the fantastic deceptions Cagliostro practices on his dupes. He exhorts his readers:

> Figure now all this boundless cunningly devised Agglomerate of royal-arches, death's-heads, hieroglyphically painted screens, *Columbs* in the state of innocence; with spacious masonic halls, dark, or in the favourablest theatrical light-and-dark; Kircher's magic-lantern, Belshazzar hand-writings, of phosphorus: 'plaintiff tones,' gong-beatings; hoary beard of a supernatural Grand Cophta emerging from the gloom;—and how it acts, not only indirectly through the foolish senses of men, but directly on their Imagination; connecting itself with Enoch and Elias, with Philanthropy, Immortality, Eleutheromania, and Adam Weisshaupt's Illuminati, and so downwards to the infinite Deep: figure all this; and in the centre of it, sitting eager and alert, the skillfulest Panourgos, working the mighty chaos, into a creation—of ready-money. (*CW* 28: 291)

The verbal phantasmagory of this passage, with its agglomeration of fragmented images and its evocation of confusion, nicely complements the visual phantasmagory created by "Kircher's magic-lantern." But both kinds of phantasmagory are artificially created and self-contained: while the dupes exist within the confusion, Cagliostro stands outside it as stage manager and engineer of the visual effects, and Carlyle stands outside it as the satirist, in control of his text's significations, denouncing both Cagliostro and his gulls. In "The Diamond Necklace" and on a larger scale in *The French Revolution*, Carlyle creates a series of "Real-Phantasmagories" (*CW* 28: 379), where the realm of uncertainty becomes far less easily contained by the authorial consciousness. The combination of the new and corrosive form of phantasmagory with the old and established form of allegory contributes to making Carlyle's artistic-historical writings the formal counterpart to his complex vision of the French Revolution.

The critical process by which Carlyle comes to distinguish these two divergent, yet kindred, forms can be traced in "Life and Writings of Werner" (1828), in "Goethe's *Helena*" (1828), and in Carlyle's commentary on his translation of Goethe's *Das Märchen* (1832). In the first of these studies, Carlyle examines Zacharias Werner's drama *Die Söhne des Thals* (The Sons of the Valley) as an inartistically fashioned "wild phantasmagoria," a work "of a most loose and formless structure; expanding on all sides into vague boundlessness" (*CW* 26: 94). Here he uses the term phantasmagory pejoratively to describe a text which ostensibly aims to present an allegory—a clear "apologue" or "typical vision" or "emblem" of human existence—but which effectively offers only "glimmerings of meaning," the "dark Sybilline enigmas" of an "inane fever-dream" (*CW* 26: 103, 112–113). He presents the "dark symbolical figures" incapably assembled in Werner's drama, together "with such expositions" as he can "gather from the context," and attempts to shape a clear allegory from them. Yet he suspects that his reading may be only an allegorical projection on an incompletely realized phantasmagoric text. "Perhaps . . . our whole interpretation may be thought little better than lost labour," he writes, "a reading of what was only scrawled and flourished, not written; a shaping of gay castles and metallic palaces from the sunset clouds, which, though mountainlike, and purple and golden of hue, and towered together as if by Cyclopean arms, are but dyed vapour" (*CW* 26: 95, 114). Carlyle does not finally know whether to characterize Werner's drama as an undisciplined phantasmagory or as a failed allegory; his interpretive dilemma is aggravated, he concludes, by the faulty construction of the text itself.

When Carlyle turns to the dramatic phantasmagory *Helena* and the narrative phantasmagory *Das Märchen*, he depicts their difficulty not as the accidental product of incomplete artistic execution but as an essential feature of a deliberately chosen and necessarily complex kind of literary art. Every artistic vision, Carlyle argues, has its own particular formal expression: as long as the artist has a "deep" and "genuine" meaning, "the proper form for embodying this, the form best suited to the subject and to the author, will gather round it almost of its own accord." The form of Goethe's phantasmagories, with their "scattered glimmerings of significance," has "its own appropriateness," inasmuch as it encourages, through its very difficulty, the "active coöperation" of the reader in reconstructing Goethe's vision: "His words are so many symbols, to which we ourselves must furnish the interpretation; or they remain . . . a dead letter: indications they are, barren in themselves, but, by following which, we also may reach, or approach, that Hill of Vision where the poet stood, beholding the glorious scene which it is the purport of his poem to show others" (*CW* 26: 148–150, 152). Carlyle therefore praises in Goethe the phantasmagoric qualities of symbolic complexity and apparent formlessness that he denigrates in Werner. In approving of Goethe's symbolic complexity, he values multiplicity of meaning far more highly than does Macaulay, who in his essay on Bunyan treats plurisignation only as a natural flaw and byproduct of allegory.[2] And while Carlyle's opposition of such a polyvalent form as phantasmagory to the univalent form of allegory is by no means unprecedented—note Blake's distinction between vision and allegory in his "Vision of the Last Judgement" and Coleridge's distinction between symbol and allegory in his *Statesman's Manual*—it does mark a bold assertion of the artist's right to concealment, indirection, and inconclusiveness.[3] Indeed, even so sympathetic a reader of Carlyle as G. H. Lewes, who dedicates his life of Goethe to him as the man "who first taught England to appreciate Goethe," finds the apology for symbolic complexity in "Goethe's *Helena*" objectionable.[4]

In that essay, Carlyle depicts *Helena* (identified in its own subtitle as a *klassischromantische Phantasmagorie*) as an "enigmatic" work, whose necessary vagueness and "dreamlike character" force the reader to apprehend "both the dream" of the author "and its interpretation." He demonstrates how the text becomes increasingly "dim, fluctuating, unsubstantial," and "chaotic," and how, offering "glimpses of all things, full vision of nothing," it moves "into a phantasmagoric region, where symbol and thing signified are no longer clearly distinguished." He maintains, finally, "that *Helena* is not an Allegory, but a Phantasmagory; not a type of one thing, but a vague fluctuating fitful adumbration of many." "This is no Picture painted on canvas, . . . but rather it is like the Smoke of a Wizard's Caldron, in which, as we gaze on its flickering tints and wild splendours, thousands of strangest shapes unfold themselves. . . ."[5] In exploring the genre of *Helena*, Carlyle moves considerably closer than in the Werner essay toward a favorable valuation of phantasmagory. Using "phantasmagory" as a specific generic designation, rather than as a broadly descriptive critical term, he gives his clearest formulation to date of his distinction between phantasmagory and allegory.

Carlyle restates this distinction in his commentary on *Das Märchen*, where that work's fictitious translator D. T. (Diogenes Teufelsdröckh) and equally fictitious editor O. Y. (Oliver Yorke) engage in a spirited debate over the meaning of Goethe's symbols. O. Y. and D. T. agree on calling Goethe's tale a phantasmagory. In his introduction to D. T.'s critical commentary, O. Y. states that *Das Märchen* "presents a phantasmagoric Adumbration, pregnant with deepest significance." D. T. similarly terms it a "Phantasmagoric Poem," whose elements are "chaotico-creatively jumbled together." *Das Märchen* "is no Allegory," he insists, "which, as in the *Pilgrim's Progress*, you have only once for all to find the key of, and so go on unlocking: it is a Phantasmagory, rather; wherein things the most heterogeneous are, with homogeneity of figure, emblemed forth; which would require not one key to unlock it, but, at different stages of the business, a dozen successive keys" (*CW* 27: 448–450). O. Y. and D. T. disagree, however, on the extent to which specific meanings can be applied to the symbols of Goethe's tale. D. T., despite his recognition of *Das Märchen* as a phantasmagory, works frenetically to determine a meaning for each character and object in the story; of Goethe's snake, for example, he writes: "I know not well what name to call it by; nay, perhaps, in our scanty vocabularies, there is no *name* for it, though that does not hinder its being a thing, genuine enough. . . . Were I bound, under legal penalties, to give the creature a name, I should say, THOUGHT rather than another." "But what if our Snake," he continues,

> and so much else that works here beside it, were neither a *quality*, nor a *reality*, nor a *state*, nor an *action*, in any kind; none of these things purely and alone, but something intermediate and partaking of them all! In which case, to *name* it, in vulgar speech, were a still more frantic attempt: it is unnameable in speech; and remains only the allegorical Figure known in this Tale by the name of Snake, and more or less *resembling* and shadowing-forth somewhat that speech has named, or might name. It is this heterogeneity of nature, pitching your solidest Predicables heels-over-head, throwing you half-a-dozen Categories into the melting-pot at once, —that so unspeakably bewilders a Commentator, and for moments is nigh reducing him to *delirium saltans*. (*CW* 27: 450)

O. Y., for his part, remains aloof from D. T.'s bewilderment, noting sardonically that "there is risk of the too valiant D. T.'s bamboozling himself in this matter." When D. T. tentatively identifies three figures in the tale as "Faith, Hope, and Charity," O. Y. responds caustically: "Faith, Hope, and Fiddlestick!" (*CW* 27: 453, 468).

In the debate of D. T. and O. Y. over what is nameable and "unnameable" in the "scanty vocabularies" of human speech, Carlyle depicts again the problem he has previously faced in assigning meanings to the confused figures of Werner's *Die Söhne des Thals*. Yet in the progression from the Werner essay to the Goethe studies, we can trace a marked advance in his distinction between phantasmagory, which is boundless, fluctuating, and chaotic, which appears in the forms of enigmas and dreams, and which displays an apparent lack of authorial control over meaning, and allegory, which is contained, constant, and clear, which appears in the forms of apologues and emblems, and which manifests strong authorial control. He has come to recognize phantasmagory as a valid literary form, whose difficulty is an essential and definitive part of its very nature. Most important (for our consideration of *The French Revolution*), he has come to understand, by studying a series of works that are not in any obvious way consistently allegorical or phantasmagoric, the possibilities of a mixed form that can provoke in its reader, through an elusive alternation between homogeneity and heterogeneity of meaning, the apprehension of a complex vision. Carlyle characteristically reuses in his art the genres examined in his critical essays, suggests or identifies their presence through generic clues or explicit designations, and transposes them from their original literary provenance to an ostensibly extraliterary context. In *The French Revolution* he uses his conception of allegory, derived from the Bible and Bunyan, and his conception of phantasmagory, derived from the interlude of Faust and Helen and the fabulous world of the *Märchen*, to portray the quite unliterary reality of French kings, *philosophes*, and revolutionaries.

II

The appropriateness of these two forms for Carlyle's history of the Revolution lies in their common symbolic basis as manifestations of the eternal reality underlying historical change. *The French Revolution*, like *Sartor Resartus*, presents modern figures as the makers and dismantlers of symbols, inhabitating a "fictile" universe where "Ideals do realise themselves; and grow, wondrously, from amid the incongruous ever-fluctuating chaos of the Actual" (*FR* 1: 6, 10). This symbolic universe, Carlyle writes, is a "Shoreless Fountain-Ocean of Force . . . ; wherein Force rolls and circles, billowing, many-streamed, harmonious; . . . beautiful and terrible, not to be comprehended: this is what man names Existence and Universe; this thousand-tinted Flame-image, at once veil and revelation, reflex such as he, in his poor brain and heart, can paint, of One Unnameable, dwelling in inaccessible light" (*FR* 2: 103). Allegory derives from what is distinctly revealed in history, from what can be clearly pictured in discrete symbols of the relation of human actions to eternal truth. Phantasmagory derives from what is veiled, from the "Unnameable," "inaccessible," and incomprehensible elements of human history which have not yet been contained in clear symbols. The allegorical impetus of Carlyle's text is best represented by its emblem of the phoenix, the mythic figure which encompasses the upheaval and conflagration of the French Revolution in a static delineation of the "Death-Birth of a World" (*FR* 1: 212–213). The text's phantasmagoric thrust is represented by the fluctuating and uncontained "thousand-tinted Flame-image," the confusing "reflex" of the "One Unnameable," which resists containment, stasis, and fixed interpretation.

In the allegorical passages of *The French Revolution*, characters are removed for a short time from the fluctuating process of history to static moral pictures. Their internal complexities are temporarily suspended so that an isolated dominant characteristic of their strength (purity, valor, resolution) or, more often, their weakness (vanity, cowardice, indecision) can be depicted; their historical roles—their relation to the processes of history, their adherence to or apostasy from the truth of nature—are clearly registered in static emblems, which together form an extended "Apologue or emblematic Fable" (*CW* 27: 327). Carlyle's emblems treat primarily the aimlessness and irrationality of French political life. Yet even when his allegorical figures portray folly, self-delusion, self-destruction, and chaos in the actions of their human subjects, their clarity of form and control of meaning suggest reason, stability, and cosmos in the thoughts of their author. The contained and controlled form of allegory reflects the degree to which the corrosive madness of the French Revolution can be encompassed by the sane and reflective historical mind.

With its insistent sense of cause and consequence—its concern with the beginning, middle, and end of human actions—allegory contributes to the overall pattern of Carlyle's history, and to the architectonic clarity of his tripartite volume division. The first volume, "The Bastille," presents the ineffectual and impercipient French monarchy in the emblem of Louis XV as ostrich, in the portrayal of him as a "drift-log" on "the wind-tossed moon-stirred Atlantic" (*FR* 1: 21), and in the horrific description of Versailles courtiers dancing their "light life-minuet, over bottomless abysses, divided from [them] by a film" (*FR* 1: 25). The fatal abdication of control by the government of Louis XVI is shown by the portraits of his ministers Maurepas, whose government "gyrat[es] as the weather-cock does, blown about by every wind" (*FR* 1: 37), and Loménie de Brienne, "a sinking pilot" who "will fling out all things, his very biscuit-bags, lead, log, compass and quadrant, before flinging out *himself*" (*FR* 1: 107). While the first volume fittingly presents the downfall of the French monarchy, it also pictures the incapacity of the various alternatives to monarchy. The era of hope predicted by the *philosophes* and constitutionalists is in reality "Cloud-vapour with rainbows painted on it, beautiful to see, to sail towards,— which hovers over Niagara Falls" (*FR* 1: 36). Here as in others of Carlyle's emblems the historical subjects' perception of their own significance is radically contrasted with the estimate of the historian, and the scheme of the dash is used to emphasize that a final and indispensable portion of the *pictura* is yet to be revealed. The futility found in this emblem of Niagara recurs in Carlyle's later emblem of Abbé Sieyes, "the Sieyes who shall be System-builder, Constitution-builder General; and build Constitutions (as many as wanted) skyhigh,—which shall all unfortunately fall before he get the scaffolding away" (*FR* 1: 144). Yet again, the dash demarcates the distance that separates self-perception from historical reality. In another emblem, the French nobles, displaced from allegiance to the king and newly allied with the constitutionalists, are portrayed as having "drifted far down from their native latitude, like Arctic icebergs got into the Equatorial sea, and fast thawing there!" (*FR* 1: 146). Meanwhile, the anarchic power of the French populace fills the vacancy left by the lack of government from above: after the insurrection of women, "Boundless Chaos of Insurrection presses slumbering round the Palace [of Versailles], like Ocean round a Diving-bell" (*FR* 1: 277), while in a related figure "the royal Life-boat" floats "helmless, on black deluges of Rascality" (*FR* 1: 288).

At the beginning of the second volume, "The Constitution," the implicit threat contained in these nautical emblems is made explicit in the twin figures of Louis XVI as an unmenacing Medusa and as a pathetically impotent scarecrow tormented by the very Sansculottic crows it was made to frighten off. "Royalty was beforehand so decrepit, moribund, there is little life in it to heal an injury,"

Carlyle writes. "How much of its strength, which was of the imagination merely, has fled; Rascality having looked plainly in the King's face, and not died! When the assembled crows can pluck up their scarecrow, and say to it, Here shalt thou stand and not there; and can treat with it, and make it, from an infinite, a quite finite Constitutional scarecrow,— what is to be looked for?" (*FR* 2: 1–2). Since royalty is dying, its emblems in this volume center on motifs of incapacity: the doomed Louis sits, "as he had ever done, like clay on potter's wheel; perhaps the absurdest of all pitiable and pardonable clay-figures that now circle under the Moon" (*FR* 2: 182–183). While the French monarchy goes "reeling and spinning, one knows not whitherward, on the flood of things" (*FR* 2: 257), the Princess de Lamballe, confidante of Marie Antoinette, becomes engulfed by a "black World-tornado" which "will whirl *her*, poor fragile Bird of Paradise, against grim rocks" (*FR* 2: 227). While the Sansculottic crows, unrestrained by fear and increasingly ungoverned, move toward the anarchy of the Terror, the constitutionalists endeavor in vain to create a "finite Constitutional scarecrow." Their efforts are depicted throughout by characteristic Carlylean emblems of impotence and futility. As in the emblem of Voltaire, "found always at the top, less by power in swimming, than by lightness in floating" (*CW* 26: 426), Carlyle writes that "the Revolution-element works itself rarer and rarer; so that only lighter and lighter bodies will float in it; till at last the mere blown-bladder is your only swimmer" (*FR* 2: 19). The philosophic age of hope comes to consist of "beautiful far-stretching landscapes" painted by man "on his strait prison-walls" (*FR* 2: 34). Without government, France is shipwrecked: the dead Mirabeau, the one revolutionary capable of creating a new order for France, is "a ship suddenly shivered on sunk rocks," and because of his death "much swims on the waste waters, far from help" (*FR* 2: 148).

The emblems of the third volume, "The Guillotine," continue to depict the futility and self-destructiveness of the new government. A disempowered legislative assembly becomes "a floating piece of wreck" to which "certain things, persons, and interests may still cleave" (*FR* 3: 4). The Committee of Public Salvation becomes a whirlwind, only apparently governed by the "Cloud-compellers" Robespierre, Couthon, and Saint-Just (*FR* 3: 231), while the National Convention is a ship without a pilot, able only "to veer, and trim, and try to keep itself steady; and rush, undrowned, before the wind" (*FR* 3: 291). The theme of self-annihilation and the motif of peril at sea reappear in the most powerful summative emblem of Volume III, the depiction of France as a fireship bound for extinction. "The Fireship," writes Carlyle in explanation of his figure, "is old France, the old French Form of Life; her crew a Generation of men. Wild are their cries and their ragings there, like spirits tormented in that flame. . . . Their Fireship and they, frightening the world, have sailed away; its flames and its thunders quite away, into the Deep of Time" (*FR* 3: 120).

Carlyle's emblems contribute, to some extent, to an impression of radical discontinuity in his text. The emblem's stasis interrupts any sense of straightforward narrative progression, while its continual intrusion of abstruse and bizarre visual motifs breaks any illusion of a consistent mimetic representation of the world. As Henry James astutely observes, Carlyle constantly exhorts his reader to "look at realities and not at imitations, . . . but all the while he gives us the sense that it is not at things themselves, but straight into this abysmal manner of his own that he is looking."[6] Their discontinuity notwithstanding, Carlyle's emblems contribute as well to his sense of the continuity of his subject. The emblem's fusion of history's successive occurrences in a solid, simultaneous form unites a particular personage or event with Carlyle's architectonic pattern of beginning, middle, and end, while the recurrent emblematic motifs of sea, wind, and fire and moral themes of aimlessness, mistaken perception, and self-annihilation suggest a continuous bardic voice. Furthermore, the application to doomed revolutionaries of motifs originally applied to doomed royalists reinforces the structural parallels of Carlyle's history. The motif of people as ostriches applied in Volume I to Louis XV is transferred in Volume II to the revolutionaries, who "can, when the Truth is all-too horrible, stick their heads ostrich-like into what sheltering Fallacy is nearest; and wait there, *à posteriori*" (*FR* 2: 189). The gyration of the royalist minister Maurepas is transferred to the revolutionary Brissot, a "man of the windmill species, that grinds always, turning towards all winds; not in the steadiest manner" (*FR* 2: 206). And the downfall of the French monarchy, which renders Louis XVI a Medusa who will not turn humans into stones and a scarecrow pecked at by crows, is mirrored by the downfall of Sansculottism, rendered similarly impotent: "The dormant lion has become a dead one; and now, as we see, any hoof may smite him" (*FR* 3: 310). Emblems from the earlier portions of Carlyle's history anticipate the destructive patterns of its later movements, while emblems from the later parts make explicit the menace latent in its opening pages.

Carlyle's emblematic figures suggest by their number and coherence the possibility of reading *The French Revolution* as a sustained allegory of the dismemberment of French society. Such a reading is suggested by Harrison, who terms it a "lyrical apologue"; by Cazamian, who finds it to be "at once a drama and a sermon";[7] and, most extensively, by Froude. The French Revolution was for Carlyle "the last and most signal example of 'God's revenge.' " Froude maintains that

> he desired to tell the modern world that, destitute as it and its affairs appeared to be of Divine guidance, God or justice was still in the middle of it, sternly inexorable as ever; that modern nations were as entirely governed by God's law as the Israelites had been in Palestine—laws self-acting and inflicting their own penalties, if man neglected or defied them. And these laws were substantially the same as those on the Tables delivered in thunder on Mount Sinai. You shall reverence your Almighty Maker. You shall speak truth. You shall do justice to your fellow-man. If you set truth aside for conventional and convenient lies; if you prefer your own pleasure, your own will, your own ambition, to purity and manliness and justice, and submission to your Maker's commands, then are whirlwinds still provided in the constitution of things which will blow you to atoms. . . . Modern society . . . breeds in its own heart the instruments of its punishment. The hungry and injured millions will rise up and bring to justice their guilty rulers, themselves little better than those whom they throw down, themselves powerless to rebuild out of the ruins any abiding city; but powerful to destroy, powerful to dash in pieces the corrupt institutions which have been the shelter and the instrument of oppression.[8]

Carlyle's text certainly affords much evidence for an allegorical reading: in addition to its moral pictures derived from legend and fable, it contains much exhortation, dehortation, and moral statement on quackery, obsolete formulas, and cant. And it manifests the pattern of cause and consequence—of apostasy and destruction—which is central to much allegorical writing.

Yet to consider the allegory of *The French Revolution* without regard to its contending phantasmagory is to emphasize the elements of Carlyle's historical vision that can be cast in clear types and emblems at the expense of elements which he conceives to be fluctuating, inaccessible, and unnameable. Carlyle himself insists that Sansculottism is an "immeasurable Thing" which cannot be reduced "to a dead logic-formula" (*FR* 1: 213), and concedes that his history offers only a "faint ineffectual Emblem of that grand Miraculous Tissue, and Living Tapestry named *French Revolution*" (*FR* 2: 185). However much Carlyle works to create an allegory, the "type of one thing," his history often more nearly approaches phantasmagory, the "vague fluctuating fitful adumbration of many" things. The clear and discrete allegorical figures of the text are therefore combined with contending figures that are "mixtiform," "many-coloured," "dim-visible," "anomalous," "sansformulistic," and "topsyturvied."[9] *The French Revolution* engages its reader in the challenging alternation between homogeneity and heterogeneity of symbolic meaning hinted at in Carlyle's critical discussions of allegory and phantasmagory. Some of the same critics who suggest the didactic and allegorical nature of the work also recognize its phantasmagoric nature. It is termed a "historical phantasmagoria" by Harrison, a "nightmare-piece" by Cazamian, and a "spectral" history by Froude: "Spectral, for the actors in it appear without their earthly clothes: men and women in their natural characters, but as in some vast phantasmagoria, with the supernatural shining through them." Another critic, Paul Elmer More, goes so far as to identify phantasmagory as the dominant quality of the entire work. "The men and women of his pages are spectres hounded by the loud Furies," writes More in an arresting Carlylean description of the text: "The vision of the whole is as it were pictures of fire thrown on a curtain of seething cloud."[10]

Whereas allegory presents human figures in static moral pictures as distinct and individually responsible beings, phantasmagory depicts humans as evanescent phantasms, whose identity is obscured by the elements of fire, dream, fever, and chaos in which they move. In allegory, individuals are isolated for moral examination; in phantasmagory, different kinds and classes of men are chaotically yet creatively jumbled together, and individuals are lost in masses. The court life of Versailles before the Revolution "is a hollow phantasmagory, where like mimes [the courtiers] mope and mowl, and utter false sounds for hire" (*FR* 1: 18). The affair of the Diamond Necklace reveals "the highest Church Dignitaries waltzing, in Walpurgis Dance, with quack-prophets, pickpurses and public women;—a whole Satan's Invisible World displayed; working there continually under the daylight visible one; the smoke of its torment going up for ever" (*FR* 1: 57). At the beginning of the

Revolution, Paris resembles "some naphtha-lighted City of the Dead, with here and there a flight of perturbed Ghosts" (*FR* 1: 183). The taking of the Bastille is a "vision (spectral yet real)," "prophetic of . . . other Phantasmagories, and loud-gibbering Spectral Realities" (*FR* 1: 189). The National Assembly, which vainly attempts to create order from the powers unleashed by the Revolution, is a "Phantasm-Reality" (*FR* 2: 200), while the Legislative Assembly, its equally ineffectual successor, is "confused, unsubstantial, you might call it almost *spectral*: pallid, dim, inane, like the Kingdoms of Dis" (*FR* 2: 240). During the savage massacres of September 1792, Paris presents a "dim Phantasmagory of the Pit," in which "few fixed certain objects" appear (*FR* 3: 27). As the Revolution enters its final phases of anarchy and destruction, the inhuman National Convention becomes "a kind of Apocalyptic Convention, or black *Dream become real*" (*FR* 3: 70), while the savage Revolutionary Tribunal appears "Dim, dim, as if in disastrous eclipse; like the pale kingdoms of Dis! Plutonic Judges, Plutonic Tinville; encircled, nine times, with Styx and Lethe, with Fire-Phlegethon and Cocytus named of Lamentation! The very witnesses summoned are like Ghosts: exculpatory, inculpatory, they themselves are all hovering over death and doom" (*FR* 3: 194–195).

The phantasmagoric passages listed here differ markedly in texture from the allegorical emblems cited above. The nature of their difference can be characterized by an analysis of the following representative, and contrasting, examples. Take first Carlyle's allegorical rendering of the historical character of Loménie de Brienne, a minister of the king who inadvertently contributes, through his own incompetence, to the onset of the Revolution. "Flimsier mortal was seldom fated to do as weighty a mischief," writes Carlyle. "*Fired*, as the phrase is, with ambition: blown, like a kindled rag, the sport of winds, not this way, not that way, but of all ways, straight towards *such* a powder-mine,—which he kindled" (*FR* 1: 110). Here we have a static delineation of the historical role and moral character of a single individual. The two symbols of which the picture consists both have a simple one-to-one correspondence to the meanings they represent: the kindled rag stands for Brienne, the ignited powder-mine for the conflagration of the French Revolution. Because each symbol is the "type of one thing," the meaning of the picture as a whole is strongly controlled by its author: folly and misplaced ambition in government lead to political destruction. The stance that the author adopts toward his subject is one of detachment and retrospection: from the perspective of a later time, the author juxtaposes cause and consequence to produce a significance of which the subject, trapped within the perspective of his present concerns, is unaware.

Compare the following phantasmagoric passage, in which the topic addressed by the emblem of Brienne, misgovernment, receives a strikingly different treatment. In the chapter "Executive that Does Not Act," from Volume II, Carlyle presents the ill-advised abdication of government ministers in the face of a threat posed by the menacing and destructive Fédérés:

> It is true, some ghost of a War-minister, or Home-minister, for the time being, ghost whom we do not name, does write to Municipalities and King's Commanders, that they shall . . . turn back the Fédérés by force of arms: a message which scatters mere doubt, paralysis and confusion; irritates the poor Legislature; reduces the Fédérés . . . to thin streaks. But being questioned, this ghost and the other ghosts, What it is then that they propose to do for saving the country?—they answer, That they cannot tell; that indeed they, for their part, have, this morning, resigned in a body; and do now merely respectfully take leave of the helm altogether. . . . Other complete Cabinet-ministry there will not be; only fragments, and these changeful, which never get completed; spectral Apparitions that cannot so much as appear! . . .
>
> And so these thin streaks of Fédérés wend Paris-ward through a paralytic France. . . . And yet, thin and feeble as these streaks of Federates seem, they are the only thing one discerns moving with any clearness of aim in this strange scene. Angry buzz and simmer; uneasy tossing and moaning of a huge France, all enchanted, spellbound by unmarching Constitution, into frightful conscious and unconscious Magnetic-sleep; which frightful Magnetic-sleep must now issue soon in one of two things: Death or Madness! (*FR* 2: 268–270)

Here anonymity and blurring of identity supplant the discrete individual: the abdicating cabinet ministers, ghosts "whom we do not name," are as anonymous and spectral as the "thin streaks of Fédérés." Fitful and unclear signification replaces univalent emblematic meaning, while frenetic movement replaces pictorial stasis and control. As Carlyle's use of the present tense in this passage indicates, the author's stance is immediate and contemporaneous, rather than detached and retrospective. An expansive and highly evocative depiction replaces the brief and conceptually limited form of the emblem.

Allegory tends to enclose and delimit the possible meanings of human experience; in its striving for univalence, it establishes a hierarchical supremacy of selected meanings deriving from a certain juxtaposition of images over the possible alternative meanings deriving from the same images. Furthermore, allegory presupposes authorial control of, and detachment from, the phenomena it depicts. Carlyle's history, concerned with portraying the "Real-Phantasmagory" of existence (*CW* 28: 328), frequently eschews such control and detachment. Rather than establishing facile one-to-one equations between things and their meanings, it depicts historical phenomena as fluctuating adumbrations of many significations. Allegory is analogous, in a political sense, to the hierarchical systems embodied in the destroyed social institutions of France: by effecting the subordination of possible meanings and orders to a limited group of meanings, it recalls a traditional world of degrees and correspondences. Phantasmagory is, by way of contrast, insistently revolutionary and anarchic. Phantasmagory derives from the juxtaposition and agglomeration of competing aspects of experience, rather than from the subordination of parts to a clearly defined whole; its mode is incompleteness, fragmentation, and suggestion, not architechtonic pattern and definite demarcation. Consequently, its texture presents bold contrasts rather than harmonious arrangements, and its style adopts grammatical fragmentation and interruption rather than clear and graceful syntactical subordination. The voice of the phantasmagorist is, unlike the calm and homologized voice of the allegorist, fragmented, probing, and uncertain. The phantasmagorist, whose "point of vision" (*FR* 1: 214) is shifting and incomplete, is unlike the allegorist subservient to time and space. Thus, while allegory's clear delineation of cause and effect reinforces the tripartite architectonic structure of *The French Revolution*, the less closed and less certain form of phantasmagory resists and subverts it. Carlyle's intermingling of antithetical modes of symbolic presentation is a compelling sign of his determination to make form radically accountable to vision and, if necessary, to transgress the boundaries of decorous literary discourse. The allegory and the phantasmagory in his savage and irregular history are not in any simple sense consistent either with each other or with the variegated form of the whole.

NINE

The Liberation of Epic

Carlyle's disimprisoned epic, by its insistent offering of literary analogues, evokes the matrix of the literary traditions it seeks to supersede. It explores the circumference of previous generic codes and then explodes beyond them, forcing the reader to rechart the literary universe and trace a new orbit for a wild and powerful new creation; yet in its Copernican thrust it inevitably recalls its Ptolemaic inheritance. Because of its mixed form and its allusiveness, *The French Revolution* suggests a bewildering variety of sources and analogues for its artistry. These include the work's historical sources—such as the *Histoire Parlementaire*, the memoirs of Besenval, and the travel diaries of Arthur Young—as well as a multiplicity of more overtly literary forms: the Bible, classical epic (Homer and Virgil), vernacular epic (Camoëns, Dante, Tasso, Ariosto, Milton), Teutonic epic (the *Nibelungenlied*), modern epic (Voltaire's *Henriade*, Goethe's *Hermann und Dorothea*, Wilkie's *Epigoniad*, Glover's *Leonidas*), epic novel (*Tom Jones*, *Tristram Shandy*, *Don Quixote*, *Wilhelm Meister*), historical novel (Scott), allegory (Spenser and Bunyan), satire (the elder Samuel Butler and Swift), biography (Boswell), autobiography (Rousseau and Goethe), and history (Gibbon and Hume).

Even if we confine ourselves to nineteenth-century experiments in epic form, our efforts to chart the place of Carlyle's text in literary history remain problematic, for other experiments manifest strongly divergent approaches to the features that he identifies as crucial for any believable modern epic: a credible argument, a mythic form congruent with modern vision, and a justifiable use of literary convention.[1] William Blake, in his *Milton* and *Jerusalem*, combines biblical and Miltonic themes and characters with an intricately developed personal mythology. In Blake's poem "The French Revolution," as in Carlyle's later treatment, we see the mythification of history, reflected, as Harold Bloom notes, in Blake's "radical simplification and condensation of events into one crucial day," in "his vision of pre-Revolutionary history as a tyrannous slumber of a thousand years," and in "his mingling of historical and fictive personages."[2] William Wordsworth, in *The Excursion* and *The Prelude*, resists inherited mythic conventions and, like Carlyle after him, argues for the visionary potentialities of contemporary life.[3] John Keats—in Carlyle's estimation a lachrymose and ineffectual poet—attempts a reanimation of Greek mythological figures and Miltonic themes in his epic fragments *Hyperion* and *The Fall of Hyperion*. Byron uses legendary matter for *Don Juan*—a work of which Carlyle approves—but in a highly iconoclastic manner, so that his self-styled epic becomes, as William Hazlitt characterizes it, "a poem written about itself."[4] Tennyson, while attempting a long work of "parabolic" significance to modern society,[5] adopts the medieval legends of Arthur and his knights as the basis of the *Idylls of the King*. In the estimation of some critics, he becomes trapped between his modern purpose and his traditional materials: Algernon Charles Swinburne observes that Tennyson writes not the *Idylls of the King* but the *Morte d'Albert*, or *Idylls of the Prince Consort*, while Gerard Manley Hopkins quips that the *Idylls* might be appropriately retitled *Charades from the Middle Ages*; Carlyle characterizes the poem as a series of lollipops doled out to eager children.[6] Robert Browning, influenced by Carlyle and his historical concerns, bases *The Ring and the Book* on Italian history, eschewing supernatural poetic machinery for a study of human perception and the shaping power of art. William Morris, in *The Earthly Paradise*, *The Life and Death of Jason*, and *Sigurd the Volsung*, uses a variety of classical and medieval myths and legends, as befits a writer so heavily influenced by Carlyle and Browning, to give focus to an examination of modern states of mind.

In order to place Carlyle more clearly in the literary galaxy of the nineteenth century, I shall compare *The French Revolution* with a series of epic experiments, of varying provenance and stature, which help to illuminate Carlyle's conceptions of modern form: Edward Bulwer-Lytton's *King Arthur*, Shelley's *The Revolt of Islam*, Hardy's *The Dynasts*, Melville's *Moby-Dick*, and Whitman's *Leaves of Grass*. In varying ways, all of these works treat the theme of social change and address the problem of what to do with traditional poetic machinery in a long modern work.

I

King Arthur (1848, revised 1870), a delightful and entertaining poem in its own way, is nearly antithetical in its aims and execution to *The French Revolution*. Whereas Carlyle attempts to register the complexity of social conflict and his own inability to choose sides in a confusing contemporary struggle, Bulwer-Lytton—whom Carlyle alternately pillories as a dandy or praises as a disseminator of German culture—presents a view of the world which is racially, politically, and religiously self-assured. He depicts the triumph of the Christian Britons, led by Arthur, over the heathen Saxons as the birth of British political liberty and British world supremacy. He pits Odin against Christ and shows how, at the end of the conflict, "The North's fierce idol, rolled in pools of blood, / Lies crushed before the Cross of Nazareth" (book 12, stanza 164).[7] Whereas Carlyle engages himself in conscious antagonism with literary tradition and resists obsolete machinery, Bulwer-Lytton is content to use the ideal knights and stainless beauties of a thin and vapid medievalism. Unlike Tennyson, who works conscientiously with Sir Thomas Malory's account of Arthur, Bulwer-Lytton fabricates his own story and creates his own Arthurian tradition, rejecting Malory and his French sources as Gallic encrustations on an essentially British legend. Consequently, when Arthur moves "thro' the artful door / Masked in the masonry, adown a stair / That coiled its windings to the grottoed floor / Of vaulted chambers desolately fair" (book 11, stanza 132), we sense ourselves caught within the architectural trappings of a Gothic thriller; we feel that we are dealing neither with modern life nor with the life of the Middle Ages, but with a medievalism entirely of the mind.

When Carlyle returns to the chivalric world of the Middle Ages, as in the crucial opening chapter of "The Diamond Necklace," he does so to present a world which was, like our own, fraught with problems, but which was nevertheless capable of producing a romantic vision of life. As he demonstrates the presence of adultery and hunger and constipation in medieval life, he simultaneously posits the existence of ideal beauty and heroism in the apparently unromantic nineteenth century. His principal point is that the past is not as unlike the present as our nostalgia would lead us to believe. Bulwer-Lytton, by way of contrast, presents the chivalric age as a time of romance now unavailable to us except through the powers of memory. He therefore engages in unfocused nostalgia for the Middle Ages, and finds in them the enchantment so lacking, to his mind, in Victorian society and culture. In book 1, Bulwer-Lytton recalls the "Fair time, yet floating before haunted eyes," when "King Arthur reigns, and song is in the skies" (book 1, stanza 3). He depicts Arthur's subjects in "gentle groups, discoursing gentle things;— / Or listening idly where the skilful bard / Woke the sweet tempest of melodious strings" (book 1, stanza 6). And he places Arthur in an age of idyllic peace and innocent chivalry:

> Fair shines the sun on stately Carduel;
> The falcon, hoodwinked, basks upon the wall;
> The tilt-yard echoes with the clarion's swell,
> And lusty youths come thronging to the call;
> And martial sports, the daily wont, begin,
> The page must practice if the knight would win.
>
> Some, spur the palfrey at the distant ring;
> Some, with blunt lance, in mimic tourney charge;
> Here, whirrs the pebble from the poised sling,
> Or flies the arrow rounding to the targe;
> While Age and Fame sigh, smiling, to behold
> The young leaves budding to replace the old.
> (book 1, stanzas 73–74)

Bulwer-Lytton repeatedly bemoans the passing away of romance and its "young illusions beautiful" (book 7, stanza 61). In the final book of his epic, he asks the spirit of romance to detain him a little while longer "among the lovely throng / Of forms ideal"(book 12, stanza 2), and he laments the loss of the poetic vision previously embodied in chivalric romance:

> Alas! the sunsets of our Northern main
> Soon lose the tints Hesperian Fancy weaves;
> Soon the sweet river feels the icy chain,
> And haunted forests shed their murmurous leaves;
> The bough must wither, and the bird depart,
> And winter freeze the world—as life the heart!
> (book 12, stanza 4)

In the final stanza of the poem he consigns Arthur to the lost and obscure realms of poetry, the remote conventional world peopled by unreal heroes which Carlyle repeatedly decries in his critical miscellanies:

> What gallant deeds in gentle lists were done,
> What lutes made joyaunce sweet in jasmine bowers,
> Let others tell:—Slow sets the summer sun;
> Slow fall the mists, and closing, droop the flowers;
> Faint in the gloaming dies the vesper bell,—
> And Dream-land sweeps round golden Carduel.
> (book 12, stanza 201)

The contrast between this dreamy stanza and Carlyle's conception of a modern factual romance could hardly be more striking. Whereas Bulwer-Lytton helplessly bemoans the loss of fancy, Carlyle attempts to interlace the products of fancy, the vestiges of epic and myth, with modern understanding to produce the elastic and inclusive modern work of reason. Whereas Bulwer-Lytton regrets the absence of romance in modern life, Carlyle gives to contemporary history a hypermagical cast and attempts to demonstrate, albeit in a characteristically perverse fashion, that the age of romance has not ended.

One final difference between Carlyle and Bulwer-Lytton concerns their uses of the symbol. Carlyle makes the symbol an overt concern of *The French Revolution* and engages in a struggle between the opposed symbolic modes of allegory and phantasmagory. Bulwer-Lytton presents a straightforward and thinly veiled allegory, in which Arthur is the type of Christian heroism and British political liberty and in which various characters and events prefigure in a univalent way the nineteenth-century issues of the British Empire, laissez-faire economics, geology and the extinction of species, the machine, utilitarianism, and democracy. There is one episode in *King Arthur* that might loosely be called phantasmagorical, when Arthur sees the specters of the future march before him in a pageant; yet this episode is, in Carlyle's terms, clearly allegorical, for the characters and symbols presented in it are patly and unequivocally equated to their significances. Milton, who stops by for a brief chat, addresses Arthur as the "Type of the Hero-Age" (book 7, stanza 75), while Arthur witnesses at the end of history, as the culmination of his efforts to unite Briton and Saxon, the era of Queen Victoria, constitutional monarchy, and the British Empire:

Mild, like all strength, sits Crownëd Liberty,
Wearing the aspect of a youthful Queen:
And far outstretched along the unmeasured sea
Rests the vast shadow of her throne; serene
From the dumb icebergs to the fiery zone,
Rests the vast shadow of that guardian throne.
(book 7, stanza 79)

Such an orderly parade of phantasms reinforces, rather than threatens, the allegorical superstructure of the poem. It is separable from what surrounds it in the text; unlike Carlyle's phantasmagories, it does not enter into the text unexpectedly, through any syntactical crevice, and unsettle the effect of the whole. For Bulwer-Lytton, the notion of composition includes the etymologically related idea of being composed, or settled. Consequently *King Arthur* is, both in its style and in its thought, a safe work, unlike *The French Revolution*, which is dangerous and anarchic.

The Revolt of Islam (1818) has a more contemporary and problematic theme than *King Arthur*, and therefore more nearly approximates the artistic dilemmas faced by Carlyle in *The French Revolution*. In his twelve cantos of Spenserian verse, Shelley addresses the issue of what happened to revolutionary fervor in the postrevolutionary era, "When the last hope of trampled France had failed / Like a brief dream of unremaining glory" (canto 1, stanza 1).[8] More unequivocally an advocate of revolution than Carlyle, he considers how the premature uprising in France might be followed by a more deeply founded European revolution. His speaker, a persona of himself as revolutionary poet, rises from his "visions of despair" at the failure of the French Revolution to recreate, within a dream vision, the tale of Laon and Cythna and their fight against oppression. Despite the disparity in temperament between Shelley and Carlyle, reflected in the latter's repeated dismissals of his predecessor, and despite their divergent views of revolution, the two authors share certain thematic concerns— order and chaos, eternity and mutability, ignorance and knowledge—and they share the emblematic patterns in which these concerns are embodied. In Shelley's poem, as in Carlyle's prose history, the star of truth remains as an eternally present yet unperceived power behind the clouds of custom and error; and because they cannot see the star, humans—mariners lost in the sea of time—founder.

Shelley and Carlyle differ most markedly in the different kinds of fiction they employ for their visions. Shelley's poem is set within the framework of a dream vision, and is therefore dependent on the powers of the imagination in a way that Carlyle, voluntarily constrained by the limits of a documentary form, does not countenance. Moreover, Shelley's account of revolution is cast almost entirely in the form of Spenserian allegory: while he does not completely ignore historical time, Shelley refers the experience of revolution to an internal, allegorical, imaginative time in which states of mind thoroughly and spontaneously transform external space. In *The Faerie Queene* Una, the figure of truth, can tame ravenous lions or restrain lecherous satyrs by her very presence; in *The Revolt of Islam* Cythna, Una's counterpart, can walk unharmed past a fierce guard sent to arrest her (canto 4, stanza 19) or win the admiration of a band of rude mariners (canto 7, stanza 41). In Spenser, an internal state, pride, immediately determines an external action, confinement in Orgoglio's dungeon; in Shelley, Laon is similarly imprisoned and subjected to tyranny the moment he feels anger and wants to kill his oppressors. When the inhabitants of Shelley's Golden City are seized by the power of good, they build in a single night a monument to human sympathy which extends into the clouds (canto 5, stanza 40); when they are conquered by fear, however, they raise in one day a similarly commanding monument to tyranny, the pyre on which the revolutionaries Laon and Cythna are to be burned (canto 10, stanza 42). The successful revolution of the future itself takes place within the mind, in a calm, trancelike disavowal of the power of tyranny. Shelley's conceit that political states change when states of mind change is undeniably compelling, yet it to some extent necessarily precludes a sense of the torment and confusion and uncertainty involved when revolutions take place in historical time and space: the stasis of Shelley's revolutionary moment contradicts the violent movement conveyed by such artistic renditions of revolution as Carlyle's history or Eugène Delacroix's fiery painting of Liberty leading the people. Carlyle, unlike Shelley, is willing to adopt allegory only as an intermittent poetic mode, unexpectedly entering into and departing from his text. Whereas Shelley willingly adopts sustained poetic fictions, Carlyle is elusively and intermittently fictitious. Finally, whereas Shelley has recourse to the fictional device of an overworld, the Temple of the Spirit into which Laon and Cythna are taken after death, Carlyle rejects a discrete separation of world and overworld, preferring that they interpenetrate each other in a real-phantasmagory.

Shelley's poetic division of world and overworld reappears in

Hardy's "epic-drama" of the Napoleonic wars, *The Dynasts* (1904–08), a much later work than Carlyle's and yet, paradoxically, a work less consistently modern and experimental in its form and techniques. Hardy shares with Carlyle a desire to unite historical accuracy with artistic truth: *The Dynasts* is, like *The French Revolution*, which Hardy much admired,[9] an artwork with footnotes. He further shares Carlyle's obsession with the perspective, or "point of vision," from which history is to be narrated: witness, for instance, the following stage direction which moves, telescopically, from considering the entire continent of Europe as a person to considering its individual citizens:

> The nether sky opens, and Europe is disclosed as a prone and emaciated figure, the Alps shaping like a backbone, and the branching mountain-chains like ribs, the peninsular plateau of Spain forming a head. Broad and lengthy lowlands stretch from the north of France across Russia like a grey-green garment hemmed by the Ural mountains and the glistening Arctic Ocean.
>
> The point of view then sinks downwards through space, and draws near to the surface of the perturbed countries, where the peoples, distressed by events which they did not cause, are seen writhing, crawling, heaving, and vibrating in their various cities and nationalities. ("Fore Scene" to "Part First")[10]

This remarkable passage calls to mind Carlyle's portrait of France as a writhing paralytic, uneasily "tossing and moaning, . . . spellbound by unmarching Constitution, into frightful conscious and unconscious Magnetic-sleep" (*FR* 2: 269–270); it recalls as well his insistent changes of perspective from the complete and panoptic to the fragmentary and limited. Hardy, like Carlyle, seeks to ferret out the underlying causes of things, and arrives at a similar overriding antithesis between mechanical and organic conceptions of the world. He embodies the former in the Spirit of the Years, which relies exclusively on experience, and which regards the universe as a giant clock; the latter in the Spirit of the Pities, which embraces human hope and imagination, and which looks for the workings of a "Great Heart" in history. While Hardy's use of dialogic voices to underscore our uncertainty in determining the meaning of history is broadly reminiscent of Carlyle, the creation of "impersonated abstractions" to present them points up a fundamental difference in the two authors' practice. *The Dynasts,* unlike

The French Revolution, clearly divides the earthly realm from the spiritual and, hence, the events of history from their interpretation: it establishes, even in its *dramatis personae*, a distinction between "Persons" and "Phantom Intelligences" that contravenes Carlyle's standards for credible poetic machinery. Hardy's overworld, with its choruses of spirits, calls up the neat cosmology of classical epics, and suggests the residual, unbelieved machinery denigrated by Carlyle in his literary criticism. Carlyle adopts a more complex procedure than Hardy by making one list of names double for both persons and phantoms: whether Louis XVI and Desmoulins and Robespierre will serve primarily as historical characters or as phantasmal illusions depends on the context and texture of individual sentences. What differentiates both Shelley and Hardy from Carlyle, in their poems based on history, is their artistic separation of divergent aspects of experience: Shelley separates the actual failed revolution of France from the visionary revolution of the future, while Hardy separates historical events spatially from the spirits which interpret them. Carlyle's technique is to bring opposites into the closest possible proximity, and therefore to demand a closer and more plastic reading of the text than is customarily expected.

II

This technique of yoking opposed modes of discourse recurs in *Moby-Dick* (1851), another attempt, shaped partly by a reading of Carlyle, to reconcile a contemporary theme with inherited literary forms.[11] Melville's novel and Carlyle's history share an obsession with the symbolic nature of the universe. Ishmael echoes Carlyle's and Emerson's assertions that the whole world is emblematic when he notes, in connection with the doubloon Captain Ahab has nailed to the mast of the *Pequod*, that "some certain significance lurks in all things, else all things are little worth, and the round world itself but an empty cipher, except to sell by the cartload, as they do hills about Boston, to fill up some morass in the Milky Way."[12] In Melville, as in Carlyle, reading the text and reading the universe become contiguous activities. Since the American author is, like his British contemporary, intrigued by the plurisignation of the universe, and consequently by the uncertainty of human interpretation, he explores the multiple meanings of symbols and juxtaposes contending modes of symbolic discourse. The doubloon becomes the subject of various exigeses performed by the demented captain, by his mates, and by his pagan harpooners. The figure of the whale, too, is subjected to various scrutinies and interpretations. "Champollion deciphered the wrinkled granite hieroglyphics," remarks Ishmael, while contemplating the head of the Sperm Whale:

> But there is no Champollion to decipher the Egypt of every man's and every being's face. Physiognomy, like every other human science, is but a passing fable. If then, Sir William Jones, who read in thirty languages, could not read the simplest peasant's face in its profounder and more subtle meanings, how may unlettered Ishmael hope to read the awful Chaldee of the Sperm Whale's brow? I but put that brow before you. Read it if you can. (292–293)

Ishmael's challenge—"Read it if you can"—offers a convenient refrain for Melville and Carlyle, who are both obsessed with the interpretation of textual hieroglyphs, and who both explore the uncertain foundations of our symbolic forms. In Melville, as in Carlyle, we have a constant shifting among three various modes of discourse, which we can broadly designate document, symbol, and allegory.[13] The first of these—which appears in Melville's extended discourses on the anatomy of whales, in his criticisms of previous literary and artistic efforts to delineate them, and in his minute discussions of the whale hunt—corresponds to the documentary mode in Carlyle's history, with its footnotes, its discussions of evidence, and its basic factual concern with who does what to whom. The second, which appears most prominently in Melville's celebrated explication of the polyvalence of "The Whiteness of the Whale," corresponds to Carlyle's evocative symbols of fire and flood. The third, which arises ironically and unexpectedly from the other two, corresponds to Carlyle's recurrent emblematic figures and his fragmentary suggestion of a sustained allegory underlying the disparate phenomena of history.

What makes the symbolic methods of *Moby-Dick* so strongly analogous to those of *The French Revolution* is the abruptness with which they leave and enter the text: without announcement or prefiguring, document gives way to symbol and symbol to allegory. Take the long central portion of the novel where the *Pequod* lumbers along, balancing a sperm whale on one side and a right whale on the other. The transportation of two quite different species of whale serves initially as a pretext for a discourse on cetology, and Melville uses it in an unrepentantly long discussion of the two species. Yet at times our assurance that his subject is whales is undermined by a sense that the whales are figures in an allegory of life. Before the right whale was hoisted up, Ishmael remarks, "the Pequod steeply leaned over towards the sperm whale's head," but "now, by the counterpoise of both heads, she regained her even keel. . . . So, when on one side you hoist in Locke's head, you go over that way; but now, on the other side, hoist in Kant's and you come back again; but in very poor plight. Thus, some minds for ever keep trimming boat. Oh, ye foolish! throw all these thunder-heads overboard, and then you will float light and right" (277). The whales' heads become the emblems of contending philosophies, while a discourse on whaling gives way to an ironic (and Carlylean) exhortation to the reader to abandon arid modes of thought. A few chapters later, Ishmael remarks in a similarly perverse vein: "This Right Whale I take to have been a Stoic; the Sperm Whale, a Platonian, who might have taken up Spinoza in his latter years" (284). The movement from physical object to emblematic figure characterizes the abrupt transitions of Melville's text and the lateral, disjunctive processes of his mind. This movement is repeated shortly afterward, when the harpooner Tashtego inadvertently falls into the oily well of the sperm whale's head and nearly drowns. "Now, had Tashtego perished in that head," Ishmael states,

> it had been a very precious perishing; smothered in the very whitest and daintiest of fragrant spermaceti; coffined, hearsed, and tombed in the secret inner chamber and sanctum sanctorum of the whale. Only one sweeter end can readily be recalled—the death of an Ohio honey-hunter, who seeking honey in the crotch of a hollow tree, found such exceeding store of it, that leaning too far over, it sucked him in, so that he died embalmed. How many, think ye, have likewise fallen into Plato's honey head, and sweetly perished there? (290)

The leap from whaling in the South Pacific to gathering honey in Ohio is sufficiently abrupt in itself, but it at least can be explained by the traditional device of the epic simile, which can in the cause of inclusiveness enlist wide-ranging and bizarre analogies. The movement from the whale's head and the honey tree to the philosophy of Plato, however, defies easy explanation.

In Melville's text, a whale can be at one minute a whale, at the next an allegorical figure of Platonic philosophy; it can, as well, be a polyvalent symbol, as in the chapter on "The Whiteness of the Whale," where it suggests a host of divergent possible meanings, from the innocence of virginity to the terror of the polar bear. Given the text's abrupt and unanticipated transitions, it comes as little surprise that Melville shares Carlyle's conscious attention to fragmented and ironic forms. The extracts from whale lore with which the novel begins are, generically, fragments piled together in an inartistic epic catalogue. As assembled by the Carlylean persona of the "Sub-Sub-Librarian," they are a series of "random allusions" and "higgledy-piggledy whale statements," mere hints at "veritable gospel cetology" (2). They are thrown together, like Henry Mackenzie's pieces of gunwadding and Carlyle's scraps of Teufelsdröckh's biography, in such a way that they dimly suggest a more rounded and coherent larger form. The fragment as a genre is consistent with the overall formal fragmentation of the text. As Richard Brodhead writes, using a critical language that works equally well for Carlyle,

> Hawthorne's and Melville's novel form is insistently a mixed medium. Instead of trying to subsume varied material into a unifying and homogeneous narrative mode they compose novels by placing alongside of one another different kinds of fiction. These authors are fundamentally unwilling to delegate to any one style of vision or organization the exclusive right to represent their world. As a result they generate in their works a conflict of fictions, and the reality of their imagined world, rather than lying in any one of these fictions, comes into existence in their interaction.[14]

The French Revolution, like *Moby-Dick*, is shaped by the interaction of contending fictions, none of which is intended ultimately to prevail.

The love of variety and formal experimentation that marks these works also characterizes *Leaves of Grass* (1855–92), Whitman's discontinuous epic of contemporary America. Since Whitman read Carlyle, published brief notices of his works (including *The French Revolution*), admired his audacious style, and lauded his resolute criticism of modern society, it is not surprising that he absorbed much of Carlyle's experimental spirit.[15] Just as Carlyle asserts that an accurate history of the French Revolution will be the grand poem of his era, Whitman announces confidently that "The United

States themselves are essentially the greatest poem" (*Prose* 2: 434) and promises an "epic of Democracy" (*Prose* 2: 714). Both *The French Revolution* and *Leaves of Grass* dedicate themselves to an accurate representation of modern facts within the framework of a liberated epic vision. Both works simultaneously use and resist the conventions of heroic literature with such insistence that their critics, though unable to use the term "epic" without considerable qualification, can never afford to ignore the context of epic tradition. Both Carlyle's depiction of European revolution and Whitman's effort to express in verse the reality of the American Revolution are shaped by an awareness of radical change in society, in individuals, and in literary form. Because of this awareness, both works are highly self-reflexive: *The French Revolution,* like *Sartor Resartus,* highlights the virtuosity of its own creation, while *Leaves of Grass* encompasses both the great poem of America and the manifesto describing the nature and importance of that poem.

The most fundamental common artistic problem for Carlyle and Whitman is an awareness of the need for a radical change in literary practice to correspond to revolutionary historical and political change, the need for new modes of expression to manifest the transcendent reality of modern historical experience. And the most important common pattern in their works is an accommodation of the romantic forms of poetic fiction to the factual demands of reality, which for both authors is potentially grander than fiction. While Carlyle experimented in the mid-1830s with historically based romance, or "True Fiction," Whitman wrote in the mid-1840s in a prose form that he called the "Fact-Romance." Their experiments in shorter forms anticipated *The French Revolution* and *Leaves of Grass,* attempts to demonstrate the romantic significance of modern history on an epic scale.[16] Epic tradition demands that the establishment of a new heroic vision embrace within itself a concerted criticism of the vision of previous epics. Carlyle and Whitman exemplify this retrospective tendency in epic by inviting the specters of past epics into their own works and allowing them to struggle with the figures of their modern imagination. In *The French Revolution,* the Dantons and Mirabeaus and Robespierres of modern French history coexist with the characters and conventions of classical and vernacular epic. Carlyle's indecorous mingling of the mythical and the historical superimposes epic allusions, symbols detached from the reality they originally signified, on contemporary events which are moving, through Carlyle's artistry, toward mythic stature. Carlyle's juxtaposition of new and antiquated mythus forces the reader to apprehend the imprisoned epic of modern history which his work is in the process of liberating, while it readmits to the text the epic machinery that the informing fact-centered aesthetic of Sauerteig ostensibly forbids.

Leaves of Grass, too, enacts the struggle of new and antiquated myths, in its proud statement of its epic theme— traditional in form, yet antitraditional in intent—"The Modern Man I sing" ("One's-Self I Sing," 8), in its wrestling with "the theme of War" as the "one theme for ever-enduring bards" ("As I Ponder'd in Silence," 9–10), and in its epic celebration of the past epic tradition which it both perpetuates and supersedes:

> An ancient song, reciting, ending,
> Once gazing toward thee, Mother of All,
> Musing, seeking themes fitted for thee,
> *Accept for me*, thou saidst, *the elder ballads,*
> *And name for me before thou goest each ancient poet.*
>
> (Of many debts incalculable,
> Haply our New World's chiefest debt is to old poems.)
>
> Ever so far back, preluding thee, America,
> Old chants, Egyptian priests, and those of Ethiopia,
> The Hindu epics, the Grecian, Chinese, Persian,
> The Biblic books and prophets, and deep idyls of the
> Nazarene,
> The Iliad, Odyssey, plots, doings, wanderings of Eneas,
> Hesiod, Eschylus, Sophocles, Merlin, Arthur,
> The Cid, Roland at Roncesvalles, the Nibelungen,
> The troubadours, minstrels, minnesingers, skalds,
> Chaucer, Dante, flocks of singing birds,
> The Border Minstrelsy, the bye-gone ballads, feudal tales,
> essays, plays,
> Shakspere, Schiller, Walter Scott, Tennyson,
> As some vast wondrous weird dream-presences,
> The great shadowy groups gathering around,
> Darting their mighty masterful eyes forward at thee,
> Thou! with as now thy bending neck and head, with courteous
> hand and word, ascending,
> Thou! pausing a moment, drooping thine eyes upon them,
> blent with their music,
> Well pleased, accepting all, curiously prepared for by them,
> Thou enterest at thy entrance porch. ("Old Chants")[17]

A striking instance of this struggle between old and new, and an intriguing Whitmanian parallel to Carlyle's artistry, is the "Song of the Exposition," in which Whitman implores the muse of his poem to abandon the stock themes of European epic for the vibrant realities of America. "Come Muse migrate from Greece and Ionia," he says: "Cross out please those immensely overpaid accounts, / That matter of Troy and Achilles' wrath, and Aeneas', Odysseus' wanderings, / Placard 'Removed' and 'To Let' on the rocks of your snowy Parnassus" (15–18). And in a magnificent elegiac passage he announces the death of traditional epic:

> Ended for aye the epics of Asia's, Europe's helmeted warriors, ended the primitive call of the muses,
> Calliope's call forever closed, Clio, Melpomene, Thalia dead,
> Ended the stately rhymthus of Una and Oriana, ended the quest of the holy Graal,
> Jerusalem a handful of ashes blown by the wind, extinct,
> The Crusaders' streams of shadowy midnight troops sped with the sunrise,
> Amadis, Tancred, utterly gone, Charlemagne, Roland, Oliver gone,
> Palmerin, ogre, departed, vanish'd the turrets that Usk from its waters reflected,
> Arthur vanish'd with all his knights, Merlin and Launcelot and Galahad, all gone, dissolv'd utterly like an exhalation;
> Pass'd! pass'd! for us, forever pass'd, that once so mighty world, now void, inanimate, phantom world,
> Embroider'd, dazzling, foreign world, with all its gorgeous legends, myths,
> Its kings and castles proud, its priests and warlike lords and courtly dames,
> Pass'd to its charnel vault, coffin'd with crown and armour on,
> Blazon'd with Shakspere's purple page,
> And dirged by Tennyson's sweet sad rhyme. (40–53)

Whitman's evocation of mythic splendor, his indulgence in what he elsewhere calls the "perfumed, arras-and-gold Nature" of Tennyson's Arthuriana (*Prose* 2: 485), gives to the "void, inanimate, phantom world" he elegizes a very real presence in his text, strangely coupled with his subsequent prosaic depiction of his own muse at the Exposition, "By thud of machinery and shrill steam-whistle undismay'd, / Bluff'd not a bit by drain-pipe, gasometers, artificial fertilizers, / Smiling and pleas'd with palpable intent to stay, / . . . install'd amid the kitchen ware" (56–59). Whitman, like Carlyle, brings his insistent awareness of the division between past and present to the surface of his text, and reflects their discontinuity in the bold contrasts of his work. His gasometers and kitchen ware, when daringly juxtaposed with the enticing beauty of his elegy for epic, challenge the reader to accept the text's incongruity by reference to a belief that the poetic spirit of past ages lives on in modern life or (in Carlyle's terms) that the "Age of Romance has not ceased" (*CW* 28: 324). In Whitman, as in Carlyle, we encounter a consciously paradoxical treatment of literary tradition, for *Leaves of Grass*, like *The French Revolution*, is peopled by the "vast wondrous weird dream-presences" ("Old Chants," 19) of epic fiction.

Carlyle's and Whitman's experiments in epic form are evidence of a shared feeling that, in Friedrich Schlegel's words, "the classical poetical genres have now become ridiculous in their rigid purity" (*Fragments* 150). Carlyle's prose history with footnotes and Whitman's discontinuous lyrics show little of the prescriptive formulas of neoclassical epic theory. Yet the nineteenth-century sense of generic disintegration which Carlyle and Whitman share does not imply any simple disavowal of genre, for they, like other nineteenth-century authors, mix, modify, and challenge established genres, rather than ignore them. In turning to the epic, Carlyle and Whitman select a genre which, being progressive and self-conscious, is already somewhat suited to a theme of radical change and modern self-awareness. What Thomas Greene writes of the problems of Renaissance epics (which are themselves "imperfectly coherent, uncertainly unified, divided by powerful forces not altogether controlled and understood") comes close to describing the situation of Carlyle and Whitman with regard to epic: "in its quest for epic the Renaissance was engaged in the quest for self-definition. It was forced to modify Homer and Virgil, to modify them in ways characteristically modern, and thus to discover in the modern age what was new and individual." Yet whereas Renaissance epic is forced, as Greene notes, to make "a series of adjustments between a Christian society and antique forms,"[18] the nineteenth-century treatments of revolution by Carlyle and Whitman must mediate between a post-Christian, postmonarchical society and epic conventions structured by the assumptions of a hierarchical worldview. Consequently, for those authors the epic is a genre to be disimprisoned: the "Epic Poem of the Revolution" (*Letters* 7: 306) by Carlyle and the "epic of Democracy" (*Prose* 2: 458) by Whitman reflect only in a severely displaced and often incongruous form the previous centuries' veneration of epic as "the greatest work which the soul of man is capable to perform."[19]

What Carlyle and Whitman both seek is a text that is as revolutionary in form as it is in theme. Neither author will accept a political revolution that does not also become a personal and stylistic revolution. As the figures of contemporary reality struggle with the specters of poetic mythology in the foreground of the text, its underlying revolutionary tensions enter into its variegated surface texture: the revolutionary form of the work becomes (in Carlyle's terms) not the clothing of its revolutionary vision, but its "skin," "the product and close kinsfellow of all that lies under it; exact type of the nature of the beast: *not* to be plucked off without flaying and death" (*Letters* 9: 228). Thus Carlyle describes *The French Revolution* as "a wild savage Book, itself a kind of French Revolution" (*Letters* 9: 116), and Whitman, in words which are almost equally applicable to Carlyle, states of *Leaves of Grass*: "as I have lived in fresh lands . . . and in a revolutionary age, . . . I have felt to identify the points of that age, these lands, in my recitatives, altogether in my own way. Thus my form has strictly grown from my purports and facts, and is the analogy of them" (*Prose* 2: 473). Whitman refuses to apologize for the lack of decorum which a revolutionary aesthetic produces, as he notes in "Spirit that Form'd this Scene, Written in Platte Cañon, Colorado," a late response to hostile critics of his style:

> Spirit that form'd this scene,
> These tumbled rock-piles grim and red,
> These reckless heaven-ambitious peaks,
> These gorges, turbulent-clear streams, this naked freshness,
> These formless wild arrays, for reasons of their own,
> I know thee, savage spirit—for we have communed together,
> Mine too such wild arrays, for reasons of their own;
> Was't charged against my chants they had forgotten art?
> To fuse within themselves its rules precise and delicatesse?
> The lyrist's measur'd beat, the wrought-out temple's grace—
>   column and polish'd arch forgot?
> But thou that revelest here—spirit that formed this scene,
> They have remembered thee.

Here, as in Carlyle, we have the opposition of the natural "formless wild arrays" to the architectonic "column and polish'd arch." Here too we see expressed the dependence of literary form on individual vision, which makes *Leaves of Grass*, like *The French Revolution*, a wild savage book, itself a kind of American Revolution in verse. With their subjection of form to vision— with their indecorous juxtapositions, variegated texture, abrupt transitions of tone, and insistent repudiation of stylistic elegance—the works of Carlyle and Whitman demand to be treated according to an aesthetic quite other than that offered by the "superannuated *unities* of Aristotle, or the French school" (Carlyle, *Collecteanea* 65) or by the "rules precise and delicatesse" of neoclassicism.

In the middle of "Song of Myself," Whitman blurts out, rather unexpectedly, "To be in any form, what is that?" (611). While Carlyle would likely have greeted with reticence Whitman's particular response, that "To touch my person to some one else's is about as much as I can stand" (618), he would undoubtedly have recognized the question as being central to nineteenth-century life and literature. Writing during a time of agitation for political reform, when the "Condition of England" question was gaining prominence in British social thought, Carlyle often invoked an era of "paradisaic Unconsciousness," when life was "a pure, perpetual, unregarded music; a beam of perfect white light, rendering all things visible, but itself unseen" (*CW* 28: 2). The implied formal counterpart, in art, of this mythical era, is a naturally classical aesthetic of purity, composure, and harmony. But "a pure, perpetual, unregarded music" is unavailable in the transitional nineteenth century, for the artificial classicism of the eighteenth century, with its "light life-minuet" (*FR* 1: 25), is degraded and obsolete, while the romanticism that replaces it is a revolutionary "carmagnole complète" (*FR* 3: 230) as yet unconstrained by order. By mixing minuet and carmagnole–the thesis of the *ancien régime* and the antithesis of the Revolution—Carlyle works to create the artistic synthesis heralded by the regenerate classicism of the modern Germans and to realize his dream of a new epic wholeness in literature and society; but, obsessed with the goal of producing a representative form and haunted by the divisions of his age, he leaves full record in *The French Revolution* of the nineteenth century's scars and dissonances.

NOTES

Preface

1. G. P. Gooch, *History and Historians in the Nineteenth Century* (London: Longmans, 1952), 225. Gooch quotes Lord Acton's dictum that "No man feels the grandeur of the Revolution till he reads Michelet, or the horror of it without reading Taine." The revolutionary histories of both authors postdate Carlyle.

2. Jules Paul Seigel, ed., *Thomas Carlyle: The Critical Heritage* (New York: Barnes and Noble, 1971), 47. Reprinted from Lady Sydney Morgan's unsigned review of *The French Revolution* in the *Athenaeum* (20 May 1837), 353–355.

3. "*The French Revolution: A History*," *Literary Gazette* 1062 (27 May 1837): 330–332.

4. Patrick Brantlinger provides an invaluable account of the British political context of *The French Revolution* in *The Spirit of Reform: British Literature and Politics, 1832–1867* (Cambridge: Harvard Univ. Press, 1977), 61–79. He rightly insists that, "like *Chartism* and *Past and Present, The French Revolution* should be read as an essay written in hard times about the politics of hard times" (74).

5. James Anthony Froude, *Thomas Carlyle: A History of his Life in London 1834–1881*, 2 vols. (New York: Scribner's, 1884), 1: 76. Brantlinger argues in *Spirit of Reform*, 61–79, that Carlyle's apparent objectivity, or his lack of allegiance to one political party, stems from his failure to come to terms with politics of any kind.

6. John Ruskin, "The Nature of Gothic," *The Stones of Venice*, 3 vols. (New York: Thomas Y. Crowell, n.d.), 2: 171.

7. G. B. Tennyson, *"Sartor" Called "Resartus": The Genesis, Structure, and Style of Thomas Carlyle's First Major Work* (Princeton: Princeton Univ. Press, 1965), 5.

Chapter One

1. "*The French Revolution*: A History," *Literary Gazette* 1062 (27 May 1837): 330–332.

2. John Clubbe, "Carlyle as Epic Historian," *Victorian Literature and Society*, ed. James R. Kincaid and Albert J. Kuhn (Columbus: Ohio State Univ. Press, 1984), 119–145. The quotation is from page 120.

3. Carlyle's difficulty stems from his prophetic role, which demands not just that he teach but also that he undermine inadequate notions of

truth. David J. DeLaura discusses Carlyle's development of a prophetic role as a response to the social crisis of the 1830s in "Ishmael as Prophet: *Heroes and Hero-Worship* and the Self-Expressive Basis of Carlyle's Art," *Texas Studies in Literature and Language* 11 (1969): 705–732.

4. *Sordello* 5: 635 (*The Poems*, ed. John Pettigrew, completed by Thomas J. Collins, 2 vols. [Harmondsworth: Penguin, 1981]). William Irvine and Park Honan note that Browning may have read as a preparation for his poem "Carlyle's recently published *French Revolution*, which the final *Sordello* resembles very much in its vivid evocation of a past century" (*The Book, the Ring, and the Poet: A Biography of Robert Browning* [New York: McGraw–Hill, 1974], 78). I am not aware whether or not an explicit connection has been made elsewhere between Carlyle's and Browning's conceptions of the brotherly bond between author and reader.

5. Carlyle's status and frustrations as an author during the writing of *The French Revolution* are thoroughly and helpfully discussed by Fred Kaplan in *Thomas Carlyle: A Biography* (Ithaca, NY: Cornell Univ. Press, 1983), 202, 207–210, 215–222.

6. Seigel, 85. Reprinted from Herman Merivale's unsigned review of *The French Revolution*, *Edinburgh Review* 71 (July 1840): 411–445.

7. "*The French Revolution*: A History," *Examiner* 1546 (17 September 1837): 596.

8. "N.," "Stray Thoughts on Carlyle," *Yale Literary Magazine* 7 (February 1842): 171.

9. Augustine Birrell, *The Collected Essays and Addresses of the Rt. Hon. Augustine Birrell, 1880–1920*, 3 vols. (London: Dent, 1922), 2: 29.

10. Hill Shine, *Carlyle's Early Reading, To 1834, with an Introductory Essay on his Intellectual Development* (Lexington, KY: Margaret I. King Library, 1953).

11. *William Allingham's Diary* (Carbondale, IL: Southern Illinois Univ. Press, 1967), 211.

12. Allingham, 225.

13. Philip Rosenberg, *The Seventh Hero: Thomas Carlyle and the Theory of Radical Activism* (Cambridge: Harvard Univ. Press, 1974), 3–4.

14. Tennyson argues "that Carlyle's methods and ideas in *Sartor* are to be sought in his work of the previous decade and that his successes in the essays as well as his failures in the early fiction were necessary undertakings in the disciplining of his literary skill and imagination before *Sartor* could be written" (*"Sartor" Called "Resartus,"* 126–127).

15. Albert J. LaValley, *Carlyle and the Idea of the Modern: Studies in Carlyle's Prophetic Literature and its Relation to Blake, Nietzsche, Marx, and Others* (New Haven: Yale Univ. Press, 1968), 20–21.

16. See especially her chapter on *Sartor Resartus* (Anne K. Mellor, *English Romantic Irony* [Cambridge: Harvard Univ. Press, 1980], 109–134).

17. J. A. Heraud, "T. Carlyle's French Revolution," *Fraser's Magazine* 16 (1837): 85–104. I follow here the attribution of *The Wellesley Index to Victorian Periodicals*, ed. Walter Houghton, 4 vols. (Toronto: Univ. of Toronto Press, 1966–87), 2: 357.

18. Kathleen Wheeler, ed., *German Aesthetic and Literary Criticism: The Romantic Ironists and Goethe* (Cambridge: Cambridge Univ. Press, 1984), 10.

19. James Russell Lowell, *My Study Windows* (London: Walter Scott, n.d.), 170–171.

20. John Clubbe, "Carlyle as Epic Historian," 131.

21. This quotation from Anne K. Mellor's discussion of Friedrich Schlegel (*English Romantic Irony*, 17) is in this instance applicable to Carlyle's reading of Goethe.

22. The various stages of Carlyle's reception, and the various guises in which he has been cast, are helpfully summarized by G. B. Tennyson in "Carlyle Today," *Carlyle Past and Present: A Collection of New Essays*, ed. K. J. Fielding and Rodger L. Tarr (London: Vision Press, 1976), 27–50.

23. Certainly, Bakhtin's critical language of heteroglossia, self-parody, and indeterminacy works well for the novelized or generically problematic epic Carlyle writes. See, for instance, Bakhtin's essay "Epic and Novel," *The Dialogic Imagination*, trans. Michael Holquist and Caryl Emerson, ed. Michael Holquist (Austin: Univ. of Texas Press, 1968), 3–40.

24. Birrell, *Collected Essays and Addresses*, 2: 312.

25. A. Abbott Ikeler, in his useful and detailed account of the internal contradictions in Carlyle's literary vision, argues that "Carlyle's divided consciousness, his inability to resolve the tension between art and the exigencies of the contemporary world, presage the schizophrenic temper of mid-Victorian romanticism" (*Puritan Temper and Transcendental Faith: Carlyle's Literary Vision* [Athens, OH: Ohio Univ. Press, 1972], 206). Ikeler's binary division of Carlyle's thought into "Puritan temper" and "Transcendental faith" is unduly polar, and it excessively diminishes the elements of conscious self-contradiction, irony, and paradox in Carlyle's writings.

Chapter Two

1. Laurence Sterne, *Tristram Shandy*, ed. Howard Anderson (New York: Norton, 1980), 132.

2. Le Bossu's prodigious reputation is discussed by A. F. B. Clark in *Boileau and the French Classical Critics in England (1660–1830)* (1925; reprint, New York: Burt Franklin, 1970), 243–261; and by Stuart Curran in the introduction to his edition, *Le Bossu and Voltaire on the Epic* (Gainesville, FL: Scholars' Facsimiles and Reprints, 1970), v–xi.

3. Among the many helpful discussions of German generic systems are Hans Eichner's *Friedrich Schlegel* (New York: Twayne, 1980); Ralph W. Ewton's *The Literary Theories of August Wilhelm Schlegel* (The Hague: Mouton, 1972); and Kathleen M. Wheeler's introduction to *German Aesthetic and Literary Criticism*.

4. For discussions of Carlyle and the modern Germans, see Hugh Walker, *The Literature of the Victorian Era* (Cambridge: Cambridge Univ. Press, 1910), 22–79; René Wellek, *Confrontations: Studies in the Intellectual*

and Literary Relations Between Germany, England, and the United States During the Nineteenth Century (Princeton: Princeton Univ. Press, 1965), 34–81; Charles Frederick Harrold, *Carlyle and German Thought: 1819–1834* (1934; reprint, London: Archon Books, 1963); and Rosemary Ashton, *The German Ideal: Four English Writers and the Reception of German Thought 1800–1860* (Cambridge: Cambridge Univ. Press, 1980), 67–104. Harrold's study remains an invaluable guide to Carlyle's readings and misreadings of German authors, but his contention that Carlyle owes little to the Germans in his aesthetic principles—"There is no evidence that he ever went to the Germans for any artistic purposes" (6)—is surely overstated. While the emphasis of most previous scholars on the moral and philosophical content of Carlyle's German borrowings (self-renunciation, the open secret, the divine idea of the world) is justified, the failure to appreciate fully the suggestions of literary influence has been regrettable. We as yet lack an accurate assessment of the importance to Carlyle of the German works on aesthetics he read and discussed: Schiller's treatise on the naive and sentimental, the correspondence of Goethe and Schiller, the essays of the Schlegels, Richter's *Vorschule der Aesthetik*, and so on.

5. A translation of this essay can be found in Goethe's *Essays on Art and Literature*, trans. Ellen von Nardroff and Ernest H. von Nardroff, ed. John Gearey (New York: Suhrkamp, 1986), 192–194.

6. Wheeler, *German Aesthetic and Literary Criticism*, 79.

7. Jean Paul Friedrich Richter, *Horn of Oberon: Jean Paul Richter's "School for Aesthetics,"* trans. Margaret R. Hale (Detroit, MI: Wayne State Univ. Press, 1973), 196.

8. The phrase "lyrical drama" is taken from the subtitle of *Prometheus Unbound*; the Dryden quotation is from *Essays of John Dryden*, ed. W. P. Ker, 2 vols. (New York: Russell, 1961), 2: 154.

9. In *The Victorian Critic and the Idea of History: Carlyle, Arnold, Pater* (Cambridge: Harvard Univ. Press, 1979), Peter Allan Dale examines the historicist principles underlying Carlyle's criticism. Dale identifies Carlyle's "application of his ideas on historical process to the study of poetry," together with his "introduction of German literature to England," as a central contribution of his criticism (16). Dale is less ready than I am to consider Carlyle as a student of particular artforms: Carlyle, he writes, "characteristically dismisses the whole question of artistic form as beneath the serious critic's concern" (17).

10. *Correspondence Between Goethe and Carlyle*, ed. Charles Eliot Norton (1887; reprint, New York: Cooper Square, 1970), 191.

11. The triad of unity, plurality, and totality is discussed by Eichner, *Friedrich Schlegel*, 35; and by Ewton, *The Literary Theories of August Wilhelm Schlegel*, 85–95.

12. Henry Fielding, *Joseph Andrews*, ed. Martin C. Battestin (London: Methuen, 1965), 7–8; *Correspondence Between Schiller and Goethe*, trans. L. Dora Schmitz, 2 vols. (London: George Bell, 1877–79), 1: 189–190,

243, 420; Richter, *Horn of Oberon*, 165; Georg Wilhelm Friedrich Hegel, *The Philosophy of Fine Art*, trans. F. P. B. Osmaston, 4 vols. (London: George Bell, 1920), 4: 171.

13. Anne K. Mellor discusses the workings of romantic irony in *Sartor Resartus* in *English Romantic Irony*, 109–134. I would suggest that her glancing reference to the works after *Sartor* creates an unduly sharp division between the early and the late Carlyle: "In later works, this increasingly sublime egotist shed the motley of the buffooning romantic ironist and donned instead the sombre robes of the Victorian sage" (134).

14. Ruskin, "The Nature of Gothic," *Stones of Venice*, 2: 158.

15. Richard Hurd, *Letters on Chivalry and Romance* (London: 1762; reprint, New York: Garland, 1971), 56, 65; William Blake, *The Poetry and Prose of William Blake*, ed. David W. Erdman, comm. Harold Bloom (Garden City, NY: Doubleday, 1965), 267. The Gothic in literature is treated extensively by Paul Frankl in *The Gothic: Literary Sources and Interpretations through Eight Centuries* (Princeton: Princeton Univ. Press, 1960).

16. Emerson writes to Carlyle about *The French Revolution* in 1837: "I insist, of course, that it might be more simple, less Gothically efflorescent. You will say no rules for the illumination of windows can apply to the aurora borealis" (*The Correspondence of Emerson and Carlyle*, ed. Joseph Slater [New York: Columbia Univ. Press, 1964], 167). Emerson's imagistic contrast between the artificial and the natural recalls Carlyle's own critical metaphors and underscores the conscious roughness of his art.

17. *CW* 26: 214; 27: 450; 28: 49, 75. The "death of poetry" in Victorian Britain is discussed by Lionel Stevenson in "The Key Poem of the Victorian Age," *Essays in American and English Literature Presented to Bruce Robert McElderry, Jr.*, ed. Max F. Schulz, William D. Templeman, and Charles R. Metzger (Athens, OH: Ohio Univ. Press, 1967), 260–289; David J. DeLaura in "The Future of Poetry: A Context for Carlyle and Arnold," *Carlyle and his Contemporaries: Essays in Honor of Charles Richard Sanders*, ed. John Clubbe (Durham, NC: Duke Univ. Press, 1976), 148–180; and Richard Jenkyns, *The Victorians and Ancient Greece* (Cambridge: Harvard Univ. Press, 1980), 21–38.

18. The nineteenth-century spirit of generic experimentation which I outline in this chapter resonates with some of the intriguing developments in twentieth-century genre criticism: the creation of multiple schemas of forms, concern with the development of forms through time, and investigation into the relations of historical and theoretical genres. Particularly interesting, in the context of *The French Revolution*, are Paul Hernardi's argument for "a polycentric conceptual framework" which resists "the illusory promise of unity and simplicity held out by most summary classifications" (*Beyond Genre: New Directions in Literary Classification* [Ithaca, NY: Cornell Univ. Press, 1972], 153); Tzvetan Todorov's contention that every literary "transgression" depends on the existence of a literary "norm" (*The Fantastic: A Structural Approach to a Literary Genre*, trans.

Richard Howard [Ithaca, NY: Cornell Univ. Press, 1975], 8) and that "every great book establishes the existence of two genres, . . . that of the genre it transgresses . . . and that of the genre it creates" (*The Poetics of Prose*, trans. Richard Howard [Ithaca, NY: Cornell Univ. Press, 1977], 43); and E. D. Hirsch's account of *Don Juan* (which Carlyle admired—see *CW* 26: 269) as a poem which depends upon established epic conventions, but which has a "genre idea" all its own (*Validity in Interpretation* [New Haven: Yale Univ. Press, 1967], 106).

Chapter Three

1. Tennyson, *"Sartor" Called "Resartus,"* 9, 173.

2. George Levine, *The Boundaries of Fiction: Carlyle, Macaulay, Newman* (Princeton: Princeton Univ. Press, 1968), 21–22. See also Levine's "The Use and Abuse of Carlylese," in *The Art of Victorian Prose*, ed. George Levine and William Madden (New York: Oxford Univ. Press, 1968), 101–126; and the references to *The French Revolution* in his book *The Realistic Imagination: English Fiction from Frankenstein to Lady Chatterley* (Chicago: Univ. of Chicago Press, 1981).

3. Gerry H. Brookes, *The Rhetorical Form of Carlyle's "Sartor Resartus"* (Berkeley: Univ. of California Press, 1972), 8–9.

4. Lionel Stevenson, *The English Novel: A Panorama* (Boston: Houghton Mifflin, 1960), 228; Alastair Fowler, *Kinds of Literature: An Introduction to the Theory of Genres and Modes* (Cambridge: Harvard Univ. Press, 1982), 123. See also Jerry A. Dibble, *The Pythia's Drunken Song: Thomas Carlyle's "Sartor Resartus" and the Style Problem in German Idealist Philosophy* (The Hague: Martinus Nijhoff, 1978).

5. George Saintsbury, *Corrected Impressions: Essays on Victorian Writers*, 2nd ed. (London: Heinemann, 1895), 45.

6. Although "Count Cagliostro" has been largely ignored, it has been used recently by Lee C. R. Baker ("The Diamond Necklace and the Golden Ring: Historical Imagination in Carlyle and Browning," *Victorian Poetry* 24 [1986]: 31–46) and by John D. Rosenberg, who states that the work "radiates an extravagant gaiety of negativity" (*Carlyle and the Burden of History* [Cambridge: Harvard Univ. Press, 1985], 33). The Count himself has been the subject of much attention, primarily because of his interest in the occult. My source for his life is Roberto Gervaso's *Cagliostro: A Biography*, trans. Cormac Ó Cuilleanáin (London: Victor Gollancz, 1974).

7. The *Oxford English Dictionary* defines *pasquil* as "any circulated or published lampoon" and cites Carlyle as its sole source for the corresponding adjective *pasquillic*.

8. Carlyle refutes the didactic conception of history in his 1830 essay "On History" (*CW* 27: 83–95).

9. "The Diamond Necklace" has garnered much appreciation, but there has been little detailed study, apart from Carlisle Moore's article "Carlyle's 'Diamond Necklace' and Poetic History," *PMLA* 58 (1948): 537–557.

10. For a discussion of romance in *Sartor Resartus* see Patrick Brantlinger's "'Romance,' 'Biography,' and the Making of *Sartor Resartus*," *Philological Quarterly* 52 (1973): 108–118.

11. These two passages are quoted from *Last Words of Thomas Carlyle* (London: Longmans, 1892), 193–194, 200.

12. From a letter to James Stanier Clarke, 1 April 1816 (*Jane Austen's Letters*, ed. R. W. Chapman, 2nd ed. [1952; reprint, Oxford: Oxford Univ. Press, 1979]), 452–453.

13. From Scott's review of *Emma* in the *Quarterly Review* 14 (1815–16), as reprinted in *Sir Walter Scott on Novelists and Fiction*, ed. Ioan Williams (London: Routledge and Kegan Paul, 1968), 230.

14. Thomas Carlyle, *Lectures on the History of Literature* (London: Ellis and Evey, 1892), 111–112.

Chapter Four

1. Seigel, *Critical Heritage*, 52. From John Stuart Mill's unsigned review of *The French Revolution* in the *London and Westminster Review* 27 (July 1837), 17–53.

2. Sir William Davenant and Sir Richard Blackmore in J. E. Spingarn, ed., *Critical Essays of the Seventeenth Century*, 3 vols. (Oxford: 1908–9; reprint, Bloomington: Indiana Univ. Press, 1957), 2: 3, 11, 56.

3. Edward Gibbon, *An Essay on the Study of Literature* (London: 1764; reprint, New York: Garland, 1970), 26.

4. The Novalis quotation is taken from Harrold, *Carlyle and German Thought*, 167; the Schelling quotation is taken from M. H. Abrams, *Natural Supernaturalism: Tradition and Revolution in Romantic Literature* (New York: Norton, 1971), 223–224. For a general discussion of Carlyle and the Germans on history as revelation, see Harrold, 164–168. Given Carlyle's insistent attention to the literary forms in which history casts itself, it is surprising that Hayden White does not make greater use of him in *Metahistory: The Historical Imagination in Nineteenth-Century Europe* (Baltimore: Johns Hopkins Univ. Press, 1973). Lee C. R. Baker does discuss Carlyle in the context of White's ideas in "The Diamond Necklace and the Golden Ring," 131–132.

5. Alfred Cobban, "Carlyle's *French Revolution*," *History* 48 (1963): 306. Rosemary Jann provides a valuable general account of Carlyle's place in Victorian historical writing, locating him in the nineteenth–century debate over the relative merits of scientific and artistic history (*The Art and Science of Victorian History* [Columbus, OH: Ohio State Univ. Press, 1985]). For other general treatments, consult the early studies of C. F. Harrold ("Carlyle's General Method in *The French Revolution*," *PMLA* 43 [1928]: 1150–1169; "The Translated Passages in Carlyle's *French Revolution*," *Journal of English and Germanic Philology* 23 [1928]: 51–66), Louise Merwin Young (*Thomas Carlyle and the Art of History* [Philadelphia: Univ. of Pennsylvania Press, 1939]), and Emery Neff (*The Poetry of History: The Contribution of Literature and Literary Scholarship to the Writing of History Since*

Voltaire [1947; reprint, New York: Octagon Books, 1979]). See also the Cobban essay cited here, G. M. Trevelyan's essay on "Bias in History" (*An Autobiography and Other Essays* [London: Longmans, 1949], 68–81), and Hedva Ben-Israel's book *English Historians on the French Revolution* (Cambridge: Cambridge Univ. Press, 1968). Specific aspects of Carlyle's practice are treated in H. M. Leicester's article "The Dialectic of Romantic Historiography: Prospect and Retrospect in *The French Revolution*," *Victorian Studies* 15 (1971): 5–17; in Robert W. Kusch's article "The Eighteenth Century as 'Decaying Organism' in Carlyle's *The French Revolution*," *Anglia* 89 (1971): 456–470; and in recent studies by Lee C. R. Baker ("The Diamond Necklace and the Golden Ring"), Lowell T. Frye ("Chaos and Cosmos: Carlyle's Idea of History," *Victorian Newsletter* 65 [1984]: 19–21), Tom Lloyd ("Madame Roland and Schiller's Aesthetic: Carlyle's *The French Revolution*," *Prose Studies* 9 [1986]: 39–45), and Beverly Taylor ("Carlyle's Historical Imagination: Untrue Facts and Unfactual Truths," *Victorian Newsletter* 61 [1982]: 29–31). Both Baker and Lloyd consider Carlyle's historical method in the light of German aesthetics.

6. Christopher Hibbert, *The Days of the French Revolution* (New York: William Morrow, 1980), 212.

7. Hibbert, 213–214.

8. Pierre Victor, Baron de Besenval, *Mémoires du Baron de Besenval*, 2 vols. (Paris: 1821), 1: 365. The *barrières* were government custom posts on the outskirts of Paris, detested by the insurgents and therefore a prime target of attack.

9. Thomas Greene, *The Descent from Heaven: A Study in Epic Continuity* (New Haven: Yale Univ. Press, 1963), 7.

10. Homer, *The Iliad*, trans. Alexander Pope, ed. Maynard Mack, Vols. 7 and 8 of *The Poems of Alexander Pope* (London: Methuen, 1967), 24: 207–212, 221–222, 225.

11. William Shakespeare, *The Second Part of King Henry IV*, Arden edition, ed. A. R. Humphreys (London: Methuen, 1966), 1.1.68–73.

12. The brevity of Carlyle's truncated epic simile runs counter to the leisure which is repeatedly cited as a distinguishing feature of epic narrative by German aestheticians such as Goethe, Schiller, the Schlegels, and Richter, and which figures so prominently in Erich Auerbach's famous account of "Odysseus' Scar" in the opening chapter of *Mimesis: The Representation of Reality in Western Literature*, trans. Willard R. Trask (Princeton: Princeton Univ. Press, 1953).

13. Jules Michelet, *History of the French Revolution*, trans. Charles Cocks, ed. Gordon Wright (Chicago: Univ. of Chicago Press, 1967), 165–166.

14. J. B. Bury, "The Science of History" (1903), *Selected Essays*, ed. Harold Temperley (Cambridge: Cambridge Univ. Press, 1930), 4.

15. Allingham, *Diary*, 241.

16. Lee C. R. Baker states the case splendidly when he argues as follows: "Carlyle and Browning are at odds with the traditional conventions of historiography, for even though they base their own poetic reconstructions

on sound historical data, they realize that the means of interpreting this data inevitably involve personal vision, at its best expressed by poetic genius, which allows imagination or romantic sympathy to project itself onto the historical field and to fill up the lacunae of the historical record with motives, reasons, and a sense of narrative direction" ("The Diamond Necklace and the Golden Ring," 37). Baker successfully links Carlyle's view of historical writing with Friedrich Schlegel's complex conception of romantic irony: Carlyle, he writes, "recognizes . . . the enormous and unbridgeable abyss between the actual historical event and the historian's depiction of it" (39).

17. The relation of Carlyle to the historical novel is discussed by Avrom Fleishman in *The English Historical Imagination, Walter Scott to Virginia Woolf* (Baltimore: Johns Hopkins Univ. Press, 1971), 116; John Maynard in "Broad Canvas, Narrow Perspective: The Problem of the English Historical Novel in the Nineteenth Century," *The Worlds of Victorian Fiction*, ed. Jerome H. Buckley, Harvard English Studies No. 6 (Cambridge: Harvard Univ. Press, 1975), 248–249; and Andrew Sanders in *The Victorian Historical Novel 1840–1880* (London: Macmillan, 1978), 74.

18. Among the many scholars who have addressed the Carlyle–Dickens relationship, see Michael Goldberg, who argues that "*A Tale of Two Cities*, both in its form and content, owes almost everything" to Carlyle (*Carlyle and Dickens* [Athens, GA: Univ. of Georgia Press, 1972], 101); and Jonathan Arac, who offers a penetrating comparative analysis of *The French Revolution* and *Bleak House* (*Commissioned Spirits: The Shaping of Social Motion in Dickens, Carlyle, Melville, and Hawthorne* [New Brunswick, NJ: Rutgers Univ. Press, 1979], 114–138). See also *Dickens Studies Annual* 12, ed. Michael Timko, Fred Kaplan, and Edward Guiliano (New York: AMS Press, 1983), which contains brief studies of Carlyle and Dickens by Murray Baumgarten, Richard J. Dunn, Elliot L. Gilbert, Michael Goldberg, Carol Hanberry Mackay, Branwen Bailey Pratt, Michael Timko, and Chris R. Vanden Bossche.

19. In Carlyle, writes John D. Rosenberg, "the Apocalypse has been relocated in historical time. Much of the power of *The French Revolution* lies in the shock of the transposition, the explosive interpenetration of modern fact and ancient myth, of journalism and scripture" (*Carlyle and the Burden of History*, 50).

20. The question of Carlyle's possible debt to Hegel has been inconclusively debated. A. L. Le Quesne strikes a convincing balance when he compares the two authors' views of history: "In . . . replacing a faith in the Bible with a faith in History, Carlyle had good nineteenth-century company—most notably, Hegel and Marx, though he was never aware of the parallel. Nor, indeed, is the parallel by any means complete, since to both Hegel and Marx history was a progressive phenomenon. The theme of progress does sometimes occur in Carlyle's writings (especially the earlier ones), but it is very muted and eventually disappears altogether" (*Carlyle* [Oxford: Oxford Univ. Press, 1982], 33).

21. Hugh Blair, *Lectures on Rhetoric and Belles Lettres*, 3 vols. (London: 1785; reprint, New York: Garland, 1970), 3: 205. British theory of the epic is well treated in Raymond Dexter Havens, *The Influence of Milton on English Poetry* (1922; reprint, New York, Russell, 1961); H. T. Swedenberg, *The Theory of the Epic in England 1650–1800* (Berkeley, 1944; reprint, New York: Russell, 1972); and Donald M. Foerster, *The Fortunes of Epic Poetry: A Study in English and American Criticism, 1750–1950* (Washington: Catholic Univ. of America Press, 1962).

22. LaValley, *Carlyle and the Idea of the Modern*, 139.

23. Friedrich Schlegel, *Lectures on the History of Literature, Ancient and Modern*, trans. John Frost (Philadelphia: Moss, 1872), 179; Richter, *Horn of Oberon*, 170; Madame de Staël, *De L'Allemagne* (Paris: Garnier, n.d.), 150–151, 172.

24. Hegel, *Philosophy of Fine Art*, 4: 147–148, 191.

25. To treat *The French Revolution* as an epic was a nineteenth-century commonplace; the most important twentieth-century studies of Carlyle's history as epic are by Albert J. LaValley, John Clubbe, and John D. Rosenberg. See also Sara Gragg, "The Artistic Unity of Thomas Carlyle's *The French Revolution*" (Ph.D. diss., Univ. of Arkansas, 1971).

26. John D. Rosenberg, *Carlyle and the Burden of History*, 57.

27. Chris R. Vanden Bossche treats this problem of voice in his article "Revolution and Authority: The Metaphors of Language and Carlyle's Style," *Prose Studies* 6 (1983): 274–289. Vanden Bossche argues that in *The French Revolution* the narrative voice becomes "a multitude of voices, the babble of the democratic millions proclaiming their own authority" (284).

28. John Milton, *Paradise Lost*, ed. Merritt Y. Hughes (New York: Odyssey, 1962), 9: 28–29.

29. Heraud, "T. Carlyle's French Revolution," 85, 101–102; John D. Rosenberg, *Carlyle and the Burden of History*, 7 ("The hero of *The French Revolution*—if it has a hero other than its author—is the demonic Paris mob"); John Clubbe, "Epic Heroes in *The French Revolution*," *Thomas Carlyle 1981: Papers Given at the International Thomas Carlyle Centenary Symposium*, ed. Horst W. Drescher (Frankfurt-am-Main: Peter Lang, 1983), 165–185.

30. John P. Farrell, examining Carlyle's "strange but meaningful juxtaposition of dissimilar genres," argues that "Carlyle exploited the idea of genre by intimating, on the one hand, that there are separable and ideal structures, and, on the other, that life is a conflation of the distinct realities that literary forms abstract from experience." These general comments on Carlyle and genre are splendid. Yet Farrell seems to work against the impetus of his own insights when he maintains that *The French Revolution* is tragedy rather than epic. "The French Revolution did not achieve epic harmony as a political event," he concludes, "and it does not do so in Carlyle's symbolic retelling either" (*Revolution as Tragedy: The Dilemma of the Moderate from Scott to Arnold* [Ithaca, NY: Cornell Univ. Press, 1980], 190, 215).

31. Jenkyns, *Victorians and Ancient Greece*, 24.

32. Greene, *Descent from Heaven*, 19.
33. Dryden, *Essays*, 2: 174.
34. Blair, *Lectures on Rhetoric and Belles Lettres*, 3: 208.

Chapter Five

1. The seventeenth-century debate over epic machinery is well summarized by Clark, *Boileau and the French Classical Critics in England*, 308–325.

2. Edmund Burke, *The Works*, 12 vols. (London, 1887; reprint, New York: George Olms, 1975), 3: 331. Burke writes: "It is now sixteen or seventeen years since I saw the queen of France, then the Dauphiness, at Versailles; and surely never lighted on this orb, which she hardly seemed to touch, a more delightful vision. I saw her just above the horizon, decorating and cheering the elevated sphere she just began to move in,—glittering like the morning-star, full of life and splendor and joy."

3. The coupling of *tempus* with *templum* is not original with Eliade, but he uses it extensively to characterize the mythic or religious sensibility. See Mircea Eliade, *The Sacred and the Profane: The Nature of Religion*, trans. Willard R. Trask (New York: Harcourt, Brace, and World, 1959), 73–76.

4. Hesiod, *Hesiod*, trans. Richmond Lattimore (Ann Arbor: Univ. of Michigan Press, 1959), 211–225.

5. Oscar Browning, in a paper first delivered in 1886, questions Carlyle's treatment of fact in this episode and concludes "that almost every detail is inexact, some of them quite wrong and misleading. This is the danger of the picturesque school of historians. They will be picturesque at any price" (*The Flight to Varennes and Other Historical Essays* [London: Swan Sonnenschein, 1892], 76). John Nichol responds, in Carlyle's defense, that his "object was to convey the soul of the Revolution, not to register its upholstery" (*Thomas Carlyle* [New York: Harper, 1904], 181). The inaccuracies and biases in Carlyle's account of the Revolution are discussed by two of his editors, C. R. L. Fletcher (*The French Revolution*, 3 vols. [London: Methuen, 1902]) and John Holland Rose (*The French Revolution*, 3 vols. [London: George Bell, 1902]).

6. As these mythical allusions are well documented by D. Heggie (*How I Read Carlyle's "French Revolution"* [Toronto: William Briggs, 1902]), Helen C. Flint ("Indications in Carlyle's 'French Revolution' of the Influence of Homer and the Greek Tragedians," *Classical Journal* 5 [1910]: 118–126), and Albert J. LaValley (*Carlyle and the Idea of the Modern*, 121–182), I shall deal with them in summary fashion.

7. LaValley writes that Carlyle's "epic for moderns is also a heightened version of mock-epic, . . . in which the Titans war upon the Olympian gods and dethrone them forever" (*Carlyle and the Idea of the Modern*, 142). Carlyle is not entirely consistent in designating the royalists as Olympians and the revolutionaries as Titans, however; he reverses his usual procedure in *FR* 1: 47, 83; 2: 27.

8. Robert Langbaum, "Browning and the Question of Myth," *PMLA* 81 (1966): 575–584.

9. Robert Langbaum, *The Poetry of Experience: The Dramatic Monologue in Modern Literary Tradition* (New York: Random House, 1957), 13–14.

10. See James Kissane's "Victorian Mythography," *Victorian Studies* 6 (1962): 5–28.

11. The continuity of *The French Revolution* with epic tradition is discussed by LaValley, *Carlyle and the Idea of the Modern*, 139; John D. Rosenberg, *Carlyle and the Burden of History*, 46–47; and Mark Cumming, "Carlyle, Whitman, and the Disimprisonment of Epic," *Victorian Studies* 29 (1986): 207–226 (especially 215–217).

Chapter Six

1. Tasso, in his *Discourses on the Heroic Poem*, lauds the epicist's ability to create "a little world" within the confines of a single tightly unified action (trans. Mariella Cavalchini and Irene Samuel [Oxford: Clarendon Press, 1973], 78). John Dryden maintains that the epic poet must supplement his "universal genius" with "universal learning": "the knowledge of the liberal arts and sciences, and particularly moral philosophy, the mathematics, geography, and history" (*Essays* 2: 36, 43). Alexander Pope, similarly daunted by the breadth of learning required of the epic poet, portrays Homer as an epicist who uses "the whole Circle of Arts, and the whole Compass of Nature to supply his maxims and reflections; all the inward Passions and Affections of Mankind to furnish his Characters, and all the outward Forms and Images of Things for his Descriptions" (preface, *The Iliad*, ed. Mack, 5). John Stuart Mill writes of epic inclusiveness in a passage cited below, and Thomas Greene includes "expansiveness" among the determining characteristics of epic (*Descent from Heaven*, 9–10).

2. From Mill's review of *The French Revolution* (Seigel, *Thomas Carlyle: The Critical Heritage*, 58). Mill discussed the Revolution extensively with Carlyle, lent him source materials, and (to make amends for his role in the accidental burning of Volume 1) gave him financial support. See Kaplan, *Thomas Carlyle*, 196–197, 200, 203, 214–215, 217–222.

3. Mill, *Autobiography and Literary Essays*, ed. John M. Robson and Jack Stillinger, vol. 1 of *Collected Works of John Stuart Mill* (Toronto: Univ. of Toronto Press, 1981), 352.

4. Burke, *Works*, 3: 244.

5. Matthew Hodgart, *Satire* (New York: McGraw–Hill, 1969), 12, 13, 214.

6. Andrew Miles Ruth offers a more extensive account of Carlyle as satirist in *The French Revolution* than I attempt here. Ruth sees *The French Revolution* as the height of Carlyle's achievement in the form, and places him in a conservative satiric tradition which mistrusts attempts to build new commonwealths based solely on human reason. See his "Thomas Carlyle as Satirist in *The French Revolution*," Ph.D. diss., Univ. of Rochester, 1980.

7. Hodgart, *Satire*, 121–122.

8. Hodgart, 118–119, 248.

9. Heggie helpfully points to the first ode in Book I of Horace's *Odes*: ' "Sublimi feriam sidera vertice' ('I shall smite the stars with my lofty head')" (*How I Read Carlyle's "French Revolution,"* 50). In *Gulliver's Travels*, the Lilliputians address their emperor as the "Monarch of all Monarchs: Taller than the Sons of Men; whose Feet press down to the Centre, and whose Head strikes against the Sun" (ed. Herbert Davis [Oxford: Basil Blackwell, 1965], 43). Carlyle's ambivalent attitudes toward satire in general and Swift in particular are addressed by Sidney M. B. Coulling, "Carlyle and Swift," *Studies in English Literature* 10 (1978): 741–758.

10. This passage is not without its engaging comic elements, which balance or complement its overriding pathos. Note, for instance, the oddly translated nickname "Towhead" and the comically inappropriate description of death: "needs no combing."

11. Again, Carlyle's elegy has a comic or parodic undercurrent. "Mirabeau lies dead" is parodied by "Théroigne lies living," and her living death is commemorated by a trivial application of traditional elegiac motifs.

12. *FR* 1: 186; 2: 147, 265; 3: 194, 280, 283.

13. Joseph Addison, *Critical Essays from "The Spectator,"* ed. Donald F. Bond (Oxford: Clarendon Press, 1970), 73–74.

14. LaValley, *Carlyle and the Idea of the Modern*, 147.

Chapter Seven

1. Curran, *Le Bossu and Voltaire on the Epic*, 79, 86–87.

2. Addison, *Essays*, 64.

3. John Holloway, *The Victorian Sage: Studies in Argument* (1953; reprint, New York: Norton, 1965), 27.

4. Levine, *Boundaries of Fiction*, 49.

5. Tennyson, *"Sartor" Called "Resartus,"* 51, 99, 127.

6. Abrams, *Natural Supernaturalism*, 74.

7. Levine, *Boundaries of Fiction*, 68; Tennyson, *"Sartor" Called "Resartus,"* 167.

8. The recent interest in Carlyle and typology has produced several valuable studies. George P. Landow explores Carlyle's role in creating an iconography of crisis in *Victorian Types, Victorian Shadows: Biblical Typology in Victorian Literature, Art, and Thought* (London: Routledge and Kegan Paul, 1980) and *Images of Crisis: Literary Iconology, 1750 to the Present* (London: Routledge and Kegan Paul, 1982). Barry V. Qualls, in *The Secular Pilgrims of Victorian Fiction: The Novel as Book of Life* (Cambridge: Cambridge Univ. Press, 1982), establishes a vital link from Bunyan and Quarles through Carlyle to Victorian fiction. See also Herbert L. Sussman's *Fact into Figure: Typology in Carlyle, Ruskin, and the Pre-Raphaelite Brotherhood* (Columbus, OH: Ohio State Univ. Press, 1979) and Chris

Brooks' *Signs for the Times: Symbolic Realism in the Mid–Victorian World* (London: Allen and Unwin, 1984).

9. Peter M. Daly, *Literature in the Light of the Emblem: Structural Parallels between the Emblem and Literature in the Sixteenth and Seventeenth Centuries* (Toronto: Univ. of Toronto Press, 1979), 88.

10. Daly, *Literature in the Light of the Emblem*, 32. Daly is quoting Albrecht Schöne, *Emblematik und Drama im Zeitalter des Barock*, 2nd rev. ed. (Munich: 1968), 48.

11. See Peter M. Daly, "Goethe and the Emblematic Tradition," *Journal of English and Germanic Philology* 74 (1975): 388–412. In this study (made particularly relevant to the present discussion by Carlyle's praise for Goethe's "emblematic intellect") Daly warns against unwary application of the term *emblem* to modern literature. Daly's first objection to seeing Goethe's work as continuous with the emblematic tradition concerns the question of sources and influence: the "case for Goethe's association with the emblematic tradition remains unproved," he contends, because of the "broken or missing links in the chain" of transmission (407). His second objection addresses the nature of Goethe's literary preoccupations: "Emblems as such were evidently not important to Goethe at any stage in his career," he argues, and the word *emblem* is not part of his working critical vocabulary (412). His third objection concerns a blurring, on the part of some critics, of the distinction between emblem and symbol. The following pages in my argument are designed partly to show how the case of Carlyle diverges from the case of Goethe, as it is presented by Daly.

12. *FR* 1: 6, 51, 52, 60, 134, 143, 189, 206, 214; 2: 4, 40, 66, 103, 185, 193; 3: 152, 207, 227, 312.

13. Francis Quarles, "To the Reader," *Emblemes* (1643), in *The Complete Works in Prose and Verse*, ed. Alexander B. Grosart, 3 vols. (New York: AMS Press, 1967), 3: 45. Ralph Waldo Emerson, *Nature* (1836), in *Nature, Addresses, and Lectures*, ed. Robert E. Spiller and Alfred R. Ferguson, vol. 1 of *The Collected Works of Ralph Waldo Emerson* (Cambridge: The Belknap Press of Harvard Univ. Press, 1971), 21.

14. See Quarles' *Emblems Divine and Moral* and Bunyan's *A Book for Boys and Girls*. The first edition of Bunyan's volume was not illustrated, but the subsequent editions which Carlyle might have known were.

15. Daly, *Literature in the Light of the Emblem*, 72, 87–89.

16. The poems referred to here can be found in *CW* 26: 469–476 and in *The Love Letters of Thomas Carlyle and Jane Welsh*, ed. Alexander Carlyle, 2 vols. (London: John Lane, 1909), 2: 341–360. G. B. Tennyson's "Carlyle's Poetry to 1840: A Checklist and Discussion, a New Attribution, and six Unpublished Poems," *Victorian Poetry* 1 (1963): 161–181, remains the standard study of these works.

17. John Bunyan, *The Poems*, ed. Graham Midgely, vol. 6 of *The Miscellaneous Works of John Bunyan* (Oxford: Clarendon Press, 1980). It has been pointed out to me that Goethe uses the same motif of the moth and the candle, though to different effect, in "Selige Sehnsucht" ("Blessed

Longing"). See also Goethe's "Fliegentod" ("Death of a Fly"). The originals of these poems, together with facing translations, can be found in Goethe's *Selected Poems*, trans. Michael Hamburger, et al., ed. Christopher Middleton (Boston: Suhrkamp, 1983), 206–7, 190–191.

18. E. Beresford Chancellor, *Literary Types* (London: 1895; reprint, Port Washington, NY: Kennikat Press, 1970), 91.

19. G. B. Tennyson discusses the fragment and *Sartor Resartus* in *"Sartor" Called "Resartus,"* 223–231. More general comments on the fragment as genre can be found in Robert Preyer's "Victorian Wisdom Literature: Fragments and Maxims," *Victorian Studies* 6 (1963): 245–262; Thomas McFarland's *Romanticism and the Forms of Ruin: Wordsworth, Coleridge, and Modalities of Fragmentation* (Princeton: Princeton Univ. Press, 1981); and Wheeler's *German Aesthetic and Literary Criticism* (see especially 9–11).

20. Henry Mackenzie, *The Man of Feeling*, ed. Brian Vickers (London: Oxford Univ. Press, 1967), 5, 7.

21. The precise extent of Carlyle's indebtedness to Richter has remained a matter for debate. J. W. Smeed goes so far as to argue that "*Sartor* owes its essential form and style to the novels of Jean Paul" ("Thomas Carlyle and Jean Paul Richter," *Comparative Literature* 16 [1964]: 226–252, quotation from 231).

22. Tennyson, *"Sartor" Called "Resartus,"* 224.

Chapter Eight

1. In *On Heroes*, Carlyle rejects theorists who argue that pagan religions grew out of the allegorical impulse: "The *Pilgrim's Progress* is an Allegory, and a beautiful, just and serious one: but consider whether Bunyan's Allegory could have *preceded* the Faith it symbolises! The Faith had to be already there, standing believed by everybody;—of which the Allegory could *then* become a shadow. . . . The Allegory is the product of the certainty, not the producer of it; not in Bunyan's nor in any other case" (CW 5: 6).

2. Thomas Babington Macaulay, "John Bunyan" (1831), *Critical and Historical Essays*, 2 vols. (London: Dent, 1907), 2: 399–410.

3. Blake, "A Vision of the Last Judgement," *Poetry and Prose*, 544; Coleridge, *The Statesman's Manual* (London: Gale and Fenner, 1816). For analogous distinctions between allegory and symbol in German aesthetics, see Wheeler, *German Aesthetic and Literary Criticism* (especially 9–11).

4. G. H. Lewes, *The Life and Works of Goethe*, 2 vols. (London: David Nutt, 1855), 2: 432–433. Matthew Arnold evidently shared Lewes' doubts about Carlyle's defence of Goethe: see David J. DeLaura, "Arnold and Carlyle," *PMLA* 79 (1964): 124.

5. *CW* 26: 151–152, 181, 192, 195–196.

6. Henry James, "The Correspondence of Carlyle and Emerson," *Century* 26 (1883): 265–272. The quotation is from page 272.

7. Frederic Harrison, *Studies in Early Victorian Literature* (London: Edward Arnold, 1910), 53; Louis Cazamian, *Carlyle*, trans. E. K. Brown (New York: Macmillan, 1932), 158.

8. Froude, *Thomas Carlyle*, 1: 12, 77.

9. *FR* 1: 274; 2: 62, 66, 74; 3: 190, 259.

10. Harrison, *Studies in Early Victorian Literature*, 53; Cazamian, *Carlyle*, 167; Froude, *Thomas Carlyle*, 1: 78; Paul Elmer More, *Shelburne Essays*, First Series (New York: Putnam's, 1904), 92.

Chapter Nine

1. Brian Wilkie's *Romantic Poets and Epic Tradition* (Madison: Univ. of Wisconsin Press, 1965) remains a standard discussion of the genre's development in the early nineteenth century.

2. Blake, *Poetry and Prose* (comm. Bloom), 864.

3. Like Carlyle, Wordsworth both supersedes and uses the vestiges of literary tradition. In book 6 of *The Prelude*, for instance, he recounts his repeated experience of a particular tree during his stay at Cambridge:

> Often have I stood
> Foot-bound uplooking at this lovely tree
> Beneath a frosty moon. The hemisphere
> Of magic fiction, verse of mine perchance
> May never tread; but scarcely Spenser's self
> Could have more tranquil visions in his youth,
> Or could more bright appearances create
> Of human forms with superhuman powers,
> Than I beheld loitering on calm clear nights
> Alone, beneath this fairy work of earth.

(*The Prelude: A Parallel Text*, ed. J. C. Maxwell [1971; reprint, Harmondsworth: Penguin, 1975], 6: 85–94.) Here he introduces the standard of "magic fiction," as exemplified by Edmund Spenser, ostensibly to demarcate the limitations of his own art. Yet he asserts that his vision of a contemporary scene is not less magical than that embodied in antiquated and overtly fictional works: like Carlyle, he rejects literary mythologies as the central focus of his long work in favor of the supernatural power inherent in natural forms, and forces the reader to a reconsideration of the "hypermagical" aspects of reality. As in Carlyle, however, the rejected literary mythologies remain rhetorically necessary to the impact of the entire passage, for the natural supernaturalism of the poet recalls the supernatural characters of romance, and the picture of the tree as a "fairy work of earth" takes its emotional coloring from the crucial reference to *The Faerie Queene*. John D. Rosenberg compares the two works in a rather different manner: "The epic journey inward into autobiographical time that Wordsworth began in *The Prelude* finds its analogue in the epic journey backward into historical time that Carlyle began in *The French Revolution*" (*Carlyle and the Burden of History*, 19).

4. William Hazlitt, *Complete Works*, centenary edition, ed. P. P. Howe, 21 vols. (London: Dent, 1930–34), 11: 75.

5. See Hallam Tennyson's *Alfred Lord Tennyson: A Memoir*, 2 vols. (London: Macmillan, 1897), 2: 127.

6. John D. Jump, ed., *Tennyson: The Critical Heritage* (London: Routledge and Kegan Paul, 1967), 334, 339; and Carlyle's letter of 27 January 1867 to Emerson, *Correspondence of Emerson and Carlyle*, 552–553.

7. Edward Bulwer-Lytton, *King Arthur: A Poem*, rev. ed. (Toronto: Hunter, Rose, 1871). All subsequent references are to this edition.

8. Percy Bysshe Shelley, *Poetical Works*, ed. Thomas Hutchinson, rev. G. M. Matthews (1970; reprint, London: Oxford Univ. Press, 1973). All subsequent references are to this edition.

9. See *Thomas Hardy's Personal Writings*, ed. Harold Orel (Lawrence: Univ. of Kansas Press, 1966), 107–109, 125, 272n.

10. Thomas Hardy, *The Dynasts: An Epic–Drama of the War with Napoleon* (London: Macmillan, 1965). All subsequent references are to this edition.

11. The Carlyle-Melville relationship is discussed by Jonathan Arac (*Commissioned Spirits*, 139–163) and by Linden Peach (*British Influence on the Birth of American Literature* [New York: St. Martin's Press, 1982], 138–161).

12. Herman Melville, *Moby-Dick*, ed. Harrison Hayford and Herschel Parker (New York: Norton, 1967), 358. All subsequent references are to this edition.

13. The last of these three forms is discussed at length by Bainard Cowan in *Exiled Waters: "Moby-Dick" and the Crisis of Allegory* (Baton Rouge: Louisiana State Univ. Press, 1982). Cowan's complex conception of allegory differs from the more straightforward Carlylean definition I employ here.

14. Richard H. Brodhead, *Hawthorne, Melville, and the Novel* (Chicago: Univ. of Chicago Press, 1976), 20.

15. The Carlyle-Whitman relationship is summarized in Kaplan, *Thomas Carlyle*, 528; and in Cumming, "Carlyle, Whitman, and the Disimprisonment of Epic," 209–212. To the studies cited in my article, add Peach, *British Influence on the Birth of American Literature*, 162–193.

16. James E. Miller calls *Leaves of Grass* "America's epic," whose hero, "unlike the hero of past epics, discovers his heroic qualities not in superman characteristics but in the *self-hood* common to every man" (*A Critical Guide to "Leaves of Grass"* [Chicago: Univ. of Chicago Press, 1957], 259, 261). See also Ferner Nuhn's essay "*Leaves of Grass* Viewed as an Epic," *Arizona Quarterly* 7 (1951): 324–338. The quotation is from Walt Whitman, *The Early Poems and the Fiction*, ed. Thomas Brasher (New York: New York Univ. Press, 1963), 319.

17. From Walt Whitman, *Leaves of Grass, Comprehensive Reader's Edition*,

ed. Harold W. Blodgett and Sculley Bradley (New York: Norton, 1965). All subsequent references are to this edition.

18. Greene, *Descent from Heaven*, 4–5.

19. Dryden, *Essays*, 2: 154.

INDEX